UNSAYABLE ABSENCE

Deborah G. Dunleavy

◆ FriesenPress

One Printers Way
Altona, MB R0G 0B0
Canada

www.friesenpress.com

Copyright © 2021 by Deborah G. Dunleavy
First Edition — 2021

All rights reserved.

No part of this publication may be reproduced in any form, or by any means, electronic or mechanical, including photocopying, recording, or any information browsing, storage, or retrieval system, without permission in writing from FriesenPress.

This is a work of fiction and the characters in it are solely the creation of the author. All photographs come from family archives.

Credits and Acknowledgements:

First and Foremost: Howard Alexander

Editorial Assistance: Dr. Kathleen Arthur

Photographer for Deborah Dunleavy: Jan Murray

www.deborahdunleavy.com

Brockville Museum; Dorset Heritage Museum, Dorset, Ontario; Muskoka Heritage Museum, Huntsville, Ontario; Northern Ontario Railroad Museum, Capreol, Ontario; West Parry Sound District Museum; Parry Sound Public Library; Doug Smith, Dr. Kathleen Arthur.

ISBN
978-1-03-911249-0 (Hardcover)
978-1-03-911248-3 (Paperback)
978-1-03-911250-6 (eBook)

1. Family & Relationships, Life Stages

Distributed to the trade by The Ingram Book Company

Dedicated to the memory of my mother Ernestine,
and her siblings Jack and Grace.

"Listen, and feel the beauty of your separation, the unsayable absence."

Rumi, translated by Coleman Barks

PART ONE

For life and death are one, even
as the river and sea are one.

Khalil Gibran

1

July 1930 **The Asylum**

What day is it?

The morning light creeps across the floor. Una sits on the edge of her bed, the crumpled sheets and coarse woolen blanket tossed aside to reveal the blood-stained mattress.

Other women's menstrual blood.

Other crazy women.

I am not crazy.

This is Una's second silent week.

Voices seep into the room from outside. Una walks over to the third-floor window on her ward and peers through the cold metal bars. Below, several patients, all men, pull weeds with their bare hands. Others break up clumps of earth with their spades. One man in a straw hat waters the new summer crop with a long garden hose.

Did I water my plants?

She glances beyond the trees, mostly oak, some maple, to where the grounds of the asylum slope toward the cliff that hovers over the river. It all seems strangely serene to Una. Today there is no breeze to dance in the leaves and the river looks as clear as glass. But tomorrow the river might rage like a monster.

Don't trust the river.

Again, Una hears the men muttering.

Secrets, lies, profanities. Their garden hose is much smaller than the one they use on us, much smaller. The nurse tells us lies. Water therapy, she says, it's good for you. You'll feel better.

The sting of the water does not make Una feel better. Last week the explosion from the hose knocked a patient over. If she could she would tell someone how the nurse ties them to the chairs.

No one will listen to me, no one.

Una is the only one who hears the aching that stays stuck in her throat. The psychiatrists want her to say something, anything. But Una has no words to spill from her heart; no words that will bring her husband back to her.

2

April 1905

"You do not eat that berry Nika."

Rachel Little Feathers shows Una a blue berry hanging from a vine. "Birds, they can eat it but not you. You will be very sick Little Goose. It may even choke you. Come this way."

Rachel Little Feathers leads Una out of the woods and across the farmer's field, a shortcut to the spring. It is a long hike from her camp to fetch water. The farmer has chased Rachel Little Feathers away more times than there are kernels on a cob of corn. Once he even set his dogs after her. They liked the bits of dried moose meat she threw at them.

"Later I will show you where to find the real blueberry, the one the bears eat. We will leave some for them. Should we do that? What do you think Nika?"

"I think so Nokomis." Una runs ahead of Rachel through the open field.

"Watch out for that snapping turtle. It will bite your big toe right off."

Rachel calls after Una who disappears in the tall hay. "It'll swallow you whole," shouts Rachel.

Una leaps above the hay like a jack rabbit. She sings back, "No Nokomis, no big snapping turtle going to get my toe. No big snapping turtle going to get my toe."

Rachel Little Feathers is not Una's Nokomis, not her bloodline grandmother. But five-year-old Una has called her Nokomis since forever.

Today Una will stay with Nokomis. Again. Her brothers and sister have gone to the log schoolhouse and can't keep an eye on their younger sister. Una's mother, Maud, has asked Rachel to look after Una. She needs to help her husband, Duncan, unload the scow. They have a delivery of building supplies to take across the bay to a construction site. A company from Toronto is building a sanatorium for those suffering from tuberculosis. Everyone on the lake is hoping to get some work there. Building, cooking, cleaning.

Maud has always found plenty of reasons to pass Una over to Rachel. But Una doesn't mind. She loves being with Nokomis. Nokomis tells great stories, and she shows Una so many things in the woods and around the lake. She tells Una why birds fly south, why stars fall from the sky, why mosquitoes buzz. And why one should avoid snapping turtles.

Rachel finally catches up to Una who squats beside the spring. The waters burble up only a few feet from the shore. Una squishes the clay laden soil between her fingers.

"Minnows." Una points to a school of tiny fish zigzagging in the shallow water.

"In a week, maybe two, they will be big enough to use as bait for fishing." Rachel fills her old tin buckets with the cold spring water.

Una swings her two tiny honey pails. They are just the right size for her small hands. She giggles as the water splashes on her pinafore and all over her bare feet.

"This way." Una gestures to a well-worn path that hugs the shoreline.

"It takes longer to get to the camp Little Goose. And we have these pails heavy with water."

"But we can see the whole lake from the lookout. We can rest. We can listen for the birds and name them. Please Nokomis. Please."

Una breathes in the sweet scent of pine and the dank aroma of moss-covered rocks. A fresh breeze wafts across the lake carrying with it a trace of burning wood from the cabins on the other side. Rachel slowly plods along over fallen stumps and uneven ground, careful not to spill the water from her buckets.

"Wait," Rachel whispers and stands motionless. "Chickadee. Look, in the bush."

"Chickadee," echoes Una in a hushed tone.

"Now that the ice has gone from the lake more birds come and build their nest. Some eggs are good to eat."

Rachel sits on a rock, the buckets at her feet. She watches Una playfully chase the waves that lap the shore. Running after them. Running away from them.

"Nika, Nika you are nibi baby. Always you play in the water. You were born on the water, born on the big nibi bay."

Una shakes the water from her feet and skips over to Rachel. "Nibi? Is nibi water?"

"Yes. Nibi is water."

"And I am Nika. You call me Nika, Little Goose. Maybe I am Nibinika."

"You are clever girl."

"But why do you call me Little Goose?"

"When your mother was pushing you out, I caught you. I catch many babies, but you know that Nika. I come to the scow. Your brothers fetch me in the dark of night, and I come to bring you into this world. You so tiny and all wet and ugly." Rachel laughs. "But you not ugly now Nika. You are beautiful girl." Rachel gestures for Una to sit beside her on the rock.

"When you were born, I wash you in this nibi, this same water here, right out of the bay, right beside the scow. And you don't even cry. You such a strong girl. Then I hear them. Geese. Soft at first then louder and closer. I look and a flock of geese land on the water close to the scow. And the sun? It is just rising in the east. I remember the color of red and pink mixed with clouds. Beautiful morning. Then one goose sit up strong and flap its wings. I think, it is one happy goose to be back on the lake. And I know this little baby I wash in the water, she going to stretch her wings one day. She going to take to flight. She going to have great life journey." Rachel smiles at Una. "So, I call you Nika, Little Goose."

Una jumps up and runs to the shore.

"Look. Look." Una points to a huge bird wading in the reeds. It lifts one of its long legs and flips a fish into its pointed beak. "Heron. Is that a heron Nokomis?"

"Yes, Mr. Fisherman, he is hungry. You hungry Nika? We will build a fire. We'll have nice fried muskrat brain and bannock when we get back."

Rachel Little Feather's camp lies nestled in a narrow rock cut valley where it is protected from the elements of nature especially the wind and the heavy snows of winter. Her shelter is part cabin, part tent. She built it from bits of scrap wood and logs that washed up on the shore. Some pieces, like the tarp and the ropes, came from the lumber yards. She traded with the men. Gave them her sweetgrass baskets. On more than one occasion she went at night and took things from the trash heap when no one was looking.

A few feet out from the tattered blanket that covers the doorway of her shelter is the summer fire pit. Over to one side is a rack for hanging up the birds and wildlife that she catches. On the other side are two stumps for sitting on and a table with three legs perched on a pile of rocks to keep it from tipping over.

The people in the village call her a squatter. They say that the land belongs to them now. She should go back and live with her own kind. But Rachel cannot go back. She married a white trapper and when he died from an accident on the trap lines one winter she was not allowed to live with her own people. It was forbidden. That's when she set up the camp in the woods. On her ancestral lands.

Local folks tell her to go. 'Go live in that Indian Village squaw. Go where you belong.' They tell her she should live with her own people, her own people who had been forced out of Muskoka years before. Driven off their own land. Banished from their hunting and fishing grounds. Now Rachel can only go to the Indian Village for feast days and only if she is invited by a cousin or other relative.

These same local folks are the first ones that send for Rachel Little Feathers to come and catch their babies, hundreds of babies. Sometimes they give her white folk's food. Flour, sugar, tea. Sometimes an old coat or blanket like the one that Una sits on now.

Una picks up one of Rachel's many baskets that lay scattered about. Baskets with sweetgrass, rabbit pelts, animal skulls, or feathers. This one is filled with clam shells. Una pulls out each shell, single ones in one pile, doubles in another. *They look like butterfly wings,* thinks Una. Her tiny fingers stroke the silky insides. She is careful. Some are cracked and sharp. She cut her foot once when she went wading in the lake. It stung for days.

July 1907

On this bright summer morning Una is glad to get out of the cramped humid quarters of the log cabin her father erected on the scow. Each April her family leaves the winter cabin, some three miles inland, and moves to the scow until the snow flies in October. During those chilly Spring months Una wears all her clothes to bed just to chase the shivers away, but this morning Una is already hot from the summer heat. She steps out of the cabin wearing only her thin cotton slip.

A huge load of timber that Una's father promises her mother that he will deliver sometime this week takes up more than half the length of the barge. At the other end Una's mother stands over an old wooden table, gutting a rabbit. And beyond that is a makeshift clothesline with a bed sheet flapping in the wind.

Una wanders over to the edge of the scow and dangles her feet in the cool morning water of the lake. She keeps them as still as possible so that the sunfish kiss her toes. In the distance a mist rises from the water toward the warming sun. A magical morning.

"Fetch the water." Una's mother holds a small knife in one hand, the body of the rabbit in the other, and blood dripping from her hands. "Don't stand there staring. Go!"

Una grabs the bucket from beside the gutting table and dips it over the edge of the scow. Water sloshes over the top. Heavy. The handle nearly slips from her fingers. She grabs it just in time. With both hands and all her strength, she hauls it out of the lake.

"Bring it here Una. Now watch. One day you will be doing this yourself." Maud is visibly pregnant with her eighth child. She swore that Una would be her last. Her two sons, and another girl, all older than Una, had survived childbirth. Three other infants had only lived for a few brief moments.

"I can do it for you Mama. I help Nokomis gut rabbits."

Maud's jaw clenches as she inserts her two fingers through the tiny slit of the rabbit's belly and pulls the skin apart. "You spend too much time with that woman."

Una knows better than to remind her mother that she is the one who always sends her to be with Rachel Little Feathers. "Yes, Mama, but we skinned a rabbit last week. I helped. I can help you."

"You can help me by doing as your told. You're too much like your father. Stubborn as a mule." Maud scoops the guts out and tosses them to one side. More blood oozes from the carcass staining Maud's already discolored apron. "Later you can row out and feed these guts to the fish." Maud stands back for a moment and holds her unborn child kicking in her womb, sighs, then returns to disemboweling the rabbit.

"Now see this, Una. See this membrane?"

Una steps closer to the table and points. "The heart and lungs are in there. Nokomis fries them. We eat them."

"No, Una, no. We do not eat them. It is not how we do it."

Maud uses a little pressure and breaks the membrane that separates the stomach and intestines then she pulls out the heart and the lungs and everything else that is in there. In silence Una watches. She has said too much already. Maud takes a large sharp knife and quickly cuts off the paws. Then starting at the belly, she separates the skin from the flesh. Suddenly the knife falls from her hand.

"Dear Lord, not now. Not now." Maud doubles over and howls in pain. Her birth water gushes onto the deck of the scow. Una stares at the puddle of fluid pouring from between her mother's legs. "Una, quick. Go. Get Rachel. Oh my God. Go."

Una runs as fast as her young legs can take her. She crosses the newly mowed hayfield beyond the landing, along the well-worn path, and through the woods. Her heart beats heavy in her chest. Her lungs ache. She leans against a tree to catch her breath. On the far side of the stream, she sees Rachel Little Feathers picking wild raspberries.

"Nokomis," she shouts. "It's Mama. She's having a baby."

"I come. You go ahead Nika. Boil some water. I come." Even though Rachel knows it will take her several minutes to get to where she can cross over on the fallen tree that spans the creek she assures Una, "Your mother, she will be fine. Baby will be fine."

Panting, Una finally arrives back at the scow. She is relieved to see that Martha, Colin, and Robert who have been fishing since early morning are paddling toward the scow.

Una calls out breathlessly, "Mama is having the baby. Nokomis is coming. She told me to boil water, but I've never started the fire in the wood stove. I don't know what to do."

Colin lands the rowboat and starts giving orders. "Robert, get the fire going. Now. Martha, help mother stay calm. Damn it, why isn't Papa home? Una, rip up that sheet on the clothesline. We need it for rags."

Colin has witnessed this before, babies being born. Two of them died. When he was little, he hid under the table and covered his ears to deaden his mother's moans and screams. The day Maud struggled to push Una into the world Colin was only eight years old. He heard his mother curse the unborn child with swear words that he'd never heard his mother use before. Rachel Little Feathers chanted and sang to try to calm Maud, but to little effect.

The next morning Colin told his mother that he had heard her say, 'God dam, Jesus, Mary Mother of God' and that she had told Rachel to go to hell. Maud, a God-fearing Christian, vehemently denied that she had ever done such a thing. It was a lie. And now once again Maud calls up every manner of blasphemy available to her lips as she fights to give birth to yet another child.

The sun sinks low over the lake sending a prism of colors to cascade across the calm evening waters. Una has rowed out alone, to dump the guts of the rabbit into the water, to feed the fish, the fish that they will catch someday, the fish they will fry and eat.

Her mother's agonizing cries of childbirth have long disappeared as have the eerie echoes that bounced off the rocks across the bay. For a brief moment Una turns her head toward the scow. Rachel Little Feathers sits on the roof of the cabin. Smoking her pipe. She too watches the blending of day into night, the subtle shifting of light to dark. Again, Una faces the western horizon just as the glowing red ball sun sinks deeper and deeper, then swallowed by the lake. When she glances back at the scow, Rachel is gone. Like a raven.

Una's father has not yet arrived home from the tavern. She knows that her father often comes home late, the smell of whiskey in his whiskers when he kisses her goodnight and calls her his *bana-phrionnsa*, his Gaelic way of calling her his little princess.

Flocks of seagulls float silently above in the darkening sky, seeking shelter until dawn. Una dips the oars into the water and rows smoothly back to the scow. She catches sight of her father, returning with a deer carcass slung over the back of his horse.

Una hollers, "It's a boy Papa, a baby boy."

"And blessed be this family." Duncan throws the deer over his shoulder and lugs it to a hook on the side of the cabin. "And your mother?"

"Sleeping Papa."

"You hungry Papa?" Una asks as she docks the rowboat and steps onto the scow. "I helped make rabbit stew with onions and potatoes and carrots. Did you catch the deer Papa? Want to see the baby? Can we call him Tom? I like the name Tom. Do you like the name Tom?"

Duncan smiles and ruffles Una's already wind-blown hair. "Come my bana-phrionnsa. Let's go see the new baby and your mother."

The next morning Maud does not rise from her bed. The birth had not been easy. Her infant son is frail, and reluctant to take to her breast. She is sullen, her eyes sunken and black, yet she is not so weak that she is incapable of ordering her children to do the chores.

Colin and Robert are sent to the trap lines to check for rabbits and grouse. Martha has been told to boil water and wash the blood-stained sheets. Una, only seven years old, is put to scrubbing the splatter on the floor around her parents' bed.

"Mama, what are you going to call him?"

"I don't know."

"Maybe we can call him, Tom?"

"I don't know Una."

"I like the name Tom, Mama. Do you like the name Tom?"

"Una, finish your work and then go help your sister. I need to sleep." Maud groans as she shifts her body under the covers.

"Are you going to be okay Mama?"

"Yes, Una. I pray to the good Lord that I do not have another baby. Now are you finished?"

"Almost."

Maud lifts her head to peer over the bed. "That's fine. You go and help Martha hang the clothes out to dry."

"Then can I go see Nokomis?"

"Yes," Maud says reluctantly, "but be back before dark, you hear. Not like the last time. Did your father come home?"

"Yes Mama. Late last night. Don't you remember? He came in here. We all did." When Maud does not answer Una kisses her mother on the cheek. "I love you Mama."

"I know. I know. I love you too Una." Maud's voice trails off as she turns her head and closes her eyes.

Una races out of the cabin to where Martha struggles to wring out the sopping wet sheets. She grabs one end and Martha holds onto the other. As they twist in opposite directions and squeeze the water out of the well-worn bedding, they sing a song they know their mother would disapprove of especially because it is Sunday, and it is not a hymn.

"The old gray mare she ain't what she used to be."

They hang the laundry to dry on the makeshift clothesline. Duncan fashioned it out of two pieces of lumber that had floated down from the mill and a length of coarse rope that once held a shipment of supplies he took over to the sanatorium. Una's father uses every bit of scrap he can get his hands on. Nothing is thrown away if it can be used again.

After they are done Una sets off like a butterfly on the breeze. She wants to hear another story from Nokomis. Maybe Nokomis will tell her how babies are made.

Baby Tom lived for two weeks. Maud tried to breast feed her wee infant, but it would not take to her teat. Rachel Little Feathers had asked around for a wet nurse, but none were to be found. She brought goat milk from a farmer across the bay. Baby Tom was not able keep it down and his emaciated body grew weaker and weaker.

It was then that Duncan crafted a crude coffin and lined it with left over cotton from the window shades that Maud had made years ago.

"That's pretty Papa." Una says looking at her father's handiwork on the miniature crate.

"Dunna say that to your mother."

"Why, Papa? Won't Mama like it?"

"Best to say nothing at all. Your mother has lost too many bairns." Duncan wipes a tear on the sleeve of his patched denim shirt. "We've both lost too many."

Martha and Una hold a white sheet over Baby Tom's lifeless body and watch in absolute silence while their mother performs her last labor of love. Maud bathes her infant's withered body and places a pair of white socks upon his tiny cold feet.

"Una, get my pocketbook, over by the organ." Maud stares blankly at her lost child.

"Why Mama?" Una asks innocently.

Martha whispers sternly to Una, "Do as your told."

Una fetches the pocketbook and hands it to her mother who retrieves two pennies. She places one coin on each sunken eyelid. Lifting Baby Tom as one might cradle a fallen sparrow, Duncan coos a soft lullaby and tenderly places his infant's lifeless body in the wee coffin.

Colin and Robert bring in buckets full of ice from the ice hut, and Duncan sets the coffin upon the ice to preserve the body until the child can be taken to be buried. Maud, who does most everything in her life by the word of the Lord, abruptly calls up an old superstition she learned from her own mother.

"When go to the church we will pass his coffin through the front window and not through the door. His soul will never be released if we do. No child of mine will be doomed to a life of eternal damnation."

Sunday. The funeral is to be held at the Anglican Church in the hamlet of Newholm, a few miles back from the family's winter cabin where Una's family spends the long winter months. On this cool summer morning everyone takes a bath in the lake. There is no splashing or playing around. More than once, Una is told to behave. She scampers into the hut on the scow shivering and clutching to a threadbare towel.

Their funeral clothes are draped over chairs and laid out on the roughly hewn pine table. Martha immediately takes hold of a freshly ironed navy-blue dress with tiny white buttons on the collar and cuffs, a handed-me-down given to the family from a cousin in Bracebridge. Pants are set aside for Robert and Colin along with a clean white shirt for each of the boys.

Una examines the dull blue frock that Maud has set aside for her. She watches longingly while here sister fusses with the collar of her dress.

Why does Martha get the pretty dress and I get the ugly one?

Begrudgingly Una pulls the pinafore over her head. She does not complain. Baby Tom is dead.

3

September 1909

School has started once again. Una dawdles about when she knows she should be getting ready. It is her third year, grade three, and it will be Colin's last year. Duncan makes the announcement over breakfast.

"You're a man now, my boy. You'll be growing a beard before the snow flies." Duncan takes a swig of his chicory coffee.

Colin stares at the floor. His teacher had filled his head with notions of going on to the high school in Huntsville and then to university. But this morning Duncan puts an abrupt end to any aspirations Colin might have had about furthering his education.

"This is your last year my son. I'll be needing you here to help with the cargo from now on. Besides, I never went to school. And you'll get lots of learning working with me my boy. Now off you go. All of you. You too Una. And no more of me having to traipse over to Rachel Little Feathers' camp because you've run away," his voice tappers off, "like you've been doing every other day this week."

"But I don't like school." Una puts on what she thinks is her most convincingly long, sad face.

"And I dunna like shoveling the horse dung, but I do it."

"I'll try Papa, I'll try."

"No, ya dunna needs to try my little bana-phrionnsa." Duncan falls back on his brogue. "Ya needs to stay put like your sister Martha. Ya needs to respect your teacher." He taps his finger on Una's nose. "Off ye go."

"Wait," says Maud who has been quiet all morning. Like most mornings lately. She hands Una her snack. A spotted apple, a square of corn bread, and a chunk of cheddar, all neatly wrapped in a red and white scrap of fabric and held together with a length of string. "Don't forget to bring the wrap and string back Una. Don't forget."

Una heads for the door when Duncan calls after her. "What do ye say to your mother now?"

Una mumbles under her breath, "Thank you Mama."

"I canna hear ye."

"Thank you, Mama." Una bolts out the door and scrambles to catch up to her brother.

"You're lucky Colin. You won't have to go to school anymore. Wish I didn't have to go to school. I hate school."

"If I could I would trade places with you. I'd love to stay in school." Six-foot Colin picks Una up by the arm pits and twirls her around. "And stop running away. You know it upsets Mama."

At school Una's legs keep moving up and down to a jig she silently sings in her head, the one that her father plays on his fiddle most nights when he is home. Jig-a-dee-jig-a-dee-jig. Her rhythmic squirming rocks the bench and shakes the table she shares with four other girls in the front row of their classroom. A chorus of giggles interrupts the spelling lesson. Martha, who sits directly behind Una, reaches over her own desk, and shoves her sister's shoulder to get her to stop, but it is too late. Mr. Fenton turns from facing the chalk board.

"Una Campbell," snaps Mr. Fenton, a pasty looking man with a handlebar moustache, a receding hairline, and a wart on his chin. Most of his students make fun of outside of school.

"To the corner young lady." Mr. Fenton points to the back of the classroom with his yard stick. "And do not turn around. No recess for you."

Una has given her teacher nothing but grief since the day he arrived in early September. She skips to the back of the classroom. Everyone laughs. Fenton, who by now is as red as a cherry bellows, "Quiet! Get back here and walk properly."

Una sulks all the way to her seat then immediately performs a grand pirouette followed by a series of ballerina tip toe steps to the back of the classroom.

During her indoor recess punishment Una hears her classmates playing outside. Some of the girls chant, "Red rover red rover can I come over?" Boys whoop and holler as they chase a ball around the yard. Her mind is made up. When Mr. Fenton rings the bell for lunch Una will not stay to have her apple, cornbread, and cheese. She will go to be with Nokomis.

Una smells something frying long before she can see through the trees to Rachel Little Feather's camp. A branch snaps under her foot.

"I hear you Nika," calls Rachel. "You can come out of the woods now."

Una pushes through the low-lying branches.

"You run away from school again? Your mother, she not be pleased with you Nika. What we going to do with you?"

"Want some goat cheese Nokomis? And some apple?" Una moves closer. "What are you frying Nokomis? It smells good."

"Muskrat brains. You want some?" Rachel stirs them with a wooden spoon.

Una joins Rachel at her makeshift table. They do not talk while they eat. Instead, they listen to the leaves shivering in the wind. They watch the squirrels scamper for acorns, their cheeks puffed out as they stuff them into their mouths.

"Big bushy tails." Rachel is the first to speak. She wipes her face with a rag, then cleans her plate with it. She takes Una's plate and fork and puts them into a pail of cold water. "Winter will be cold Nika. Look at that fat squirrel with his big fluffy tail. He's getting ready. There will be plenty of cold days ahead. Plenty of snow too."

"How do you know that Nokomis? How do you know these things?"

"You live long like me Little Goose, you learn many things. I learn from my father and my mother, and from my grandfather and my grandmother too. I learn about trees. I learn about birds. I learn about all the animals. I listen and I watch." Rachel points to her ears, then her eyes. "You will learn this way too Nika because you no learn anything in school." She laughs and scrubs the dishes in the cold lake water.

"Nokomis," Una brings the frying pan to Rachel. "How old are you?"

"Don't know."

"Don't know?

"Don't know. I know I am older than your father. Much older. I remember time before he come here. From before when those tall pine trees reached to the sky. You should have seen it Nika. So beautiful. They grow everywhere. But now they all gone. Nothing but stumps for as far as you can see. And my mother and father they have to leave. Government man give our land away. Give our land to lots of your people even before your father come here. Then more men come from down south. They cut so many trees and make houses on the shores of our lake."

Rachel vigorously scrubs the pan.

"And them silly men, not like your father, he's a good man. He understand our ways better than most. But they come here, and they try to farm around those stumps. You can't grow turnips on a rock." Rachel laughs. "Silly men, they build fences but Mister Fox, he still eat their chickens."

"So how old are you Nokomis?"

"Older than I know. But younger than this lake."

November 1909

"He hasn't come home. You best go get your father Una."

Maud peers through the front window at the fresh dusting of snow that blew in during the night. She worries that the storm may have prevented Duncan from travelling home but suspects that he most likely got into the drink again.

"He'll be at the tavern with the other hunters."

Una heads out the door, and tramples across the snow toward the road that leads to the village. The wind has blown the snow from the puddles to reveal the thin layers of ice. Una pops the white ice bubbles under the heel of her boots.

Maud calls out, "Quit your playing games Una. Get your father. We need to move inland before we get stuck out here. Get a move on Una. No time for fooling about."

Una sprints ahead for a bit then slows her pace down when the wind bites at her cheeks. She tugs her tattered hat over her ears and tightens her brother's hand-me-down wool coat with a belt that her father used to wear when he was thinner. Her bare hands tingle from the cold. She stuffs them into the holey pockets of the clumsy coat and trudges against the stiff wind.

The tavern is over five miles away and even in good weather it takes her close to an hour to get there. Una sings a song she has heard Duncan sing many times, so many times that Una knows it by heart, and it spurs her on.

> My love she's but a lassie yet, a light-some lovely lassie yet.
> It scarce wad do to sit an' woo, down by the stream
> sae glassy
> But there's a braw time coming yet, and taste the bliss of
> loves first kiss,
> When fa's the modest gloaming yet.

More than a dozen deer hang from hooks on the wall outside of the

Baysville House. It has been a good hunting season. Several men with rifles flanking their sides stand proudly next to their trophies. A newspaper photographer has been sent down from Huntsville. He leans into the camera on the tripod, his black bowler hat tipped back on his head.

"Don't move," he shouts. "Stand still."

Una rushes up to her father. "Mama wants you to come home and take us to the winter cabin, Papa."

"Those cheeks of yours make you look like a rosy, red robin. You must be chilled to the bone," Duncan says leading Una through the tavern doors. "Come in and warm yourself up."

Una follows her father inside where a glowing fire in the hearth sends a welcome heat into the room. Una rubs her hands together, the tips of her fingers still numb. Duncan orders a whiskey and places it on the stained pine table. The men brag about the biggest bucks they ever caught followed up with one tall tale greater than the other.

Duncan boasts, "My daughter Una, she has the voice of a lark she does. Come here my girl. Sing your old Da and these gentlemen a song."

"I don't know Papa. Maybe we should go home."

"We will pet. We will. But first, sing that lovely song of yours." Duncan lifts Una up onto a chair and after much cajoling and teasing by the men Una sings.

My love she's but a lassie yet, a light-some lovely lassie.

At the end, the men applaud heartily and bang their glasses on the table for another round of drinks. One of the men brings out a mandolin and another lifts his guitar from its case. Duncan borrows a violin from the bartender. The three of them tune up.

Time disappears as they play one tune after another, jigs, reels, and a few waltzes in between. Una joins in on the chorus to songs she has heard before and tries her hand at playing the spoons. And much like her father, Una is swept up in the moment of frivolity and soon forgets that there is a harsh wind howling outside the tavern windows.

"Well, my lovely bana-phrionnsa, we'd best be on our way home." Duncan tips his chair over but catches it as he stumbles to his feet. He turns to his drinking companions. "I'll come back for the stag tomorrow."

Outside the tavern Duncan leads Una to the stables at the rear of the building. "Ya can ride behind me. Old Mac, he's a good horse," he slurs, "he knows the way home even if I don't."

Duncan pulls up on the reins to stop the horse.

"Now do hear that?" He pauses for a moment and clear as a bell the music drifts across the lake from the scow.

"It's your mother. She's playing one of her hymns on that pump organ she loves so much. Listen. What's that now?" Duncan waits. "She's playing 'Jesus Keep Me Near the Cross'. She'll be wanting to have that organ moved to Newholm for the winter. Nearly broke my back on that cursed thing when I hauled it to the scow last Spring. Ah well, I loves your mother dear. I do. And if she wants it moved, then moved it shall be."

"Papa?"

"Yes, my lovely."

"Do you think maybe I could have an instrument to play so I can join in and sing along too? Maybe a guitar or mandolin?"

"Your brother Robert wants a new lacrosse stick for Christmas. I've promised Colin a new pair of boots. His feet are bigger than mine and my old boots, well, they dunna fit him anymore. Now Martha, she wants a frilly dress. Don't you want a frilly dress too Una?"

"If I have to Papa but I really would like something to strum so I can sing with it. I really would Papa. It would be so nice."

The move to Newholm for the winter takes its toll on Duncan. For now, the scow remains empty and secured to the shore at Norway Point until the ice in the bay melts again and the sap oozes from the maple trees. Then, when the days grow longer, he will move everything back to the scow once more. For years it has been this way.

Duncan settled in Newholm long before marrying Maud. At the age of nineteen, back in Glengarry County, he had nothing to lose, no prospective girl to marry, no burdens at all. So, with an immeasurable amount of courage and a head full of dreams he secured a land grant from the federal government. Two hundred acres could be his for free on the condition that he clear enough land to construct a sixteen by twelve-foot cabin. He would have to live in it for a minimum of five years. And at any time during those years the government was allowed to come onto his land and cut down the majestic pines.

Even though he left his parents behind on the farm that hugged the shores of the St. Lawrence River, he did not abandon his Scottish brogue. He'd been born in Perthshire, Scotland and came with them when he was a lad. On the day he left for Muskoka he brought along his fiddle and a heart full of the old Gaelic ballads that he had heard at the ceilidhs.

The first few winters were long and lonely until one New Year's Day when he was invited to attend a hogmanay gathering at the Anglican Church Hall. A young woman with her strawberry blonde hair held up in bows sat quietly waiting to be asked to dance. And when Duncan offered his hand to her, her face flushed yet she did not refuse his offer. Three months later they were married and Maud, who was pregnant, moved into the shanty with Duncan.

Maud added curtains to the one window. She placed evergreen boughs outside the door for Duncan to wipe the mud off his boots, and she spread an heirloom quilt on their bed. She tried to make the shanty feel like home even though she never could get warm during those freezing winter nights. Seven months later she gave birth to Colin on their nuptial bed.

At the end of the five years the government had cut down most of the trees on Duncan's land. All that remained were a few misshapen solitary pines and acres full of stumps, a forest graveyard that Duncan was perpetually struggling to remove.

Even the smaller ones proved to be a challenge. Duncan bartered with Alexander McIntyre, a neighboring landowner who had two quarter horses. Duncan was skilled at the finer things. He had made chairs and tables for his shanty. He offered to do the same for Alexander in exchange for help to remove the stumps. Still there were many that even the horses could not unearth. It took dynamite to blast the stubborn roots out of the ground. And that left huge holes. Another job for Duncan.

He piled dozens of those stumps around the shanty and fashioned a fence to define his immediate area. The rest were heaved up in the middle of the field. They made a great bonfire for the summer solstice. Folks came from miles around. They'd never seen such a blaze. They were sure that Duncan's place had burned down. But no. Duncan was just that kind of man. Bigger than life. Like the stories he told. Like the stories Una loved to hear.

Every attempt that Duncan made at gardening failed. The soil was too shallow for growing crops and any effort to raise livestock proved to be a disaster. Over the years he'd witnessed most of his neighbors giving up and moving away. But not Duncan. He saw this as an opportunity to start anew. This was his home. Besides, he had a wife and baby boy to look after.

Duncan possessed a charm that secured him a contract from a local lumber company. They engaged him to transport building supplies for the incursion of people moving north from Toronto. He bought the scow and erected a hut that they could live in. The following year he began building a house for his family in Newholm. It took years to complete and when it was done, the original shanty became a shed for goats and chickens.

December 1911

It has been snowing for several days and the drifts have grown higher than the downstairs windows and doors. The only option to go outside is for Duncan to crawl out of the upper storey window and jump down into the snow to clear a pathway to the front door.

When he finally comes through the front door, he is covered from head to toe in chunks of snow and ice. Stamping his boots on the mat, he declares, "We won't be going to church this Sunday."

Una skips joyfully across the living room floor. She finds the sermons long and tedious. Once, when she fell asleep Maud was not pleased. Another time Una asked, "I don't understand? How can you get every animal in the world in one boat?"

"It's God's word," answered Maud emphatically.

Duncan leaned over and whispered in Una's ear, "Oh, it's just a lovely story."

Last year at the baptism of her new baby sister, Beth, Reverend Wright gently poured holy water on Beth's head three times and blessed her with the cross. All the while Maud feared her newest child would cry out, but she did not. It was Una who was bawling.

"Robert hit me," Una shrieked, the blood from her nose dripping onto her white blouse.

Apparently, Colin and Robert, who were sitting in the pew on either side of Una, started pulling punches at each other. Robert accidentally smacked Una in the nose. When Una cried out Martha merely moved further down the pew.

Maud grimaced. After the final 'Amen' she handed Baby Beth to Duncan and marched swiftly down the aisle while hauling Una by the collar and escorting her outside the church.

"You're nothing but a source of embarrassment. You never do what you're told to do, and you're constantly acting out."

Una tried to explain what had happened. When Maud refused to listen, Duncan spoke up, "It's not her fault. The boys were roughhousing."

"So why didn't you do something?" Maud's anger was festering like an ingrown toenail. She did not give Duncan a chance to say another word.

"It's just like you. Always covering for her. You, making promises and never keeping them. Some days I don't know why I ever married you, Duncan Campbell. And Una is no daughter of mine. She's your daughter. You can look after her from now on. I'm finished."

Sundays at home are dull as door nails, Una mulls. *There's no playing card games, no tossing jacks, and no indoor ball bouncing. Mother won't even let us go skating.*

Duncan in his inevitable charismatic way takes Maud by the waist and spins her around. "Let the children clear the snow off the ice today so that it's ready for tomorrow. Shoveling is not playing Maudie my love. The fresh air will do them good."

And it did.

Later that afternoon Una sits at the kitchen table strumming the mandolin she got for Christmas a couple of years ago. She hums a tune she's heard the lumbermen sing at the Baysville House. The steel strings vibrate into the wooden soundboard sending shimmering tones against her chest.

> Oh, mother dear, I'm sweet sixteen and Billy the river driver,
> Has asked me if I'd marry him, he wants to be my lover,
> He is so manly, strong and brave, tomorrow he'll come over,
> To take me for a pleasant walk across the fields of clover.

Maud has heard enough. She slams the butcher knife on the cutting board with such force that it bounces back and cuts the end of her index finger. Blood drips onto the turnips.

"You know it's Sunday. You know you're not to be singing such songs. You ought not to be singing them any time. You're only eleven Una." Maud wraps her apron around the bleeding finger. "And now look what you've made me do."

Martha runs over to comfort her mother while looking back at Una as if to say, *you know that your music gets her upset.*

Colin and Robert wisely keep to themselves. At moments like this everyone can easily be blamed for things they didn't even do. Silence is best kept until Maud speaks again. But then the quiet is suddenly broken by the muffled mewing of goats and the distinct shrieks of guinea fowl in the shed adjacent to the house.

The previous summer Robert had convinced his parents that they needed to have a few goats, for the milk. "I'll manage them," he said, "Feed them, clean out the shed." And when they agreed he also suggested that they get chickens. His mother and father tried to reason with him telling him that most folks in the area had lost their chickens to invading foxes. But Robert, being a clever lad, already had a plan.

"Guinea fowl," he explained, "We'll get them too. They put up such a racket. We'd know if a fox comes around." And he went on about a classmate whose guinea hen attacked a fox to defend her brood of chicks. "Pecked its eyes right out."

"Something bad is going on over there boys." Duncan puts on his coat. "We'd best get to digging our way over to the shed. Colin, grab the water bucket. Robert, you get the roasting pan."

Maud stands frozen in time, her mouth agape at the notion that her roasting pan is about to become a shovel. "And how do you suppose I'm to roast the chicken for supper?"

"Now Maudie, my love. I know you is some upset, your finger and all, but you know we have no choice. If there be a fox in the shed, you can say good-bye to all those fresh eggs now can't you, my love." Duncan always has a soothing way of calming Maud's frantic outbursts and when he kisses her, she gives him a sideways smile.

It takes most of the morning for Duncan and the boys to clear a path to the shed. Inside they look around the cages, in the corners, and under the bench. No trace of a fox. Not even a paw print. What has triggered the cacophony are the two female goats in desperate need of milking. Their extreme discomfort had caused them to bleat and bawl repetitively. That induced the guinea fowl to chant "buck-wheat-buck-wheat-see-chee-chee", and this in turn set off the chickens who, according to Duncan, just wanted to be part of the choir.

Robert is the first to return to the house. He brings in a bucket filled with fresh milk. Next comes Colin with several eggs in the roasting pan, and finally Duncan comes in wearing a grin.

Maud, who is seated at the pump organ calls out, "Gather 'round. Beth sit still on Martha's lap. Una stand beside me, and boys, you can take your places on the other side of the organ."

"I'll be outside clearing more snow." Even though he loves music Duncan has cleverly found a way to escape the hymn singing this Sunday. "I'll bring in more firewood."

"I'll lend a hand," offers Colin.

"No," says Maud, "you need to join in. You have such a lovely tenor voice for the harmonies and Robert, you sing tenor too. Martha, you sing alto with me, and Una, you're the soprano."

For once Maud has chosen to play a hymn that Una likes.

> Shall we gather at the river
> Where bright angel feet have trod
> With its crystal tide forever
> Flowing by the throne of God?
> Yes, we'll gather at the river
> The beautiful, the beautiful river
> Gather with the saints at the river
> That flows by the throne of God.

On this beautiful winter afternoon of warm sunshine and fresh air Rachel Little Feathers and Una shuffle their way across the field to where they have set up the rabbit snares. Their snowshoes crunch against the crisp snow.

"The snow is covered in sparkling diamonds," Una calls back to Rachel.

"We wait here," gasps Rachel, "Listen. Hear the wind whistling in the trees." Rachel's chest wheezes.

"You okay Nokomis?" Una asks. "You've been coughing a lot lately."

"This way." Rachel points. "The traps are over by the pine trees. You go. I follow."

A flutter from a nearby tree startles Una. She looks up at the canopy of snow laden branches. A light dust of white flakes falls onto her eyelashes just as a cedar waxwing takes to flight.

"Any rabbits?" Again, Rachel coughs and spits the green sputum onto the snow.

"Not this time," Una says. "We should rest now. You're not well Nokomis. I'm worried."

"You no worry. I have special tea. It make me better. You no worry Little Goose."

Inside Rachel's shack the air is so thick and grey that even Una finds it hard to breath. When Rachel built her ramshackle home, she made a fire pit in the floor and cut a hole in the layers of the tar paper roof to serve as a vent for the smoke to escape. Still much of it hovers within the flimsy walls.

"I put spruce on the fire." Rachel Little Feathers tosses a branch onto the smoldering embers. Sparks shoot up toward the flimsy ceiling. "This cleans the air. Smells good. Here drink this." Rachel's voice rasps as she hands Una a chipped china cup filled with white cedar tea. "I find this in the dump. Pretty pink roses. Why someone throw it away I don't know."

"Miigwech, thank you." Una wraps her hands around the warm cup. "I am worried Nokomis. Your cough is getting worse. You need to go to the village. You need to see the doctor."

"Nokomis is her own doctor." Rachel sips her steaming tea. "I take care of myself. I no need those medicines. They will kill me. They will kill me like they kill my husband after his leg get cut in the woods."

"I will ask Papa to take you. I will go too," offers Una.

"No, Nika. I stay here."

"But it's getting colder and what if there is too much snow. What if I can't come and help you."

Rachel stirs the cinders with a stick. "You want to have some fish? Some bass? I smoke them last week. They taste real good and salty."

"Yes, please."

"You polite girl Nika. Always please and thank you. Your mother, she must be proud."

Una does not answer.

My mother is not proud of me. Martha is her favorite. I try to please her, but it doesn't make any difference. Some days I wish I had been born a boy. Maybe that would make her happy.

"I have no children Nika. My belly did not welcome a baby." Rachel rocks gently back and forth. "I tell you that many times past. Many times. But you are a gift to me Little Goose. I bring you into this world. I hold you in my arms. I give you goat milk when your mother cannot feed you hers. I tell you my stories. You are my shadow daughter. You are my - "

Una sees the tears welling in Nokomis' eyes.

"I love you Nokomis."

"Gaye niin Nika. I love you too."

Together they watch the embers of the fire and tell one another what they see. Wolf, frog, snake, eagle.

4

May 1912

The last of the winter ice has melted away beneath the warming sun. Una sits on the scow gazing into the stillness of the water. Calm. Even before the ice was out of the bay Una's family moved back to the barge, and now on this fresh morning, Una senses the turning of the season. She smells the dank manure emanating from a nearby field and out on the lake she hears the familiar warble of mating loons.

Why do I look so strange? Una cocks her head and stares at her own reflection. *Why am I so skinny?* She touches herself and feels the tiny changes in her breasts. Growing.

Suddenly, some ten feet out from the scow, a hand pushes ripples into Una's dream time. Mesmerized, Una watches the bloated, ivory-colored hand bob back and forth at the end of a man's distorted body.

At first she thinks she is imaging things, like when she sees faces in the rocks, and creatures in the ferns, but then it strikes her. This is not her imagination. It is a man floating face down, his arms and legs swollen and grotesque. Una is not frightened. Just curious.

Where did he come from? How did he die? Who is he?

"Look, look in the water," Una shouts.

"Look at what?" says Martha who sits braiding her hair.

"Water snakes going under the scow again?" Maud says while peeling potatoes and carrots.

"No, Mama. It's a man. A dead man."

Martha drops her comb and shrieks, "Oh my God, oh my God, oh my God." She rushes to see the lifeless body rolling in the water.

Maud comes over and looks down at the floating corpse.

"Lord Almighty Good Gracious Jesus of Nazareth there is a curse upon this household. Una fetch your father. Why that man has to go to the tavern every day is beyond me. Good grief Martha, at least you could have brought your breakfast up somewhere else other than on my shoes. Una don't stand there staring at him. Have some pity on the poor man's soul. Oh Jesus, Jesus, Jesus."

The account of the dead man's body washing up against the Campbell's scow made for good storytelling all that spring. Rumors of a jealous lover drowning a man because of a dispute over a pretty girl in the village circulated around the tavern. Parents warned that his disfigured ghost would come back to haunt children who wandered in the woods or stayed out too late at night. Some even swore he was an evil Wendigo who deserved to die.

Truth was that loner Old Joe McMillan, after imbibing too much whiskey at the Baysville House last winter, had tried to cross the lake to get to his cabin. But there had been an early thaw and Old Joe had slipped under the ice.

Apparently Old Joe didn't have any family to speak of, so the church community took it upon themselves to give him a proper burial. Some folks, like Maud, strongly objected.

"Who knows if he was even baptized. Besides, he never set foot in this church."

"Now Maudie," Duncan cooed, "Where's your charitable spirit?"

After the funeral Una dreamed of Old Joe for weeks. Sometimes he was all ugly and puffy and doing weird things like picking flowers or strumming a one-stringed guitar. Other times he was just the same Old Joe except he was spitting tobacco into a blueberry pie. None of it made any sense to Una and it bothered her that he wouldn't go away. Until one night.

Old Joe was standing at the end of her bed. And it wasn't a dream. Una sat up. Old Joe looked happy. When Una spoke to him, he slowly faded away like fog on the lake. From that moment on Old Joe never came back.

When Una told her mother of the visitation, Maud simply said, "You've got too vivid an imagination for your own good. Nobody sees ghosts. Nobody."

June 1912

"Everything is changing Nokomis." Una slumps on the crude bench beside Rachel's shack. "Colin has moved out. He lives in Baysville now. In a rooming house with the other lumbermen, and Robert has a job on the railroad. Martha only talks about William Banting. He's three years older than she is." Una draws circles in the dirt with a stick. "And he has a big nose. A really big, ugly nose."

Rachel Little Feathers slowly weaves a sweet grass basket with her gnarled fingers. When she speaks her lungs wheeze, and her voice sounds gravelly and rough.

"You like woodpecker bird Nika?"

"Yes, but..."

"Woodpecker bird got really big beak." Rachel clears her throat and spits on the ground. "Big beak helps woodpecker bird get ants from trees."

"I see," Una smiles at Rachel. "We are all different for different reasons."

For a long while Una and Rachel sit in the comfort of each other's silence. Una sorts stones she has found washed up on the shore. Some are smooth, and shiny when wet. One looks as if it has specks of gold on it and another is full of diamond-like shards.

"Look at this one Nokomis. There's a fish on it." Una hands the flat stone to Rachel.

"This fish stone tells a long-ago story." Rachel passes it back to Una. "Very special stone. You keep it safe."

Una tucks the stones into a small deerskin bag that Rachel helped her sew together. "Is it true what they say, Nokomis? Is there a monster in the lake?"

"What have you been told?"

"Papa says it's a really big fish, like they have in Scotland, like the Loch Ness monster. It tips over canoes with its tail, and it has ruby red eyes that glow at night. He saw it once under a full moon and he told me that it's longer than our scow. Is it true? Is there a monster in the lake or is Papa telling me one of his fairy stories again?"

"Maybe it is true. Maybe it is not true." Rachel coughs and rests a moment to catch her breath. "What is most important is what you believe to be true."

"I tell you what my grandmother tell to me, and her grandmother tell to her. There is a great water lynx in our lake. We call it Mishipeshu. It is big like dragon, and it has horns on its head. It has a long tail covered in scales and big paws like a cat. Mishipeshu uses his long tail and big paws to make rapids and whirlpools. And he breaks the ice in the winter."

"Maybe this monster drowned Old Joe?"

"Maybe Nika. Who knows? Mishipeshu been here a long, long time. Maybe even before your fish rock was made. Only one thing scares Mishipeshu. Thunderbird. But that is another story and I need to rest now. We rest.

Unsayable Absence

By the time Una arrives back home the sun is already setting beyond the horizon sending majestic colors streaming through the clouds, streaks of crimson, turquoise and rose.

Everyone has turned in for the night. Everyone except Duncan. Una sees that his horse isn't hitched to the tree on the shore. A fresh breeze wafts across the lake and blows Una's hair from her face. A quiet moment.

Papa must be at the tavern. I wonder what songs they're singing. Why Mama is so unhappy? Martha says it's because Papa made promises he couldn't keep. I don't know. I just wish I could make her happy. I try to make her happy. I do.

A loon calls for its mate to come into the shelter of the bay for the night. Una holds her hands to her mouth and blows a trill to the loon. She listens. Waits. Again, it sings a quaver that rises up toward the first evening star.

Una hears sobbing coming from inside the hut. Cautiously she opens the screen door and peers into the dimly lit room. Her mother leans against the organ, her head buried in her arms.

Crying? Mama never cries.

Una stands motionless beside her mother not knowing what to say or what to do. Maud abruptly straightens up and wipes her eyes and nose on a rag that she then tucks under the sleeves of her blouse.

"Mama? You okay Mama?"

"Una. You shouldn't sneak up on people like that. Your sisters are sleeping. Don't wake them up."

"What's wrong Mama?" Una whispers. "Why are you crying?" Una sees something in her mother's eyes. Something she has never seen before.

"It's nothing," Maud says as she stands up. "You should have been home long before this. How many times have I told you to be home before dark? It's dangerous. You know there have been bear sightings this Spring and they're hungry. They've got cubs."

Suddenly Maud sits back on the bench. "Dear God, not again, not again."

"Mama? What is it Mama? Tell me. What's wrong?"

"I'm with child. Another child, Una. One day you will have to be very careful. Very careful not to have this happen to you. I am too old for babies. Too old."

That night sleep does not come easy to Una. *Why is Mama so upset about having another baby? Mama's not that old.*

After a while Una hears her father's footsteps land heavily on the scow. He trips over a pail and stumbles through the screen door. He slurs as he sings, 'Oh my darling Clementine'.

From her cot behind the curtain Una hears her father kick off his boots. He mumbles cooing words to Maud as he rustles his way under her blanket.

"Oh, my sweet lovely."

"Not now Duncan, not now," her mother pleads.

Her father chants repeatedly, "Oh, my sweet lovely."

Then no words at all. Nothing but the steady thumping of the bed as it hits the wall over and over again. A huge moan. A sigh.

"Oh, my sweet lovely."

Una, her hair still tangled from her fitful night, slowly saunters toward the kitchen table. The smell of frying bacon has awakened her. Bacon, a rare treat for the Campbell household. And her father is doing the cooking. Another unusual occurrence.

Maud sits at the organ playing a melancholy air, singing softly.

> Pity from Thine eye let fall,
> By a look my soul recall;
> Now the stone to flesh convert,
> Cast a look, and break my heart.

"Come to the table Maudie my love. Breakfast is served."

Duncan is in fine spirits and shares the tittle-tattle he picked up the at the tavern the previous day. "Ian McDougal saw a black bear and her two cubs eating raspberries back of Brunel. He tried to shoot them, but they ran into the woods."

Duncan takes a bite of his toast and mumbles with his mouth full, "Looks like Sam McKay got himself a new banjo, but he can't play it worth a darn."

And a bit later he adds, "Finnegan built a still up back of his place. Heaven help those who drink that rot gut brew. It'll kill you fast as lightning."

Maud remains unusually subdued. As is Una. Martha excuses herself from the table and takes little Beth outside to look for worms to use as fishing bait.

"And they're still finding bodies from that Titanic ship. That ship, you remember, the luxury liner, I told you about it. It struck an iceberg. Sank like a stone. You remember me telling you don't you Maudie?"

Maud pushes back from the table. "Una help me clean up these dishes."

"Well, my lovelies," Duncan says grabbing his cap, "I best be getting the tug ready to take us across the lake. Them folks from the south are expecting a delivery of these logs today. That old steam tug has been acting up again. Should never have bought it used from the lumber company. At any rate, it's probably the pistons that needs some adjusting. Don't want to end up half way cross the bay, now do we."

Duncan leans over to kiss Maud on the cheek and when she ducks out of the way he gives her a love pat on the backside. "Cheer up Maudie. Looks like a sunny day ahead."

Outside Una washes the dishes in the lake water while Maud sits nearby sewing a patch on the knee of an old pair of Duncan's threadbare coveralls.

"Mama," Una starts.

"No need to talk about it, Una."

Una kicks at a piece of wood.

"You can go now, Una. I know where you'll be. With Rachel. Your father and I have to cross the lake, but we'll be back before dinner."

"Mama?"

"What now Una?"

"It's Nokomis. She's sick Mama. She has a horrible cough, and she can't breathe very well. Sometimes when we do things we have to stop and wait for her breath to come back. I'm worried, Mama. She won't go to a doctor. I've asked her to go but she says no because of what happened to her husband. I don't know what to do."

Maud sets the sewing aside and stands up. "I have an idea. Come."

Una follows her mother into the hut. On the shelf above the organ there are four books, a bible, two hymnals, and 'Enquire Within Upon Everything'. Maud pulls the book down and opens it to the back. She reads aloud, "Lodger, lotions, lumbago."

"Lumbago? What's lumbago?" Una asks.

"Pain in your muscles and joints, and by my age Una you will be full of lumbago like I am." Maud continues looking down the list. "Here we have it. Lungs, inflammation, remedy, see item 590."

"Where did you learn to read Mama. You didn't go to school."

"My mother taught me how to read the bible when I was your age or maybe a bit younger. It was a long time ago. Here, see what it says. Can you read Una?"

"A little."

"Then go ahead. Turn to item 590. What does it say?"

I hope I can do this. I don't want Mama to be upset.

Una carefully sounds out each word:

"'For in-flam-ma-tion of the lung avoid heavy smoke and damp sur-roun-dings. Pre-pare a de, de-mul, de-mul-cent'. Demulcent? I don't know what that is."

"A healing mixture. Go on."

"Please read it for me Mama."

Maud takes the book from Una. "'Prepare a demulcent of three parts: Peppermint, Marshmallow Root, and Echinacea. All aid in reducing mucus and inflammation. Steep together in boiling water. Add honey.'"

Maud looks up from the book. "I will ask your father to take you to Eva Stanton's place. She knows all the herbs and what they do. Hopefully, she can be of some help. But Una, Rachel is very old. I am not sure that any of this will do any good."

5

July 1913

With its lush spring garden and white picket fence Eva Stanton's house in Baysville stands apart from the other houses on the street. Una walks up the brick pathway past the ivy-covered trellis toward the wooden steps that are painted sky blue. In front of a canary yellow screen door a calico cat suns itself on a circular braided mat.

Una reaches down to pet the cat when the door opens. A tall, graceful woman with flowing white hair steps out onto the porch.

"May I help you?"

Una remains motionless, still dazzled by the unusual attractiveness of the cottage and the sudden presence of this eccentric woman. Eva Stanton dons a calf length floral dress, the likes of which Una has never seen before, not even at church.

"Azalea seems to like you," Eva says encouragingly.

Una blinks and looks around, realizing that she has been staring at her.

"Azalea is a funny name for a cat."

"I suppose it is. Puss here was born under the Azalea bush in my backyard. So, I naturally called her Azalea. Perhaps you know that the azalea is a flowering shrub in the genus Rhododendron. It belongs to the family Ericaceae?"

Eva senses that Una does not understand. She continues almost apologetically, "They bloom beautifully in the shade. Would you care to come in and join me for that cup of tea? It's rose-hip, and with a dab of honey it tastes heavenly. Besides, it is full of nutrients that ward off those nasty colds. So? Tea?"

"Yes, please." Una is in awe of this woman's peculiar prattle and strange mannerisms. "I've never had rose-hip tea before."

Eva holds open the screen door to the foyer. "Down the hall to your right." Una steps gingerly onto the plush, patterned rug that covers the shiny hardwood floor of the richly decorated parlor.

Noticing this Eva explains, "It comes from Marrakesh. My uncle brought it over after one of his adventures abroad.

Una runs her hand along the top of an oddly shaped sofa with only half a back.

"Nothing like a chaise lounge. I love stretching out on it while reading." Eva gestures. "This way. Let's sit in the kitchen, shall we?"

Eva reaches for a large kettle burbling on the electric stove. She pours the steaming water into a china tea pot with fire breathing dragons on it. "There. We'll let it steep."

"Oh, let me clear away some of these herbs from the table. So messy. I've been sorting through them and selecting the best buds and leaves for some of my special recipes. Now, I've completely forgotten my proper etiquette. What is your name my child?"

"Una Campbell, my name is Una, daughter of Duncan and Maud."

"Yes, of course, you look quite a bit like your father. He owns the scow at Norway Point, doesn't he? Delivers lumber to the Sanatorium? I hear they are adding a new wing. So, why have you come to see me?"

Una hands a sealed envelope to Eva. "It's from my mother but she says

I shouldn't ask you what it's for, and that you would know what to give her to make her feel better. But you know Miss Stanton, Mama doesn't seem sick to me."

Eva slips the envelope into the pocket on her dress.

"But that's not why I've come."

"Yes?"

"My friend is very, very sick. She coughs all the time, and she wheezes and finds it hard to breathe. She won't see a doctor and Mama thinks you might be able to help. You might have something to make her get better."

"It is a shame when a young person becomes so gravely ill." Eva pours the rose-colored tea into two delicate china cups. She offers the honey to Una who takes a heaping teaspoon and stirs it awkwardly with the ornate silver spoon.

Una grasps the teacup in her hands and not by the delicate handle. When she sees that Miss Stanton's perplexed look she inelegantly sets it back down in the saucer and sits up straight. Again, she lifts the cup by the handle and holds it precariously between her thumb and index finger.

Eva smiles. "You were telling me about your young friend."

"She's not a young person Miss Stanton. She's old. It's Rachel Little Feathers."

Startled, Eva drops her spoon onto her saucer. "You are friends with Rachel Little Feathers?"

"I call her Nokomis because she has always been like a grandmother to me, and I am really worried." Una lowers her head to her chest.

Eva speaks tenderly, "I would not be here if it hadn't been for Rachel coming to my mother's bedside when she was in labor with me. I was breached and Rachel knew how to turn me around inside my mother's womb. There were no doctors in the village back when I was born."

Eva takes a sip of her tea. "The people of this village, particularly some of those so-called righteous men, kept taunting her and chasing her away. Finally, she stopped coming to help with the births in the village."

"Can you make something for her Miss Stanton?"

"I may have the right mixture. If it's not too late."

"Is there a cost? Mama gave me some money. I hope it is enough."

"It won't cost anything for Rachel Little Feathers. I owe my life to her."

"Go through here." Eva points to the pantry at the rear of the kitchen. "It leads to the back yard. You can wait for me there. I need to look up a few things in my herb book."

Standing at the oak bureau Eva fills a paper bag with seeds from a round wooden bowl.

"Scatter these under the pine tree for the goldfinch and the sparrows. They might even sing for you. They do for me. And if you are ever so still and hold a few seeds in your hand they might feed from your palm."

Una is amazed at all the items that fill up the pantry. Sweetgrass baskets of varying shapes and sizes hang from the ceiling, and bundles of herbs dry on the cross beams. The air is saturated with the aromatic scent of sage, peppermint, and lavender. Some plants hang in the window while braids of garlic adorn each side. Floor to ceiling shelves are filled with every manner of crockery, and so many jars, all with detailed labels. Una stops. She attempts to read one of the labels. *Matricaria, Chamomilla, Roris Marini.*

Suddenly Una is aware that Eva is standing beside her. "Roris marini? That's Latin for rosemary."

"Latin?"

"Ah, yes. It is a very ancient language but if you have been taught by nuns, you get to learn Latin, which coincidentally has come in very handy when studying the medicinal powers of herbs. My, but the nuns would be ever so disappointed in me."

"I don't understand."

"Let's leave that for another time. Aren't you going to feed the birds? I'm sure they're waiting. I won't be long."

Una finds the garden as fascinating as the interior of the house. Tiny wooden bird houses painted in brilliant colors hang from the bough of a maple tree. Una looks at an ornate bird bath.

I wonder if she washes her hands in it. What else is it for?

A marble bust of a bulging-eyed woman with snakes in her hair, and her tongue sticking out sits atop pedestal. Una reads the carved letters. *Me-du-sa. Medusa? I'd hate to meet the real Medusa. Maybe Miss Stanton put her here to scare away the crows.*

Shimmering golden fish swim up to the surface of the garden pond. Una examines their huge mouths that pulsate at the surface. *You don't look like any fish I've ever seen. Are you begging for food or throwing me fish kisses?*

Walking around Una admires several flowering shrubs. She saunters over to a tiny square garden filled with pegs stuck into the ground. Each one bears a label. In a sunny open space is a strange flat metal disc with a fin sticking up in the air. It casts a shadow on the numbers around the perimeter of the disc. *This is very, very strange. Maybe Miss Stanton uses it to count her flowers.*

Una reaches into the paper bag and tosses the seeds on the ground. In a matter of seconds several small birds flutter out from the bushes and down from the trees.

You've been waiting for this, haven't you?

Una extends her hand, keeping as still as possible. She waits for a bird to nibble the few seeds in her palm. Nothing happens. Again, she tosses them on the ground and watches the birds flit about.

I'm not giving up.

Una reaches out a second time, offering more kernels to any brave bird willing to come to her. Magically, a sparrow lands on her thumb and pecks at a few seeds. Flutters away. Comes back again. *Looking for seconds are you my little friend?*

Una spends the rest of the afternoon with Eva Stanton. She listens to Eva's stories about her trips to England, and how she used to teach school in the log schoolhouse outside of Baysville until they hired a Mr. Percival to replace her.

At the piano Eva plays music for Una. She has never heard such intricate melodies and rhythms before and is drawn into the music in an inexplicable way.

Eva explains, "That one was composed by Mozart and the one before that was written by Beethoven."

"Where do they live?" Una asks naively.

"They lived long ago, in Europe." Eva responds kindly, "Their music has lasted for centuries."

The clock on the mantle chimes four times.

"I have to go, Miss Stanton. Papa is waiting for me at the tavern. Mama will be wondering where we are."

Eva goes to the herb pantry and brings back a plain paper bag.

"This is for Rachel Little Feathers. I've mixed several herbs that should help her cough up the mucus and reduce the inflammation. Put a spoonful in a pot and pour boiling water over it. If it gets too strong you can add honey. Do say hello from me, although by now she may not remember who I am."

Eva then gives Una a tightly sealed blue package. "And this one is for your mother. Make sure you don't lose this. I rarely make it for anyone."

Una puts both bags into a burlap sack that she slings over her shoulder.

"Before you leave, I was wondering if you might like to come back some time and help me with my herbs?"

"I'd like that," Una hesitates slightly, "very much."

"I know, it's a bit of a hike. I have an old bicycle that I'm not using. You can have it, Una. It's out back."

Una's eyes open wide. She races through the pantry and into the back yard where the bright green bicycle rests against the white picket fence.

"I think I will walk with this for a while. I'll try riding it when I get home," Una says excitedly. "I've never had such a beautiful thing in my life."

Una starts to move away from the house, stops, and calls back over her shoulder, "Thank you Miss Stanton. Thank you for the tea and the bird feed and the music and the bicycle and for the herbs and everything."

"You are most welcome Una," Eva laughs with a light musical trill. "Next time I expect to see you arriving on your bicycle. By the way I brought it back from England. Everyone rides over there. I have a new ladies' roadster being shipped over. Perhaps we can ride together when it arrives?"

Eva walks closer to Una and whispers seriously, "The remedy for your mother is extremely powerful. It could make her very sick before she gets better. Try not to worry."

At the tavern Duncan tells Una to go ahead, to give the bicycle a try. "Tell your mother, I'll be home shortly."

Una awkwardly straddles the bicycle, and after much waddling and swerving manages to balance and steer the two-wheeler with ease. The rush of the wind on her face sets her heart racing faster than her legs can pump the pedals.

When she arrives at the scow, she leans the bicycle against the back of the hut. The smell of a ham stew makes her mouth water.

"Mama. Mama. What are you cooking? It smells delicious. I'm so hungry. Miss Stanton gave me a bicycle and I rode it home. I rode a bicycle Mama."

Maud swiftly jerks around from stirring the pot. "Do you have it? Do you have what I asked you to get?"

Una hands her mother the sealed bag. "What is it for Mama?"

"Una, it is better not to ask questions when there is no answer to be given."

August 1913

Una sits on the stoop of Eva Stanton's house, Azalea curled up at her ankles. "Today," she says to the cat, "when Miss Stanton returns from doing her errands, I'm going to help with the herb garden." The warmth of the mid-morning sun shines down on Una. She covers her eyelids with her hands and presses down on them with each palm. Sparkling stars dance across the midnight black behind her eyes. Bright sun, black world, bright sun, black world. Una colors her morning.

No one ever talks about it. The abortion. They think I don't know what happened.

But Una cannot erase the haunting memory. After the expulsion of the fetus from her mother's womb it was never discussed. Una helped wash the blood-stained sheets in the lake. No one said a word. Her mother moaned through the night until finally she lay in her bed, ashen, withdrawn, and solemn. Una fed her mother spoonfuls of broth until she was strong enough to come to the table, her body ravaged by the experience.

Why did Mama do this? It's a sin, isn't it? She was so sick, so sick. I thought she might die. She doesn't play the pump organ anymore, not even on Sundays. At least we don't have to go to church. That's fine with me. Mama doesn't make us say our prayers at bedtime, and these days we sometimes don't say grace before dinner. Mama just sits at the table staring at nothing. I've tried to talk to her about it. But she doesn't say a word. It's as if it didn't happen, but it did. We all know it did. Even Papa knows. That must be why he goes to the tavern every day. He's always drunk when he comes home.

A bicycle bell startles Una. She opens her eyes and sees Eva Stanton riding down the street on her new roadster bicycle. Her mid-calf length burgundy dress billows out like a sail, and the brim of her floppy straw hat flips back off her face.

"Isn't it lovely," Miss Stanton says as she pedals up to the front gate. "It's called 'The Kew Flier'. I swear it must have flown across the ocean all the way from Bristol in a hot air balloon."

The wicker basket on the front handlebars overflows with packages of meat, eggs, milk, butter, and cheese. Una hopes she stopped by the village bakery to bring back fresh butter tarts or cinnamon rolls. Always a Saturday treat between chores.

"I have a special task for you today," Miss Stanton beams. "I'd like you to gather some dandelion greens. They make a lovely summer beverage."

By mid-morning Una has collected a huge bundle of dandelion leaves which she proudly dumps on the kitchen table.

"Excellent foraging Una," Miss Stanton says picking through the greens. "We have enough for a salad as well. The kettle has just boiled." She places a handful into her dragon teapot and pours hot water over them. "Let's set this aside for a few moments."

After a short while Eva serves the cooling beverage over ice chunks from the icebox. Eva takes a sip. "Just right for a hot summer afternoon," says Eva Stanton.

"Just right," echoes Una whose face reveals a slight pucker of the lips. "I think it could use a bit more honey."

Eva Stanton teaches Una how to tell what weeds to toss away and what weeds are useful. In return for her help around the garden, Eva gives Una lessons on the piano. It doesn't take long for her to play simple melodies - "My Bonnie Lies Over the Ocean" and "London Bridges". Sometimes Miss Stanton encourages Una to try to pick out tunes on her own.

"You have a good ear," she says. "Music must live in her heart."

Una rarely goes home, except to sleep. Sometimes she stays overnight at Miss Stanton's. And lately at the end of each day Una makes another excuse not to leave.

"It is too dark to ride my bicycle back to the scow now. If I stay overnight, I can help you sort herbs for that special order first thing in the morning."

Truth is Una enjoys the comforts of the fresh linen on the brass bed, the indoor running water, and especially the indoor toilet.

After dinner one night Eva tells Una that the house belonged to her parents. "It was their summer home. They called it 'The Cumberland'. That's an elaborate garden in London near to where my father worked as a banker before emigrating to Toronto. He was sent to Canada to head up the city's Bank of British North America. And when he retired my parents moved up here permanently."

"Where are they now?" Una asks innocently.

"They passed away. My father first. I guess that was about six years ago, and my mother died shortly after that. I'm their only child so 'The Cumberland' was left to me." Eva points to a portrait of her parents above the fireplace. "I still miss them."

"Why aren't you married?"

Eva smiles despite the embarrassment of Una's question. "I was in love. Once. That was in England. I was studying English Literature at Oxford. When I told Arthur that I wanted to return to Canada to care for my aging parents, he chose not to come with me."

"Do you miss him?"

"Not now. I have everything I need right here. The house, my garden, Azalea, and a helpful young woman who asks too many questions."

Una's eyebrows lift. *Young woman? Miss Stanton called me a young woman.*

"We've had a wonderful day. It's not quite dark yet. Do you want to stay over?"

"If I may. Yes, I'd like that."

Early the next morning Miss Stanton marches into the kitchen and announces, "I've bought a newspaper."

Una sits at the breakfast table, still in her nightgown. Her hair is a tangled mess, and her eyes are only half open.

"Thank goodness the Baysville House has "The Mail and Empire" sent up by rail from Toronto. Even if it does take two days to get here, it's better than not getting the news at all." She waves the newspaper vigorously in the air then unfurls it and reads the headline to Una.

"*Suffragette Killed by King's Horse at Derby*".

"Una, this is intolerable. When will we women ever share the same human rights as men?"

"What happened?"

"Emily Wilding Davison. Surely you have heard of her. She's the leader of women's rights in England. Good God, what a sacrifice. To think that she would offer up her life."

"I'm sorry Miss Stanton but I don't know this person. We don't have newspapers at home unless my brother Colin comes for a visit. He reads the news to us, but he's never mentioned her. What is her name?"

"Emily Wilding Davison."

"Why would she be on a racetrack? She must have known that it wouldn't have been a safe thing to do. Wouldn't she have known that?"

"Of course, she knew exactly what she was doing. Miss Davison is a suffragette." Eva sits beside Una at the kitchen table. "Look at this photograph." Eva places the paper on the table and slides it toward Una. "She was doing this for us, Una, for women like you and me. According to the report she tried to cross the track at the wrong time. But that is absolute rubbish. Her heroic action has finally brought attention to the plight of our sex. But at what cost?"

Eva slams her hands on the newspaper. "I must write my university friends in England. They will give me a more honest account of her tragic demise than this prejudiced report claims as the truth."

"What did you mean when you called her, what was it, a sufla, a sulfagret?"

Eva gathers her composure. "Suffragettes are those of us who believe in the emancipation of women. We consider it our equal right that we should be allowed to vote the same way that men are allowed to vote, men like your father, and like your brothers."

Una furrows her brow. "I don't understand. Why can't we vote?"

"Precisely, why shouldn't we be allowed to add our mark to the ballot."

6

Autumn 1914

One day I am going to take a ride on that steamboat. I, Una Campbell, do solemnly swear that I will.

For as long as she can remember the steamboats have come by the scow, some close, some far away. *The Mohawk* passes by on route from South Portage to Dwight. Una recognizes the long, curved hull, the grand upper and lower decks and the banner of flags that run from the bow to the captain's cabin.

Una stands on the edge of the scow, clad only in her under garments. Brazenly she waves at the people leaning on the railings of the steamboat, craning their necks toward shore. Una waves again and this time the passengers wave back. Taking a huge breath Una dives headfirst into the water. She swims until her lungs feel like they are about to burst then she surfaces, and shouts, "Good Morning!"

Several passengers applaud.

"Time to grow up young lady," Maud harshly calls out, her arms folded across her chest.

Una hauls herself up onto the scow.

"Now go and get dried off. There's something I want you to take to your brother at the lumber camp. He's been asking me to mend his flannel shirt that he wore last winter. He'll be needing it soon enough."

Una stands shivering in a puddle of water.

"Good gracious Una, what are you waiting for?" admonishes Maud. "You'll get the grip standing around like that."

It is the first time that Una has ventured this far on her bicycle and by the time she reaches the lumber camp the sun is high in the sky.

I can hardly wait for Colin to see me. Won't he be surprised. Me on a bicycle.

Una pedals past a long wagon packed with lumber being transported to the mill. After she passes by, she spots a group of lumbermen gathered along both sides of an upturned canoe that they are using as a table for their homemade lunches.

"Who do we have here?" barks a burly man with a scraggly beard.

"Now there's a lovely sight to see out here in the woods," teases another man, his cap askew and a red bandanna tied about his neck.

A third man stands up holding a mason jar in his hand. When he speaks Una detects a French accent. "What's your name, ma belle? Me, I am Maurice Dubois."

"Cut it out fellows. Leave my kid sister alone." Colin walks up to the men.

"She's no kid no more, mon ami, she is all woman by my eyes."

The men break out in laughter. Colin walks over to Una and whispers, "You'd better go back now Una. This is no place for a girl. Thank Mama."

Una hands Colin his flannel shirt. She flushes red. "Why are those men talking about me like that?"

Colin speaks directly at the men, "Because they're no good rotten heathens, that's why." And kidding, he says to Una, "Okay get going before a bear gets hold of you."

"Mon Dieu, I'd like to get hold of you. I'm a nice big bear. Give you great big bear hug."

"Shut up Maurice." Colin shakes his fist.

"You going to the dance this Friday," Maurice hollers after Una as she mounts her bicycle. "Maybe we have a dance? What do you say? Maybe a nice waltz."

Una pumps the pedals and the tires skid in the dirt. She looks back over her shoulder in time to see Colin shove Maurice to the ground. What she doesn't hear is the threat that her brother gives to Maurice if he so much as touches Una. Ever.

A dance? Maybe I can go. Maybe I can wear one of Martha's dresses.

Sometimes the rage is extreme. At breakfast Una licks her knife and her mother snaps, "Una, behave like a young lady. Why can't you be more like your sister?"

Una throws the knife on her plate and storms off the scow. She grabs her bicycle and tears down the road with such force that she nearly loses her balance.

Her moods are so unpredictable. There are times when she breaks out in uncontrollable giggles over things that any other person wouldn't find funny at all. She couldn't stop laughing when she saw the screwed-up look on the face of farmer Jessop's horse when it defecated.

But worst of all are days like today when those intense feelings of injustice that sweep over her like a hailstorm blowing in from the east. That's when Una walks around for hours with a scowl as big as a thunderhead.

Maud is at a loss. She has no notion of how to cope with her daughter's emotional kaleidoscope and the shards of fragmented words that spill out without warning. Constantly Maud compares Una to Martha and that just makes Una as fiery as a hot burning coal.

The last thing Una says as she leaves the table is, "I wish I were a fish then I wouldn't drown."

Martha never contradicts a word Mama says. She wouldn't dream of it. She always does as she's told. Stupid cow. I know when Martha lies about things, so she doesn't ruffle Mama's feathers. At least I don't lie. Maybe I should tell Mama how Martha lets the boys kiss her and touch her breasts.

Miss Stanton, who has never had children, recognizes in Una a little bit of herself. She remembers her own youthful rebellious spirit, and consequently is tolerant of Una's uneven moods. When those hormonal shifts explode from her young protege Eva usually suggests that Una drink a cup of sweetened chamomile tea to calm her nerves.

Rachel Little Feathers calls it the phases of the moon.

"It pulls at you Una. But you cannot fly into the sky. You need to keep your feet like roots of the tree. You need to let those big feelings go into the earth and leave you alone. Only you have the strength to do this, my child. But you will not always be a child, Una. You are becoming a woman."

September 1914

The shimmering sun chases the chill from the cool September morning. Normally Una would be full of energy and ready to embrace the autumn colors and damp scents of the day. But lately her heart has been weighed down with worry. Rachel Little Feathers is growing weaker, and she strains more to do the simplest things.

Today Una has promised to help Rachel collect the bright red sumac berries. As she arrives at the camp, she spots Rachel huddled on a rock a few feet away from her shack. Her gnarled fingers grip onto a walking cane that she fashioned out of a branch from a fallen tree. Her head droops down and her eyes are closed.

Overcome with fear, Una bites her knuckle.

Poor Nokomis. She can't stay out here this winter. She might die.

"My eyes are closed but my ears, they are open. I know your foot sounds, not some fox trying to steal my food." Rachel peers from beneath the wool scarf tied about her head.

"How are you Nokomis?" Una asks in a concerned tone.

Rachel coughs several times. "Old and cold like rock I sit on."

"Maybe today's not a good day to pick sumac," Una suggests cautiously.

"Maybe today is the only day." Rachel sputters up a throat full of phlegm. Her lungs wheeze as she tries to inhale.

"Do you want me to build a fire? We can go tomorrow if you like."

"Today is good day." Rachel says defiantly. "We get sumac."

"Maybe we should go to the village and see Miss Stanton. She can give you another package of herbs. You know, the ones for your breathing."

"Maybe you ask her for a tea to stop me from being old woman," Rachel says wryly. "Maybe she has a tea to make the blood come between my legs again."

Why does Nokomis want the blood between her legs? Nokomis is losing her mind."

Rachel points to the sky with her cane and says stubbornly, "I hear geese. They fly south. No time to throw away today like falling leaves."

Reluctantly Una gives in and leads the way through the woods toward an open meadow. Every few steps she looks back to make sure that Rachel isn't lagging too far behind.

"We're almost there." Una sees Nokomis sitting on a fallen tree at the edge of the woods.

"Look at the clouds Una. So many clouds. All different. And look. Over there. See. Crow chase hawk." Rachel moans in discomfort. "Sore right here," Rachel points to her hip.

"Miss Stanton can make a balm to put on it," Una says reassuringly.

"Not so bad. I get better." Rachel takes Una's arm to stand up. "Sumac. There. By the road." Rachel coughs, "What you waiting for?"

For a while it feels like things are just the same as they used to be with Rachel telling Una how to do tasks a certain way, and Una listening to Rachel's stories of when she was a girl. Una excitedly tells Rachel about the upcoming dance and for a moment Una's worries melt away. The orange golden sun warms her face, and a gentle breeze blows in her hair.

"We have plenty. We go back now, but not too fast. I not fast like you Nika."

"You can go to the dance if Colin takes you." Duncan crosses his fork and knife on his plate.

"She's not old enough to be going to dances. She's only fourteen and Lord knows what devilry those lumbermen will get up to, drinking all that spruce beer they make out at the lumber camp." Maud gestures for Martha to clear the table. "Just pile them up and take your little sister outside."

"I'll be there Maud. I can keep an eye on her." Duncan wipes his chin on his sleeve. "I'll be playing fiddle for some of the dances. Maybe Una would like to get up and sing a tune?"

"I'd like that Papa," Una looks to Colin.

"Don't worry Mama, I already set the boys straight. There won't be any nonsense."

"What nonsense?" Una asks with curiosity.

"See, she isn't old enough to know right from wrong," Maud says.

"Yes, I do Mama. I know how to be a young lady. Just last week Miss Stanton taught me how to dance." Una adds enthusiastically, "She has a Victrola and I learned how to waltz."

Una quickly jumps up and counts as she sashays: "One, two, three, one, two, three. And she says there is a new dance called the Fox Trot and everyone in New York City is doing it."

"My word Una, that woman is filling your head with all sorts of claptrap." Maud fusses with the leftovers.

"She reads the newspapers to me Mama and sometimes I read them too, a little bit anyway, and Miss Stanton says I am improving."

"Improving," Maude scoffs, "that's a matter of opinion."

"Can I go Mama? Please." Una pouts slightly. "I just want to get up with Papa and sing, and I want to dance with Colin. You'll dance with me, won't you Colin."

"With my two left feet you'd better wear good shoes. I'm bound to be stepping on your toes." Colin gives her a wink.

"Very well," Maud begrudgingly relinquishes. "You can go, but no dancing with the boys from the lumber camp. We all remember what happened to the Latham girl."

"What happened to her Mama?" Una asks.

"Let's just say she moved away last October, and she hasn't come back. Probably never will," Maud sighs. "Go ask your sister if she can lend you something respectable to wear."

"Thank you, Mama, thank you, thank you, thank you." Una spontaneously hugs her mother who just shakes her head.

"Oh, that girl. She is one of a kind. One of a kind." She glares at Duncan. "And a whole lot more like you than like me."

Even though Martha has outgrown a few of her dresses she is overtly reluctant to give one to Una, saying she is planning on taking them apart to make smocks for Beth. After much debate she offers one to Una pointing out that it has a tear under one arm and that the hem is falling out. She fails to mention the missing buttons from the cuffs which she had already removed for another dress.

Una asks, "What are you going to wear, Martha?"

"I haven't decided." Martha folds her other dresses and places them in an old suitcase for storage. She pushes it under the bed.

"Let's go together," Una offers.

"That won't be possible. I am going with Jonathon Green."

"Jonathon Green, from the tannery? That Jonathon Green." Una states in disbelief.

"Do you know of any other?" Martha fusses with her hair and brags as she looks down her nose at Una, "He's picking me up in his father's carriage and driving me there."

"Can I get a ride with you?" Una asks.

"I doubt it." Martha purses her lips. "You can always come on your bicycle you know."

"I don't care. You just don't want me to see him putting his grimy hands up your ugly skirt." Una grabs the dress and stalks away before Martha can say a word. In the kitchen table she looks for matching thread in her mother's sewing basket.

Black? No. Navy blue. Una sings a ditty to herself. *I'm going to the dance, and I don't care, going to the dance and not with you. I'm going to the dance, and I don't give a damn what you wear.*

Una threads the needle and whistles the melody of a familiar jig she often plays on the mandolin.

"Una. It's Sunday," Maud says brusquely. "How many times do I have to tell you, there is to be no whistling or sewing on Sunday. Put it away. Now."

Una sees red. "You don't believe in God anymore," she yells. "You don't even go to church anymore. So, who says I can't do what I want?"

Suddenly Maud's hand strikes Una across the face.

The shock turns from disbelief to anger. Una snatches her dress from the table and storms off the scow.

Miss Stanton will understand. She'd never hit me. I never want to come back home. Never.

"Una, this is an unexpected visit, on a Sunday, at this hour."

Eva holds the door open for Una who races into the parlor and collapses on the divan. Tears stream down her cheeks as she emotionally recounts the events of the evening.

"I really want to go to the dance and my sister, she's so mean, she gave me this old dress. I was just trying to mend it and Mama started yelling at me."

Calmly, Eva sits beside Una. "Well, let me see it." She holds the dress up to the light, turns it one way, then another. "I think we can do something with this Una. But first let's have a cup of chamomile tea before retiring for the evening. I've just made a fresh pot. Tomorrow you can tell me more about the dance. I believe it's being held at the Stones' Barn on Brunel Road. It must be the harvest dance?"

Eva hands a cup of the tea to Una.

"It's good that you're spending the night," Eva says cheerfully, "We can get started on the garden first thing in the morning. I've covered the delicate plants with old bed sheets to protect them from the frost, but it is getting colder, and I want to bring in most of the herbs as soon as possible."

Eva stops to take a sip. "So is the dance next Saturday?"

Una nods then asks expectantly, "Will you go with me Miss Stanton? We can dance together now that I know how to waltz. And I can teach you how to do the jigs, that is if you don't know them already."

"I have danced a few jigs in my time," Eva says confidently, "and a quadrille."

Una tilts her head, confused.

"Quadrille?" Eva says, "In England I participated in a dance club. We did all the old dances. The quadrille has four couples in a square."

"Like a square dance?" Una asks.

"I suppose one could say that."

Eva takes hold of the dress again. "Yes, Una, let's go together. It has been quite some time since I attended a dance. Tomorrow we shall turn this dress into something that even Cinderella would wish were hers."

Lively music spills out from the Stones' Barn. Standing at the farm gate Una nervously straightens the new lace collar on her sister's old dress, and adjusts the sparkling buttons that Eva sewed onto the sleeves.

"Are you sure my dress isn't too short Miss Stanton?" Una pulls at it anxiously. "Thank you for the new shoes. They are lovely Miss Stanton. I've never worn such lovely shoes in my life."

"You are most welcome, Una. Every young woman should have a pair of dress shoes. I am sure you will have plenty of opportunities to wear them again. And our dresses are merely a little above our ankles. That is the modern way, my dear."

Eva puts her hands on Una's shoulders. "You look absolutely divine."

"This is my first time at a dance like this," Una whispers.

"And it's been years for me," Eva admits. "Well, what are we waiting for, shall we?"

Arm in arm, Una and Eva enter through the barn doors. Right away they join in with the throng on the dance floor. Una is swept up into the merriment of the night, her heart light and joyful as she and Eva sway to the music.

After only a few dances Eva is noticeably winded. "I need to rest for a while and have an apple cider. This dancing has made me quite parched. Go on Una. Have some fun. I'll be right here at the refreshment stand."

Una strolls over to a row of chairs occupied by spinsters and one young woman who holds a baby in her arms. She sits at the end of the row and looks up to see her father playing fiddle with the other musicians.

He seems so happy. I'm glad mother isn't here. She'd say something to upset father, I just know it. And she'd probably tell me that the hem on my dress is too short. Una adjusts the rhinestone hair clip that Miss Stanton gave her. *I am a sophisticated young woman. Miss Stanton says so.*

Una glances over at Martha leaning against a wall at the far end of the barn. Jonathon Green tries to impress Martha by juggling apples which he repeatedly drops onto the barn floor. Further along Una recognizes a group of girls her age who live in the village. Their dresses reach down to their ankles. One of the girls covers her mouth with one hand and points at Una with her other hand.

Why are they snickering at me?

Unsayable Absence

Una pulls at her dress and fusses with her cuffs.

A sudden hush descends on the crowd as a group of men from the lumber camp stagger through the open doors of the barn. Though they are dressed in clean clothes, and have scrubbed faces and trimmed beards, it is clear to Una that they have been into the liquor. Maurice Dubois heads directly for the food table while the other men ask the women to dance. One by one they politely refuse the drunken offers.

"So, here you are." Colin bows. "If my little sister doesn't look like a beautiful rose. Shall we dance?" He yanks Una from her chair. They join in with a long line of couples facing each other. One by one each pair of dancers hops and skips up and down the line. Colin takes Una by the hands and prances with her to the far end.

"You dance like a horse," Una teases.

"Well, I warned you," Colin replies.

The band breaks into "The Green River Girl", a popular lumberjack waltz. The rows of dancers disperse and soon the room is filled with couples swaying in circles about the floor. Colin playfully takes the waltz pose with Una, and they bob up and down in large bouncing steps.

Several inebriated men from the lumber camp bellow out the lyrics.

> I'm one heartbroken lumber jack, my sunshine turned to rain,
> For cupid's dart has pierced my heart and turned my joy to pain.
> I'll tell you all the sad affair and tell without delay,
> 'Twas caused by that pretty Green River Girl who stole my heart away.
> I dressed her in the finest clothes in muslin silk and lace,
> And choices finest linens my fair sweetheart did embrace.

Maurice leaves his cronies and staggers over toward Una and Colin. He rudely jerks Colin by the shoulder. "Let me show this beautiful young lady how to really waltz. You clumsy oaf."

"Sit down, Maurice, before you fall down. You're drunk." Colin starts to walk away with Una, but Maurice grabs his elbow and spins him around.

"I not sit down unless you, ma belle," Maurice stumbles as he tries to take Una in his arms, "unless ma belle want to sit on my lap."

Colin puts his hand on Maurice's chest and pushes him out of the way.

Una watches in horror as Maurice falls against another couple. He recovers then comes at Colin, his fists flailing in the air. Colin ducks out of the way. Maurice trips forward onto a group of lumberjacks who have gathered around to watch the fight. They toss Maurice back toward Colin. The band stops abruptly. Everyone clears the dance floor, and the men go at it. Chairs fly about. Tables turn over. And all the woman and some of the elderly men flock for the doors. Colin strikes Maurice in the jaw.

Dead silence.

Maurice stays motionless on the floor, Colin towering over him.

"Come Una. We should leave," Eva Stanton says uneasily. "Now I remember why I stopped going to these affairs."

Una resists momentarily. All she can do is stare back at Colin as they leave the dance.

"What if he's dead? What if Colin killed him? I should have danced with that buffoon. It's my fault. It's all my fault."

Even though it has been weeks since the fight broke out at the dance, Una still feels the guilt in her gut. On the way home Miss Stanton had reassured Una that it was, as she had said, most definitely not her fault.

"Maurice is a cad," she said, "an unrefined boor, and he absolutely deserved what he got. It's the alcohol. Men get drunk and it leads to the fisticuffs."

Colin was not charged. The lumbermen sided with him and said that it had been Maurice who started the fight. And in their minds that was the truth. "So help us God," they slurred to the constable when he finally arrived.

Maurice had never been very popular at the camp. He was the sort of bloke who liked to play tricks on the men, things like putting sawdust under their bed sheets. They all agreed, he got his just desserts.

After the dance Maurice never showed up at the lumber camp. Some say he moved back to Aylmer, Quebec and went to work at the Giles lumber camp. Others say he headed out west to the Caribou in search of gold. In the end the only good thing that came of Maurice were the stories that people made up about him and the fact that he was gone.

Since that night Una has felt ashamed of her body even though she knows he was not a decent man. He did not respect her. And more and more she has no control over the changes that are happening to her body. Her breasts are sore, and they keep getting bigger. Hair sprouts on her legs, under her arms, and near her groin. Some days she feels dirty and disgusted with herself.

I hate myself. I hate that man. I hate him so much I hope he goes to hell. I wish I'd never been born. I don't want to end up like Martha always giggling around boys. And God forbid I end up like Mama. If I have to grow up, I want to be a refined woman like Miss Stanton.

In the morning as Una's dreams surface into her waking consciousness she feels an unfamiliar dampness beneath her body. Her body aches and she is consumed by a miserable discomfort. Blood.

She knows what it is. She's been waiting for it ever since it came to Martha a few years ago.

She's watched Martha and her mother wash bloody rags in the cold lake water. And today her mother gives her an old bed sheet to rip into strips, and safety pins to keep them from slipping in an apron that she is told to wear backwards in case she has a leak. The awkwardness of these items on her body only adds to her feelings of self-revulsion.

Maud offers basic instructions and emphasizes Una's clothes washing duties at this time of the month. "Soak them in cold to draw out the blood."

Martha on the other hand is too lost in her own world of wanting to get married and exhibits little if any expression of sympathy for Una's situation.

"You're growing up Una. You're a young woman now and maybe it's time you acted like one."

A few days later Miss Stanton recognizes the black circles under Una's eyes and detects the acrid scent of dried blood on her clothing. She gently explains, "We women have this cross to bear, for some unfathomable reason. We must endure such pain and suffering even if children are not to be born from the womb."

They sit down at the oak dining room table. "I have a gift for you Una." Eva hands Una a polished wooden case with a brass handle and two ornate clips that hold it closed. "Go ahead, open it."

"For me Miss Stanton? What is this?" Una is both surprised and confused.

Eva pushes the case closer to Una, "Open it and see."

Una slowly lifts the lid and upon seeing the contents she sits back in astonishment. "Oh, Miss Stanton this is so beautiful. So, so beautiful. But why are you giving me such a fine gift? A brush and comb, and all of these things?"

Eva swivels in her chair to face Una and takes Una's hands in her own.

"My dear, you are like a flower blossoming in my garden. And every girl who is coming of age deserves a little celebration. This is the first vanity case that was given to me when I was about your age or a little bit older."

Eva stops to think about how long ago that was, and how young she must have been back then. "Fourteen or fifteen perhaps. I have another one that I use daily and yet for some reason I've been keeping this one in the bottom drawer of my dresser. I haven't used it in years, and it only seems fitting now to give it to you."

"Is it real silver?" Una asks.

"Silver plated." Eva hesitates for a moment. "Una when we women bleed, sometimes we give off an odor that is not very pleasant. And, well, I thought that perhaps you'd like to have a nice hot bath. We can burn those bloody rags in the bin out back and I can give you some fresh cotton to make new ones. I can order some store-bought ones to be sent up from Toronto if you'd like."

"Miss Stanton, why are you so kind to me?" Una tries to hold back her tears.

"Oh, now Una, that is because you are so easy to be kind to." She hands Una her lace trimmed handkerchief. "Now run upstairs. Get out of those clothes and run a bath. There are clean towels in the hall closet. Call me when you're finished."

And for the first time Una throws her arms around Eva and tells her she loves her.

October 1914

The Autumn days grow shorter. Fallen leaves spread out like a soggy blanket on the ground while a slight drizzle puts a chill in the early morning air. Fog rises from the lake.

Una has been meaning to visit Rachel Little Feathers but lately most of her time has been spent helping Eva Stanton. As she approaches Rachel's camp she calls out and when there is no answer, she reaches for the flap to the hut that flickers in the wind. Una peers inside. Rachel is not there.

Ashes in the fire pit. Good sign. She's probably checking the trap line.

Una goes to where the traps are usually set, only to discover that there are no animals caught in the snares. *Maybe Nokomis has been here already. I hope she is on her way to the camp but how did I miss her?* At the sheltered cove Una is relieved to see that the canoe is out of the water and securely tied to a birch tree. *She hasn't gone fishing. Thank God. With this wind she'd* never be able to paddle alone. Una's thoughts grow darker. *What if she has fallen somewhere? What if she's hurt?*

Quickly Una strides along the shore toward a familiar cliff. She scrambles to the top of the ridge to get a better view of the surroundings. When she was small Rachel would take her there to look for animals or watch the clouds dance in the sky.

Una scans the landscape. Still no sign of Rachel. Then, just as she is about to climb back down, she catches sight of Rachel, bent over in the marsh.

"Nokomis," Una's voice echoes over the land below, "Nokomis."

Rachel slowly straightens up and waves a cattail in the air, its autumn seeds floating away with the wind.

Una swiftly retraces her way back down the side of the cliff, her feet familiar with each uneven crevice. At the bottom of the crag, she sprints over to the marsh where Rachel stands, balancing a basket on her hips.

"Nika, I am not surprised to see you," says Rachel. "We go to my camp. Today is special day, Nika. You become woman, yes?"

"How do you know, Nokomis?" Una is baffled. "How do you know? I didn't tell you about what has happened."

"Some things I just know. I see you in my dream last night. You are tall, beautiful girl-woman and you dance with bear, big brown bear, and you no afraid. Then the full moon, it send sparks of light all around you and you shine like star. I know you are woman now. So, I bring you these soft Apuk'we seeds. Soft for you to bleed on."

Una is overwhelmed by Rachel's dream message. She has listened to many of her night visions. Some tell Rachel when a baby is about be born, or when a person will die, but never a dream about herself.

Back at the camp Rachel says, "Get some dry wood Nika. We build a fire. Easy to start. See. Coals still warm."

It doesn't take long for a flame to ignite the wood. They sit close warming their hands near the fire.

"Nika, I cannot give you what my mother and grandmother give to me. You are not one of my people." Rachel waves at the smoke. Wheezing, she pulls her tattered blanket around her shoulders. "But I can give you my story and maybe one day you give my story to your children." Rachel pauses to catch her breath. "Now that you bleed you can have babies."

"I don't want babies, Nokomis."

"Not now, but one day." Rachel pokes the fire with a stick. "In my time and my mother's time and her mother's time before her, when a woman is with the moon, she has very special powers. We call it Makwa. Makwa means turning into bear. That is how I know you bleed Nika. I dream you are dancing with bear."

"How old were you when you started Makwa, Nokomis?"

"So, long ago, I forget. But I remember it all as if it happen yesterday." Rachel's voice is low and husky. "For one whole year I cannot touch a baby. My oldest sister have a new baby, but I do not want to make it sick. And I cannot cross in front of my father when he sits at the fire. It is very bad. He can be crippled or even killed, and I no want to make that happen." Rachel gasps as she speaks, "We are strong Nika. Very powerful. This is why men fear us."

"Nokomis, you are not well."

"You listen. I tell you my story." Rachel stares into the fire. "There is more."

"But you are tired."

"There is more." Rachel speaks firmly and turns her head to look directly at Una. "You need to know this story. I tell you that already."

"They build a hut for me behind where we live. It only big enough for me. I have blanket to keep me warm and water to drink. That is all. It happens with my first blood. For ten days I stay alone. No one speak to me. No one. Only my mother and grandmother bring me little food each day. Small piece of rabbit or fish. I no scared. I listen to birds. I hear the wind speak to trees."

"One night owl come and sit in the tree beside my hut and sing to me. I peak through a hole and see the stars. I dream. So many dreams. After ten days all the women from near our home come and sing to me. I have a hot cedar bath to make me clean again and then we have big feast. So much food. Good food." Rachel laughs and coughs, "I eat so much I get sick. Everybody happy for me."

"For a year I cannot pick berries. For a year I cannot touch a tree. And I am told over and over again not to touch the drum. The drum is alive, Una. The drum has spirit in it. I no want to kill the spirit."

Una stares at the fire taking in everything that Rachel has just told her. Finally, the only sound is that of the wood crackling in the flames.

Rachel breaks the silence. "I give you two things for your Makwa, Una."

Rachel reaches into a small deer skin pouch and pulls out a long leather string. Tied to it is a bear claw and a feather.

"This is a totem. Keep it close to you when you bleed. I find the body of a dead bear last spring. Hunters just leave it for the ravens and wolves. So, I take this claw. This feather is from a mother goose. When she lay her eggs in her nest, she use her feathers to keep them warm. I take it for you my Little Goose. I know this day come soon. Your breasts they tell me to do this."

Rachel leans forward and puts the talisman over Una's head.

"Bear protect you, and goose give you strength to fly, to go where you must go. Life has a journey waiting for you. Take it."

7

December 1914

"You've seen her, Una. She rarely comes in from the shed these days. I told her she could sleep in one of the bedrooms upstairs. I've offered it to her more than once," Eva says. "I even set up a cot in the kitchen, but she took the blankets off and slept on the floor."

"At least she's not at her camp," Una sighs. "I am sure Nokomis would never survive the winter. You see how frail she is. Besides, you've made the garden shed quite cozy."

"I think so. The Quebec heater keeps it warm. Although it is a big adjustment, isn't it? I mean, she doesn't need to go out hunting. She does eat the fried fish and stews that I make. And, of course, she has developed a fondness for my sweets."

Eva wraps a scone in a napkin. "Take this. It's buttered and has a dollop of raspberry jam on it. And here's some tea and honey."

"Thank you, Miss Stanton. You are so kind. I didn't know what to do when I went to see her last week. She was huddled inside her shack with no fire, and only a few bits of dried venison to eat. She was coughing so much, and I could tell that she was finding it harder to breathe. I begged her to come to your place with me. But you know she can be stubborn."

"I've noticed that." Eva warmly agrees.

"I told her that I had always listened to her and that maybe it was time she listened to me. I don't know why that worked but it did. She came here, on the condition I take her to the Indian Village in the Spring. She has family there."

"You did the right thing, Una." Eva wipes her hands on her apron. "Ask her to come inside later for some beef stew."

"Tea with honey and fresh baked scones," Una musically announces as she enters the shed and places them on the rough pine table.

"I make this basket for Miss Stanton." Rachel holds up her handiwork in her weather-worn hands. "Do you like the blue flower? I collect quills from dead porcupine. Only get eaten by vulture anyway. My grandmother teach me how to get quills." Rachel takes a bite of the scone. "I need more sweetgrass, more birch. I make baskets to sell. It cost money to go to Indian Village."

"Do you have some sweetgrass and birch at your camp?" Una pulls up a stool and sits beside Rachel.

"Yes. We go tomorrow."

"The snow is getting deep, Nokomis. Look, it's still falling." Una points to the flakes coming down on the old glass window frame that serves as a roof.

"We use snowshoes." Rachel does not look up.

"Let's see what the morning brings. Maybe I can go there for you," Una offers.

Rachel shrugs. "Maybe I go when you not here."

"Maybe you want to come in for beef stew?" teases Una.

"Maybe I do," Rachel adds mockingly. She throws a patched wool blanket over her shoulders. "Miss Stanton tell me I save her life when she is born. That's why she let me stay here. She is good woman, but not such a good cook."

Una and Rachel come in through the pantry and remove their snow-covered boots. They find Eva in the kitchen staring at a newspaper spread out on the table.

"A ceasefire. That's just fine and dandy now isn't it," Eva says sardonically. "Stop killing for a day and then go at it again the next day."

Rachel looks baffled.

"It's the war," Una explains. "Colin and Robert told me that they might enlist. Papa's too old."

"Why Canada ever had to get involved is beyond me. As if it will boost the economy. And all these young men losing their lives. And for what? Listen to this."

"'In the week leading up to the 25th, French, German and British soldiers crossed trenches to exchange seasonal greetings and talk'."

Eva shakes her head in disgust, "One day. One day free from slaughter. This is monstrous." Again, she reads the article aloud.

"'In some areas, men from both sides ventured into no man's land to mingle and exchange food and souvenirs. It is reported that some of the soldiers enjoyed a game of football with the enemy'."

"This is utterly unconscionable. When will it ever end, man's need to destroy one another over greed?"

"Stew smells good," Rachel says.

Spring 1915

"We go to my people now." Rachel stands in the kitchen holding a carpetbag packed with her few belongings. "The roads are clear. No mud to get stuck in now."

"Yes, Nokomis we leave today. Miss Stanton has arranged for Mr.

Thompson the blacksmith to take us by wagon. They should be back soon. But first I will pack us a lunch. Turkey sandwiches and dried plums."

"Finally, I will have good food, wild rice, bannock and stewed rabbit." Rachel sits at the table. "I know Miss Eva been kind to me. But I miss my people. Many years since I go to Obogawanung. Maybe my sister still alive. She is one year older than me. You never know."

"What is it like there?" Una wraps the sandwiches in brown paper.

"Many people live there, some like me. Other people too, Mohawk. Pretty place but we come from many other places. Lots of dogs, everybody got a dog."

"I thought you had to be invited to go there."

For a moment Rachel stares out the window. "We go. We sent letter. They cannot turn me away. I am born of my people. No government man take away my birth. No government man take away my death."

Rachel's words startle Una. She is about to ask Rachel what she means by no government man take away my death, when the door to the kitchen opens.

"The wagon is here." Eva hangs her cardigan on the hook by the back door. "Mr. Thompson has agreed to take you there and back, but Una, do not pay him until he has done what he said he would do. I've heard he likes to drink a bit and if he has his money too soon you might get stranded."

Eva hands a small purse to Una. "Keep this on you at all times Una. It will take two days to get there and two to get back. Thompson will drop you at a guesthouse in Port Stanley. It's run by a Mrs. Armstrong. There's enough money to pay for your board for one night each way, and for your meals. Are you sure you have packed a good lunch?"

"It's all ready," Una says with confidence. "Thank you so much Miss Stanton. Looks like I will be doing a lot of garden work when I get back."

"Yes, that's what we have agreed upon." Eva hands Una a large jar of mint tea.

Rachel steps toward Eva. "I make these for you." She holds out a pair of moccasins decorated with intricate porcupine quill flowers. "Keep your feet warm for many winters."

Eva hugs the moccasins to her chest. "They're absolutely beautiful. Thank you, Rachel." Eva gathers her composure and gives more instructions to Una. "Mr. Thompson is prepared to look after his own lodgings in Port Stanley and when you get to the Indian Village he will find a place to camp on the outskirts." She turns back to Rachel, "Do you know where you and Una will stay?"

"I have big family, many friends," Rachel says as she walks out the door. "You are good woman Eva Stanton. You no need to worry."

Eva catches Una by the arm and whispers, "This is your first overnight trip Una. Be wise. Stay close to Rachel."

"I will. I made a promise to Rachel that I'd take her to her people." Una skips down the stairs and calls back, "See you on Thursday."

The road leading out of Baysville is mottled with ruts and potholes carved out from the rain. Una and Rachel grip the rails of the bench while the wagon lurches forward and back.

Thompson hollers at his horse to keep to the road and not the ditch. Every once in a while, he breaks out in his favorite song, "The bear went over the mountain, the bear went over the mountain, the bear went over the mountain, to see what he could see."

At first Una sings along but by the third time she sighs, "Not again."

Rachel whispers, "That must be one big mountain."

By late afternoon they pull up to the guest house in the village of Port Sydney. Una helps Rachel climb down from the wagon.

"That's half the fare now," Thompson says with assumed authority.

Una clutches the purse to her side. "I am afraid you are mistaken Mr. Thompson. I have strict orders from Miss Stanton that you are to be paid upon our safe return."

"That's not what I was told." The blacksmith steps in front of Una to prevent her from going toward the guesthouse. "What if I just leave you right here?" he threatens.

"Then you get no money at all." Una stands her ground.

"Take this Mr. Thompson. Buy yourself a whiskey." Rachel hands him a few coins. "Be back when the sun comes up. We want an early start." She hands him a few more coins. "Have two whiskey. You sleep good tonight."

Grumbling, Thompson stuffs the coins into his grease-stained denim coveralls and climbs up onto the wagon. Una keeps an eye on him as he slaps the reigns and drives down the dirt road. He brings the wagon to a stop in front of The Red Lion tavern.

"Do you think that was a good idea, Rachel, giving him that money? Your money?" Una turns the bell on the front door of the guesthouse.

"He is dumb man. He thinks of one thing. Booze. Maybe two things. Booze and wild women. At least he leave us alone."

Una turns the bell again just as a hand draws back the lace curtain on the window. In the shadows a blurred face peers out at them.

I hope this is the right place. Miss Stanton said there would be someone here to let us in.

The door opens it a crack to reveal a small, round woman with her grey hair piled up in a tight bun.

"The letter did not say that a squaw was coming," the woman says curtly. "I do not allow Indians to stay in my house. I'm afraid you'll have to find some other accommodation."

"But Mrs. Armstrong? It is Mrs. Armstrong, isn't it? Miss Stanton said that -" Before she can get another word out, the woman slams the door tight.

Una calls out, "Miss Stanton made the arrangements."

No answer from the other side of the door.

"Where can we stay?" Una pleads.

The woman pulls back the curtain and snaps, "Try the tavern."

Several men downing their drinks mingle about on the veranda of the Red Lion Tavern. Una bravely takes Rachel by the hand and helps her up the wooden stairs toward the open door. She feels the men staring at her. One of the men hawks into a spittoon. Una does not look at him. With Rachel at her side Una boldly steps into the foyer.

Rachel taps Una on the shoulder and points to a sign over the stairs that lead to the second floor. "What does that say?"

"It says 'Rooms to Let. See Bartender'. Wait here. I'll be right back."

Keeping her head high Una steps through the archway and marches into the barroom. At the far end of the room the bartender stands behind a long, oak counter pouring whiskey for a couple of male customers.

"Can I help you, young lady?" The bartender winks suggestively at the men.

"We'd like a room for the night?" Una gestures to the foyer.

"Who might we be?" asks the surly man.

"My friend, my grandmother, my -" Una says tongue-tied.

"Which is it?" The bartender mutters. He rounds the corner of the bar and looks toward the foyer. "You and that old squaw want a room?"

"Yes sir. I am taking her to the Indian Village, sir." Una states plainly, her palms wet with perspiration.

"Well, it wouldn't be the first time an Indian has stayed here," he grunts, "but she's not allowed in the tavern. Them there Indians get to drinking and all hell breaks loose. And no Indians in the dining room neither. It's no good for business. We got some refined people come here for dinner and an Indian squaw ain't one of them. You understand?"

Rachel calls from the other side of the archway, "Give us the key. We cause no trouble. We just need a bed for the night."

"Payment first, then the key," he demands with gruff insistence.

Una fumbles as she undoes the clasp on her purse. She hands the bartender some money. "That includes our breakfast?"

"Yours, not hers." He gives Una a key. "Upstairs. Third door on your left. Bathroom at the end of the hall." He scratches his protruding belly. "Wouldn't go alone if I were you. We got a full house tonight. Never know what a man whose been tipping the bottle is likely to do with a pretty thing like you."

Una takes the key, her jaw stiff from an emotional cocktail of fear and anger.

At the top of the stairs a ray of light from a small window casts a yellow glint on the stained wallpaper. The stale smell of beer and tobacco reeks in the air. Una turns the key in the lock. The door creaks open.

A brass bed takes up most of the space. To one side is a plain wooden chair. On the other side is a washstand with a pitcher and bowl on top. A mottled mirror with a crack in the bottom right corner hangs precariously above the washstand.

What have I done? That Mrs. Armstrong is one horrible bitch. I'll be glad when we can get out of this place.

"It's musty in here. I'll let some fresh air in." Una jostles the wooden frame of the window that overlooks the street below. She overhears the men on the porch. Their teases and taunts float up on the black wings of swear words.

"Miss Stanton will be horrified when we tell her about this." Una bites her lip.

"No need to tell her unless she asks," Rachel advises wisely.

"Hungry?" Una asks.

"Some, but where we going to get food. Can't go fishing here." Rachel laughs.

"I'll bring something up from the dining room. Have a little rest Nokomis. I won't be long."

By the time Una arrives back with a bowl full of beef stew, Rachel is fast asleep, curled up on the floor with her head resting on the carpetbag. Una places the meal on the washstand. Exhausted from the trials of the day, she slips off her outer clothes, and crawls under the covers but she is too worried to fall asleep.

Noises from the barroom below seep into the room. She thinks of the men at the Baysville House, where on more than one occasion she has had to fetch her father. At least there, they all know who she is. Here, no one knows her, and it makes her feel uneasy when the men on the veranda talk

Unsayable Absence

about "the old squaw" upstairs.

Una is just about to nod off when she jerks awake. It's Thompson. She hears him coming down the hall singing 'Oh my darlin', Oh my darlin', Oh my darlin' Clementine'. And there's a high-pitched giggle. A woman. Una recognizes the sound of the key as it unlocks the room next door. She grabs the pillow and puts it over her ears. Nothing deadens the bang of the headboard against the thin walls. Nothing stifles the whines and moans, until finally, the woman shouts, "You cheap bastard," and slams the door on her way out.

Dawn's dull light creeps across the floor. Rachel stands over the bed, shaking Una by the shoulder. "Wake up Nika. We go now." And again louder, "Wake up."

"Where are we?" Una mumbles as she lifts herself up onto her elbows, "No, wait a minute. I know. The Red Lion."

"We better find Mister Blacksmith and get going. I wonder which room he stay in?" Rachel sits on the end of the bed, her carpetbag on the chair next to her. "You know where he is?"

"You didn't hear him last night? With a woman?" Una asks.

Rachel yawns, "I sleep like a bear."

"And you snore like a bullfrog," Una jests. "He's next door. I heard him come in last night. He was drunk Nokomis."

"We wake him up. We go."

After several hours of careening over the dirt roads Rachel speaks up, "My bones are going to fall out of me."

"We can take a break for our lunch," Una suggests, "This morning I paid the cook to make us some sandwiches and lemonade." Una pauses to build the anticipation, "and butter tarts."

Una shouts at Thompson, "We need to stop here for a rest. Pull up by that lake."

The wagon jostles over the uneven ground to a clearing not far from the water.

Thompson warns them, "You can't stay long if you want to make it to Port Carling before sundown."

"Long enough for lunch," asserts Una.

She helps Rachel down from the wagon and they follow a pathway beside the shore.

"Sit here," Rachel says breathlessly as she lowers herself onto a large log that, seasons ago, washed up on the shore.

"Hear that?" Rachel asks. "Wind whispers secrets to the trees. And see up on that branch? Mr. Kingfisher? He's looking for his lunch. Maybe a nice fish swim by for him." Rachel takes a sip of the lemonade. "We spend many years together, Nika. Like this. Looking over the water. See them dragonflies dance? See all their eyes. So many eyes. And their rainbow wings." The sweet syrup from the butter tart oozes onto Rachel's chin. "This is some good," Rachel laughs as she licks her fingers, then points. "Boochikwanish dragonfly tell me it is good that I go to my people."

Una stares at the sun-dappled water. "You taught me many things Nokomis. How to tell poison berries from the ones we can eat, and how to skin a rabbit."

"And you teach me how to be patient with wild girl who does silly things and almost drowns," Rachel teases.

"I remember. I fell out of the canoe when I stood up too fast," Una says. "Nokomis, do you remember how I played with the shells?"

"I remember."

"Do you remember telling me stories about the stars?" Una asks.

"Yes. You remember them too because sometimes you tell them back to me the next day, but in your own way."

"I remember the one about shooting stars and how they are babies," Una recalls.

"Special story." Rachel seems far away with her memories. "My grandmother tell it to me when I was little girl."

Suddenly Thompson comes up to them. "I wondered where you two had wandered off to. Time to leave this place."

Una steadies Rachel as she struggles to get to her feet. Together they walk slowly arm in arm along the shore. Una feels Rachel's hands. Cold.

Rachel raises her voice over the sound of the horse's hoofs. "There was a time when my people used to fish and hunt in these lakes and woods, but then white people come and we are made to move away, far away to land full of rock, *Mnjikaning*. No good land for my people."

Rachel tells this same story to Una; one she has told many times before. "Some go to Christian Island. You hear of it Nika? Christian Island on Georgian Bay?"

"Yes, you have told me of this place," Una says.

"I tell you this before? I no remember anything these days." Rachel laughs until she falls into a coughing fit. She pulls a rag from her pocket and spits into it. Una grimaces at the blood stains but says nothing.

"There was a time, my mother tells me, there was a time," Rachel pants, "when we never got along with the Mohawk, but you know they lost their land too, Nika. So many people lose their land. The Mohawk people, they come every year to fish where we fish. We all set up a camp. We stay there all spring and summer. What we going to do, huh? That's when the government man say he give us our own place. That is where you take me now, to Indian Village."

Rachel leans on Una, "Hope we get there soon. My butt is sore." She continues, "When I was little girl my father take me there by canoe. But my father he got real sick and die when I am only eight years old. I only remember few things, like those canoe times. He even let me paddle with him."

"How did he die?" Una asks as if she has not heard the story before.

"Coughing sickness."

83

Thompson pulls on the reins. "We're here."

Una sees several Indian women seated on benches on the dock.

Rachel gives her orders to Thompson. "You go camp somewhere else. Not here. You stay away from our village. I know men like you. You take our girls. Get them drunk and do stupid things."

Una helps Rachel climb down from the wagon. "Your carpetbag, you forgot your bag. Wait here, I'll get it for you."

Una scrambles onto the wagon. "Mr. Thompson, we want to leave by mid-morning tomorrow." Una looks around at the unfamiliar landscape and is unsure of what to tell him. Finally, "We'll meet you here. At the docks."

Thompson gripes under his breath, "I should never have agreed to do this." He slaps the reins so hard that the horse pulls away with a jolt.

Una catches up to Rachel who is more than halfway to the dock.

Immediately one of the women comes straight toward Rachel. They embrace. With laughter and tears they speak to one another in their own language.

"Una, this is Esther. She is my cousin's granddaughter." Rachel says. "She will take us to the village in her boat. See. She got big boat with little motor. Pretty fancy, huh? Take no time to get there."

At the village Esther leads Rachel and Una to one of the shacks.

"I rest here Nika," Rachel struggles for breath, "I have many questions for Esther. She tell me news about my family. You look around. Lots to see."

Una wanders about the village. She stops to watch an elderly man sitting on a wooden bench. He holds a miniature birch bark canoe on his lap. A flock of tourists barter with him. At length, a well-dressed man gives him a few coins and walks away with his souvenir of the day.

Further along, in a sunlit area, Una spots a long clapboard hut. It boasts a stand filled with the handiwork of its inhabitants. Two visiting women, dressed as if they are about to attend a Sunday picnic, chatter over which item on the ledge delights them the most. Meanwhile village children scamper in and around the onlookers.

The shadows of the day grow long and one by one the stalls close for the night. Soon all the outsiders leave the village taking with them sweetgrass baskets, porcupine quill moccasins, and other souvenirs of their excursion.

"I know you."

From behind a grove of bushes an older woman carrying a winnowing basket on her hip comes up to Una and offers her a toothless grin. "Me, I am Rachel's father's second cousin. You can call me Marie. That is my Christian name. But my birth name is Namid. It mean star dancing. You must be the girl. Rachel has told me about the white girl who stay with her on the big lake far from here. She tell me about you. Come with me."

"My name is Una."

"I know, Rachel tell me that. But she call you Nika. I know all about you. We go to the feast now. Lots of good food tonight. Me, I like fish on wild rice. You? Bet you like the maple syrup."

That evening Rachel's face glows in the light and warmth of the bonfire. Una is relieved to see such happiness in Nokomis' eyes, and delighted to know that her dear friend is so lovingly welcomed by those who surround her. Songs are sung, stories are told, and laughter rises up to greet the stars in the night sky.

The bright morning light dances like diamonds on the dew-wet leaves of the trees. Una leaves the shack and deeply inhales the fresh scent of damp pine needles. Several dogs chase after a red squirrel.

Rachel was right, there are lots of dogs.

The shack that Una slept in belongs to Namid's son. All the beds were taken by Namid, her son, his wife, and their four children, so Rachel and Una slept on the floor. It was close quarters and, in some ways, reminded Una of living on the scow where she could hear everyone's cough or snort.

Rachel appears in the doorway. "My friends are coming."

"We have to leave soon Nokomis," Una says. "You saw everyone last night."

"Yes."

"Mr. Thompson will be waiting for us. Let me help you gather your things."

"No."

Rachel puts a blanket over her shoulders and walks toward the smoldering ashes in the fire pit. "My friends are coming."

Una looks around. First one, then another, and another. The elderly woman appears from several different directions and form a circle around Rachel.

Namid is the first to speak. "Rachel is home now. She stay here, with us. We take care of her. She does not need to be out in the woods. Alone. She need her people. No one can stop us. We will hide her if they come asking questions."

"It is as they say Nika. I am home." Rachel stands face to face with Una.

"If you stay here, I won't be able to see you, Nokomis," Una pleads.

"Nika, I always see you in my heart no matter how far away you are. And one day you will go from me. One day you will start your own life with your own people. It is the way of things." Rachel holds her hand out and drops a few coins into Una's hand, "Give this to Mr. Thompson tonight and tell him to go and get drunk. You stay at the guest house okay without me. You be fine, my Nika. And me too. I be fine here."

"But."

"I be fine here."

On the return trip Una does as Rachel had suggested. When they stop for the evening, she has Thompson deliver her to the guesthouse. She gives him the coins that Rachel had handed over to her.

"This is for your whiskey or whatever you choose. Don't be late picking me up in the morning. Miss Stanton is expecting us," she reminds him, "and that's when you'll be paid."

At the guesthouse Mrs. Armstrong makes a weak attempt at apologizing for having turned them away before. Una says nothing. Her heart is breaking and her body aches from the rough ride. All she wants is a bed for the night.

She is thankful for the hot tea and porridge in the morning but finds it very unsettling to carry on a conversation with a woman who had shown so much disdain for Rachel.

By midday storm clouds roll in and the skies open up. Thompson throws Una a dank smelling tarp to put over her head, but the winds grow stronger, and the rain repeatedly lashes at her. Soon she is soaked to the bone. Hours pass before they arrive at the back door to Eva Stanton's home. Una is so chilled she can barely talk except to say simply, "She's with her people."

Autumn 1915

Most of the birds have migrated, except for that annoying raven, always heckling at me whenever I come outside.

Una stands up, mud on her gloves from pulling out the plants hit by the unexpected frost. For a moment she thinks she is talking to Rachel Little Feathers, as if she were right beside her as she works. It has been like that ever since she died.

In August, a parcel came from the Indian Village. The timing was uncanny. Una had made the final move from the scow to take up residence with Miss Stanton. In return for her room and board Una works the garden, does the laundry, and the general housekeeping. And the music lessons continue. Neither Miss Stanton nor Una were surprised by the news. Sad, yes, but somehow accepting of it. The birch box contained a braid of sweet grass, a porcupine quill basket, and a raven's feather tied with a length of beaded leather. A simple note accompanied the package, "For Nika when I go."

Una recalled the stories Nokomis had told her about raven, the trickster who brings enlightenment and calls out a time of change. This was a message. She sensed it in her heart and in her mind. She took the raven's feather and that night she hung it over her bed.

There are times when Una feels Nokomis' presence, a shiver tickling the back of her neck, or a shadow disappearing whenever she tries to see it. A comfort too difficult to explain, that Nokomis still cares from beyond.

PART TWO

Deep calls to deep
at the roar of your waterfalls;
all your breakers and your waves
have gone over me.

Psalm 42 v. 7

8

July 1930 **The Asylum**

The slap of hard soled shoes on the linoleum floor resonates down the length of the institution's corridor. A voice calls out.

"Time to go."

Una recognizes the nurse in her stiffly starched uniform standing rigid in the doorway of her room. She gestures for Una to come. Una's heartbeat quickens. Her hands turn clammy with fear.

They will spray me with the cold water again. I don't understand. Why am I being punished?

A second time the nurse summons Una, louder and with insistence, "Time to go. Come along. That's a good girl."

I am not your girl. I am not a child. Oh God, they can't find his body. They can't find Angus. And my children? Who is looking after them? I have to get out of here.

A crow cackles from the branch of the tree just beyond the window. Una looks outside to see it staring back at her.

What are you trying to tell me? What good can come of this?

In the dimly lit hall three other women wait to be cleansed of their madness. An elderly woman with stringy gray hair giggles nervously as she follows behind Una. The women shuffle down the white-washed hallway, their slippers rasping like sandpaper on a rough plank of wood.

Other patients peer suspiciously from the doorways to their rooms. One haggard-looking woman wraps her arms about her emaciated body and rocks back and forth, cooing words of comfort to an invisible infant.

Una averts her gaze, stares at the floor, and counts the steps to the shower room.

One, two three, they can't get me. Don't they know, I'm not crazy. One, two three, no not me.

In a desperate attempt to save what little is left of her dignity Una struggles to remove her clothes. Her fingers fidget with the buttons on her white cotton blouse. She gingerly takes it off and hangs it on a worn brass hook.

I do not want them staring at me. Stop it. I'm not looking at you.

Quickly she throws the beige muslin tunic over her head. She keeps her arms inside the rough gown so that she can remove her camisole without anyone seeing her breasts. She slips off her pleated skirt, then her underpants, and places them on the same hook as her blouse. Finally, she pulls off her slippers and stands barefoot. Her eyes remain transfixed on a crack on the wall hoping to find a speck to crawl into.

The sharp smell of disinfectant that hovers in the change room air catches in Una's throat. She coughs. Tears well in her eyes. Her body trembles from the dankness of the room and the fearful anticipation of another session in the water chambers.

The same nurse leads Una into the shower room.

"Sit."

She orders each woman, one after the other, expecting them to behave like obedient mongrels. Suddenly a big-boned woman lashes out. It takes three nurses to subdue her and strap her into a chair.

Una hums to herself: *I'm singing in the rain, just singing in the rain, what a glorious feeling...*

She tries to tuck her gown under her bare skin, and when she sits on the cold metal chair her urine immediately begs to be released. She clenches her legs as tight as she can while one of the nurses, who never looks her in the eyes, ties her to the chair with leather straps.

One strap goes around her waist and over her arms to keep her from trying to undo the restraints. Another goes over her lap, and two smaller straps keep each leg in a fixed position.

Across the room the hose man tips his bald head to one side as if assessing the situation. Una seems momentarily fixated on his bulging midriff and how it protrudes over his coveralls like lava flowing from a volcano. She watches as his hairy knuckles grasps the large hose. She searches for something, anything in his expressionless face.

Maybe this is a movie. Maybe I'm only dreaming.

"Ready," calls the head nurse.

Stinging jets of cold-water assault Una's body.

I can't hold it any longer. Oh no, not again.

Warm urine dribbles down her legs and pools onto the cement floor.

The head nurse chastises Una, "Do I have to keep telling you to use the toilet ahead of time. Heavens woman. Have you no shame?"

The force of the water continues to strike Una. She squeezes her eyes and drops her chin to her chest in a vain attempt to avoid the harsh spray on her face. Her dark wet curls drip straight toward the floor and her nipples protrude through the thin hospital gown.

Una bites her lip and shrieks in silence, *Drown me. Go ahead. Drown me for Christ's sake.*

The patient next to Una squirms and jerks with such agitation that her chair keels over. She smacks her head on the floor. A nurse shouts for the hose man to shut the water off. He rushes to help sit the woman back up. When there is no sign of blood, he returns to the taps, turns the nozzle, and once again aims the stinging pelts of water at the women.

Every morning, every evening, Ain't we got fun? Not much money, oh, but honey Ain't we got fun...

For Una, the onslaught goes on for what feels like an eternity.

It will cure you. Like hell it will.

The other women yell for it to stop while Una moves tighter and tighter into herself.

In the few short weeks that Una has been in the Asylum she has witness the disappearance of more than one woman from her floor. Some say they died.

Will I be next? Am I going to die here?

Soaked to the bone, Una slips deeper into the sensory memory of unreachable places. Into the blackness of Vermilion River. Into the crashing waves of Georgian Bay. Into the moon sparkling waters alongside the scow.

Una looks up. All she hears is the trickle of water seeping into the hole in the middle of the cement floor. The dribbling water and the heavy pulse of her heart pounding in her ears.

9

October 1916

A shaft of light. Sunrise breaks through the hoarfrost on the munitions factory's dormitory window. Una shivers. She purses her lips and breathes a circle on the square pane of glass, then wets her finger and draws it larger to peer outside.

I wonder when the snow will come.

Sitting on the crude wooden bench at the end of her cot she pulls on her wool work socks and recalls the day she arrived. It was still summer when the train pulled into Parry Sound. There were several young women from the Muskoka area, all eager to start work at the munitions plant.

She'd taken the steamship across Muskoka Lake to the Bala train station. In the passenger car she sat next to a girl dressed in an olive-green jumper, Emily Finlay. They giggled the whole way and found out they had much in common. Like Una, Emily had lied about her age, saying she was seventeen. Girls younger than sixteen were a liability. They discovered that they each had two older brothers who had already enlisted. And they'd seen the war posters: *To the Women of Canada* and *Buy Victory Bonds*. They agreed that it was their duty to play a part in supporting the war effort and it sure beat the hell out of being a domestic. Factory wages might be less for women than men, but it would fill their pocketbooks a whole lot quicker than any other job. Una had shared her lemonade with Emily, and Emily gave Una half of her ham salad sandwich.

"Snap to it Una," Emily stands fully dressed and halfway out the door of the dormitory. "They'll dock our pay if we're late. Want to get us fired?"

"Go ahead. I'll catch up." Una glances at herself in the mirror beside the washstand. "Go on, Em." Gazing eye to eye with her own reflection she makes a promise.

"That's it. I'm bobbing my hair on Saturday."

Every morning, like on this frost covered day, Una takes the same path to the Gun Cotton Building. And after her twelve-hour shift she takes it back to the dormitory where the women talk about the latest fashions, shorter hem lines and longer jackets to cover their hips. Some knit socks to send overseas while others talk about a new manufactured fabric called Serge and how it will just have to do, for now. A few women keep to themselves and read letters from their loved ones fighting the great war in Europe.

A couple of the women have taken to smoking cigarettes. Una wants to be like those girls with their bright red lips, short hair, and wild stories about dancing ragtime in Toronto. She tried smoking once, but it just made her cough uncontrollably.

Autumn mornings like this frigid one always come too soon. None of the girls can sleep when the temperature drops overnight. The site manager firmly stated that the heaters could not be used until after Thanksgiving. Last week a few women in her dorm saw Mr. McPherson ride by on his white horse. They ran out and begged for some firewood for the Quebec heater.

"These are stringent times," he said, "and that means stringent measures." Then he kept on doing his rounds.

Una overheard the women say that he had taken one of the girls in unit seven to be his mistress. There are plenty of rumors circulating around the plant. Some are true.

Outside Una sees Emily, already walking past the water tower. She could run to catch up, but she knows she won't be late. As fond as she is of Emily, there are times when her friend's sense of urgency outweighs any common sense. As a rule, Emily is usually the first girl on site for their day shift.

Una thinks, *it feels good to be alone for a change. I hardly ever get to be by myself.* A familiar call rises from the cornfield on the perimeter of the plant property. Geese. *Getting fat before your long flight, are you? Rachel Little Feathers would have made sure to snare one of you, wring your neck, pluck your feathers, and roast you on her fire pit.*

Una's mouth waters. She loved eating wild goose with Rachel. Now it's crude oatmeal in the canteen every morning if you give enough time to get there before your shift. Most girls save bread from dinner and keep a jar of jam stashed away under their beds. Last week a care package from Miss Stanton had arrived with lemon sage biscuits, cheese curds, and homemade raspberry preserve. Una only told Emily as she carefully hid the treats in the sock box under her bed. Things go missing in the dorms.

Steam billows from the seven smokestacks at the Powerhouse where a group of women with coke smudged faces are already shoveling the slag from the belly of the furnaces. Una is thankful she hasn't been assigned that job. Maybe it is more dangerous to be stuffing the cylinders in the Gun Cotton Plant but at least it isn't back breaking work. At least she gets to sit down from time to time.

Una walks beside the tracks that lead to the Nitric Acid Plant where a long line of box cars wait to be filled with a shipment of weapons. Everyday thousands upon thousands of bombs leave the plant.

So many bombs. So many people will die. Una tries unsuccessfully to shove the thought aside. *My brothers could die in this god damn war.*

"Well, every train needs a caboose, and it looks like you're doing a fine job of holding up the end of the line again." Doris Finnegan, the change room matron stands in the doorway, her arms folded across her chest. She looks Una straight in the face then shakes her head disapprovingly.

"Quick. Get changed. We need to fill the box cars by morning if we want to get these bombs shipped overseas. Bloody war."

As she passes by, Una gives the matron a half smile but is abruptly stopped by the sharp tug at her elbow.

"How many times do we have to tell you girls. No metal. Nothing. You want to have an explosion in here? Una, hand over the bobby pins. Gracious girl, have you not got the brains God gave you?"

"Thank you, Mrs. Finnegan. We're lucky to have you keeping an eye on us. I'd hate to be flying arse over tea kettle past Henderson's corn field." Una winks.

Dozens of blue denim kit bags filled with the workers' day clothes and personal belongings hang on the hooks in the women's change room. Una stands in front of hook number eight.

My lucky number. An even number, two zeroes, one on top of the other.

Una neatly folds her ankle length skirt, her high neck long sleeved cotton blouse, and lastly her slip. When she stuffs them into the kit bag, she wonders why she even bothered. They'd be all wrinkled by the end of the shift and besides, it would be too dark to notice the creases. She hadn't brought any valuables with her. The few that she owned, like the cameo given to her by Miss Stanton as a parting gift, were hidden in a pair of hose stuffed into her dress shoes. Her wages and those of the other women were kept in a safe in the manager's office. They could have access to their pay on Fridays if they wanted to go to the town on their one day off.

Una bends over to remove her buttoned boots and places them below her kit bag. She pulls up her one-piece khaki coveralls and tucks every strand of her hair under her mop cap. More than once a girl's hair has been caught in the machines. Balancing on one foot at a time Una sticks her toes into the government issued wooden clogs with glued leather straps.

The constant clang of machinery, and the steady clash of banging hammers is so loud it bleeds into the change room, that and the voices of people yelling to be heard over the cacophony. Every day at the end of her shift the racket in Una's ears turns to a constant ringing. It only stops when she falls asleep from exhaustion, but today she is going to try something. Before retiring the previous night, she snipped two tiny squares from the bottom of her flannel nightgown. Today she's plugged her ears with the bits of fabric.

By the time Una arrives on the factory floor most of the women have already taken their places. The acrid stench hits like a ton of bricks. The sweet, sharp tang had caused her to gag on more than one occasion that first week, but now it's just the usual odor. It's normal to feel slightly nauseous and to have her eyes water up.

Una calls to a group of women, "Gosh don't we smell lovely today ladies."

She heads toward her station where the women assemble detonators. Una passes by a tall muscular woman turning a heavy wheel used to bore out the nose of a shell. Even though it is the beginning of the shift the woman's arm pits show rings of sweat. Further on Una sees that Emily is going right at it, grinding a shell. Fan shaped sparks explode around her.

"Looks like Dominion Day," Una shouts.

Emily appears to be replying. Una only sees her lips moving. She shrugs her shoulders and points to the flannel stuffing in her ears.

Again, Emily says something and gestures that there is someone or something behind Una.

Una whips around and nearly trips into Mr. Stratton, the floor supervisor. He is a small man of not more than five feet and Una obviously towers over him.

Stratton does not look amused. He puts his hands on his hips and seems to be barking orders to Una who doesn't hear a word. She raises her eyebrows and smiles.

This makes Stratton even more irate. He wags his finger at Una, his face growing increasingly red, and his eyes bulging out like a fish as he peers over his thick wire-rimmed glasses.

Una knows if she gets caught with stuffing in her ears, she's likely to be sent packing. Promptly, she points over Stratton's shoulders. When he looks away, she pulls the cotton from her ears and hides them behind her back.

"You're needed further down the line. One of the girls got sloppy. Her apron got caught in the gears and well, she's fine, fine, don't you worry Miss, Miss?"

"Campbell, sir, Una Campbell."

"Right, well now, we need you to join the grooving crew, you know, fixing the copper strips, measuring, that sort of thing. We'll have you work with one of the men for this morning. He'll show you the ropes and you know, you should have the hang of it by noon, you know. "

He swallows a bit of his spittle. "Good then let's get you started. Never too old to learn a new trick you know, not that that applies to you. You're not old. No, not that that applies to you."

Una silently chuckles at his inability to stop rambling. She follows on his heels toward the far end of the factory floor where a stooped unshaven man in his mid-forties works the line.

"Mr. Hudson, this is Miss Campbell. She'll be taking over from now on." Stratton tugs on his suspenders in an ineffective effort to demonstrate his authority. "We don't want any more interruptions, so see to it she learns the job right. Good then. I've got more to do this morning. Good then. I'll be moving along. Right."

Hudson's jaw muscles twitch. "No place for women here, anyway. No place at all. Now, you keep your hands out of the way and watch what I'm doing. I mean it. Don't touch a thing until I say so. You got that?"

"Yeah, I got that."

Una is not about to take crap from this man or any other man on the floor. She knows he gets paid more money for doing the same job as the women. She knows that like so many of the men at the munitions factory he was likely rejected by the army for something or other, flat feet maybe. Una stares at his feet.

Bastard.

"Look lady, the last girl lost her arm because she was stupid and didn't listen to me, so if you know what's good for you, you'll do what I say, when I say it."

Una has no come back. The whole idea of someone being maimed by the machinery makes her swallow the words stuck in her throat.

Hudson bellows, "Well?"

"Right, I'm ready."

10

October 1916

Saturday morning. The women in Una's dorm are unusually chatty and giddy. Most of them are already dressed in their civilian clothes, their hair neatly arranged under hats with broad rims, all except for Maisie Matheson who wears a tight-fitting cloche with a plume sticking boldly upward, making her six-foot frame appear even taller. She says she had it made by a milliner in Toronto. To herself Una admits that it really is quite striking, but she has another mission on her mind. A haircut.

Next week the free day is Sunday, and it is expected that in the morning they will go to church, and in the afternoon, attend to their personal matters like laundry. That means waiting two more weeks to do what Una is bound and determined to do. Go to town and come back looking like a modern woman.

The crisp autumn air and golden sunrise guarantee a fine day for an outing. Several women have arranged to be transported to Parry Sound by wagon from Henderson's farm. When Una first came to the plant, she had wisely brought her bicycle with her. Today she dons a pair of knickers so that her skirt doesn't get snagged in the chain. Three of her friends, Emily, Rosie, and Evelyn agree to pedal into Parry Sound with Una, a short distance of just over six miles.

The dirt road is riddled with potholes. Una takes the lead. She swerves and calls out, "Keep to the right," and then, "keep to the left." Every once and a while one of the riders hits a rut and screams in delight. Una breaks into "Johnny Canuck's My Boy" and they all join in on the chorus.

> From where the Rocky Mountains dip
> And virgin Prairies sweep
> From Arctic rim to Scotia's tip
> Our call is o'er the deep.

As they come into the town the women pass under the newly constructed Canadian Pacific Trestle.

"It's the longest rail bridge in Ontario," quips Evelyn who always seems to be up on rare bits of news. "Let's head over to the Kipling Hotel. We can have our lunch there."

"Go ahead. I'll come along shortly." Una pulls over beside the Toronto Bank and dismounts from her bicycle. "Save me a seat." Una scans the row of stores on the other side of James Street. She had asked Maisie Matheson, who had her hair bobbed a few weeks ago, where she had it done.

Maisie had proudly fluffed her short permanent wave curls saying, "In the beauty salon, next to the barber shop, across from the bank on the main street. You can't miss it."

And there it is, a sliver of a storefront with a sign "Complete Beauty Services" hanging over the door, and a poster of a woman admiring herself in a mirror. Una grabs the handlebars of her bicycle and skips across the street to the salon. Peering through the window she can make out two women, both in long skirts, their hair neatly pinned up in buns. The taller woman is cutting a client's hair. The shorter of the two who is sweeping up the locks looks out and gestures for Una to come inside.

Tentatively Una opens the door. A small bell jingles over her head.

"I don't have an appointment, but I was really hoping that, perhaps, if it is alright, that maybe you could fit me in sometime today before it gets dark, because you see I've come in from Nobel by bicycle and, well, I only get to come to town every other Saturday and, well, I…"

"Not a problem my dear, not a problem at all. We can do it right now," says the taller woman. "Would you like to have it cut dry or washed?"

"Washed?" Una says startled at the notion. "You wash people's hair?"

"All the time. Would you like that?"

Una has no recollection of anyone ever washing her hair for her, not even her mother, although she is certain that it must have happened when she was quite young. Growing up on the scow she often washed her hair in the lake.

"Would you like that?" the taller hairdresser asks again.

"Would I?" Una beams, "Oh. Yes. I would."

Leaning over the basin Una feels as if all the worries of the world are being washed away. The delicate scent of lavender makes her think of Miss Stanton and the days of drying herbs from her garden.

If only Miss Stanton could see me now. Wouldn't she be surprised.

With towel wrapped about her head Una announces unabashedly, "Bob it. I want it short."

"You must be one of the munitionettes from the plant?" asks the shorter of the pair.

"How did you know?"

"Well, you're not from here. And you said you cycled in from Nobel. I know everyone in the Sound. I either know them or I'm related to them." She whispers into Una's ear, "You have a tinge of that yellow still on your skin."

Una flushes with embarrassment. "It doesn't wash off. I've tried."

"You're not alone, my dear," the taller woman says while clipping Una's locks. "I have a niece working at the munitions plant in Burlington. She says the yellow is from the chemicals they use when making those bombs.

But don't worry my dear, we all have a part to play, now don't we? If I were younger, I'd be there too. But I do help when I can. I collect donations for the Red Cross."

Una is so engaged in conversation she barely notices her long dark curls tumbling to the floor and when she looks up into the mirror, she is delightfully shocked. Her hair turns up perfectly under her ears.

Una sashays into the cafe at the Kipling Hotel. When her companions spot her they immediately stop everything. Like a photograph frozen in time their jaws splay open wide and their forks and knives hang suspended in mid-air. Emily's spoon slips from her fingers and clangs into her soup bowl.

"Now that's one lollapalooza of a haircut." Emily picks up her spoon and adjusts the white linen napkin on her lap.

"Do you like it?" Una twirls to give her friends a complete view of her newly coiffed hair.

"It really suits you, Una." Rosie's eyes keep blinking. "My parents would read me the riot act if I ever so much as even trimmed my hair, especially at one of those beauty salons. I hear you can get cooties from one of those places."

"Oh, eat your perch and clam up," Evelyn interrupts. "You look just like one of those Hollywood film stars. We ordered already. Sorry. We were famished. Here, take the menu. I highly recommend the creamed chicken on toast."

"It's a bit too heavy if you ask me," chirps Emily ladling her tomato soup toward her pursed lips. "I'm saving room for a chocolate éclair."

"Chocolate éclair?" Una looks puzzled.

"You've never heard of chocolate éclair?" Evelyn says in disbelief.

Una holds her head up high. She refuses to be embarrassed. "Have you ever eaten muskrat brains?"

On the ride back from town Evelyn pedals beside Una. "Muskrat brains? You're pulling my leg."

"We fried them." Una stands to pump the pedals up hill.

"That's disgusting," calls Rosie from the back.

"How do you know if you've never tried them?" Una shouts at the top of her lungs as she speeds down the other side of the hill, her feet pointing out in opposite directions.

I'm flying like a bird. Look no hands.

The bicycle pedals whip around. Una screams, "Holy jumping-jeepers!"

Una heads straight for a huge curve. With her feet flailing about she makes a desperate attempt to catch the spinning pedals. She tries to push back on the brakes, but her shoes keep slipping. The tires bounce erratically over the bumps. The handlebars jostle uncontrollably.

From the top of the hill her three companions watch in horror as Una careens directly into the ditch and flies face first into the middle of an enormous raspberry bush. They scurry to the bottom of the hill just as Una pulls herself out of her prickly entrapment. She picks up her bicycle and wipes the dust and leaves from her coat and pants.

"Just my luck. " Una holds a greasy broken bicycle chain in her hand.

It's at least another four miles to the plant site. And the sun is already below the horizon. What the heck am I going to do now?

"I guess I'll just hide it behind the bush and arrange to have it picked up later. So, who wants me to pedal standing up while you sit like a princess on your bicycle seat? Emily?"

"Why not?"

Emily mounts the bicycle and holds onto Una's waist just above her hips as they swing with the motion of the pedaling. She senses an erotic attraction to Una that she cannot explain. How she wants the ride to never end. How she longs to be naked with Una, kissing her, and stroking her body. The height of the pleasure exceeds the words in her heart.

After the cafeteria dinner of smoked ham and scalloped potatoes the four girls saunter back to their dormitory still exhilarated from their day in town. Evelyn sees it first. A poster tacked outside the door to their building. Rosie holds up her flashlight.

"Look. There's going to be a Thanksgiving dinner and dance at the Recreation Hall in the New Village."

"When?" the other three chorus together.

"Two weeks from tonight. Hallelujah. A Saturday. We can go ladies. We can go," Rosie chants brightly.

"Who's playing the music?" Una asks.

"The Alexander Brothers." Rosie makes a spotlight on their photo. "Take a gander at him. The one with the saxophone. I could really fall for him."

"Don't you have a boyfriend overseas?" asks Emily. Evelyn gives her a poke in the ribs.

"No harm in looking, is there?" Rosie flicks off the light. "Time to hit the sack girls. It's been a dilly of a day, that's for sure."

Una waits outside while her friends go inside and head toward their bunks. Craving the tranquility of a rare moment alone, she walks to the far end of the dormitory, and around to the dark side of the building. Una leans against the clapboard wall and glances up at the crystal-clear sky. The stars shimmer like diamonds.

Rachel, I wish you were here to tell me your night-sky stories, you know, the ones about shooting stars and babies.

Una strains her eyes to find the ones that both Rachel and Eva had taught her about. Pegasus, Aquarius, Venus, and traces of the Milky Way. The only sound is the wind whispering through a row of pine trees. Una takes in a slow, deep breath of the cool autumn air and holds it as long as she can.

Peace at last.

11

October 1916

"Here you go girls."

Mrs. Greenfield, a senior volunteer from the New Village, pushes aside a wisp of white hair dangling in front of her eyes.

"Lots of letters this week and a few parcels too. Thanksgiving goodies I suspect."

Twice a week mail is delivered to the plant by train. Mrs. Greenfield along with two other older women sort and deliver the letters and parcels to the dormitories. The women working in the munitions factory know that Mondays and Wednesdays are the only days of the week when their letters are taken by train to Toronto. From there they are shipped out across the province or overseas to their loved ones fighting in the war.

"You're lucky," Emily holds out a parcel and two letters addressed to Una. "Say, is that military postcard from one of your brothers?"

"It's from Colin," Una says with relief. "I've been waiting weeks to hear that he's okay."

Una turns the card over and reads the typed note:

> Nothing is to be written in this side except the date and the name of the sender. Sentences not required may be erased. If anything else is added the postcard will be destroyed.

Scrawled in pencil are a few words.

I am quite well.

Several lines are struck off with a black pen followed by:

I have received your letter of July 8, 1916. Letter to follow shortly.

More marked out lines and finally a signature and date.

Colin Campbell, September 2, 1916.

Una sighs and her shoulders drop down.
"That's good news. He's still alive," Emily says.
"Well, he damn well better be."
"Did he send you that?" Emily points to a sketch Una has pinned up on the wall over her cot.
"Colin did that when he was still at Camp Niagara with the 162nd Battalion. Remember the call from Prime Minister Borden? They needed more soldiers. Colin and a gang of the lumberjacks raised their own battalion. That's why the regimental badge that Colin drew has a pair of axes in a pine stump."
Una reads the note scribbled below the drawing. 'We'll show these German rats who's going to win this war. No one is going to beat the Timber Wolves of Parry Sound'.

Unsayable Absence

"My other brother, Robert, is with the Muskoka Cracker Jacks, the 122nd Battalion. It sure would be nice to know where he is." Una's voice waivers.

"I know. These are uncertain times." Emily moves closer and puts her arm around Una's shoulders. "Wonder what's inside the package. Cookies?"

"Wouldn't you like to know."

"Yes, I would." Emily waits. "Well, aren't you going to open it up?"

"I suppose I will. Could I have a little elbow room?"

"Where is it from? Who sent it?" Emily points to the return address. "Baysville? Oh, that must be from your friend, you know the one you told me about, oh gee-willickers, what is her name?"

"Eva Stanton. You are one nosy-parker Emily Finlay."

Una unties the string and slowly unfolds the flaps of brown paper. As soon as she lifts the lid off the box, the smell of lemon, rose petals, and honeysuckle causes Una to bring her hand to her lips and close her eyes.

"We used to make this potpourri together. We put the petals and herbs in tiny sachets and sold them at the Fall Fair in Huntsville. We gave half of the money to the hospital fund. Em, this is so lovely, smell."

Taking the potpourri in her cupped hands Emily holds it under her nose.

"Oh my, it's heaven Una." She leans over and peers into the box. "I told you. I bet your bottom dollar you've got cookies."

Una pulls out a card and reads the hand printed list: Pumpkin Sugar Cookies, Molasses Cookies, Oatmeal Cookies. Under the tin of cookies Una pulls out a neatly folded silk scarf with burgundy flowers.

"I recognize this. It's from Eva's Japanese kimono. Oh, my word she made this for me. Wait there's a note attached." Una reads silently.

"Well, what's the story?"

"She says she caught the hem of her kimono on a crate in her shed and the tear couldn't be mended so she's made two scarves, one for me and one for her. I can't wait to wear it to the Thanksgiving dance."

Emily holds the scarf and feels the silky-smooth texture against her cheek.

111

"Didn't you get a letter from your parents Em?"

Emily shakes her head. "No, not this time. Maybe next time though. My father's a professor and my mother is always volunteering with one thing or another."

"Here, take a couple of cookies and get yourself ready for bed. I want to write to Miss Stanton to thank her. Now go on."

Emily starts to saunter away but abruptly turns back and throws her arms around Una. "Thanks Una, thanks for the cookies. You're the best friend a girl could ever ask for."

"You too Em, you too. Good night."

Una watches Emily head toward her cot on the far side of the room then reaches to pick up the letter bearing a Canadian King George stamp in the top right-hand corner.

Look at that. Martha did write. Miracles never cease to happen.

Martha's letter is full of gossip and stories about her baby, a girl named Madeline.

> Maddy has the croup and barks like a dog all night long. I hardly sleep a wink these days. Thank God Jonathon is working his father's farm and not fighting overseas. No word from Robert yet. Colin sent a card. I am constantly making meals for the women who have come up here for the harvest. I wouldn't trust any of the alone with Jonathon. They're a bunch of silly biddies, giggling and fussing about. Father has gout again. You really should write to mother.

Just like Martha, always making me feel guilty. Una crumbles Martha's notepaper in her hands and shoves it under her mattress. It's getting late. Most of the women are tucked in for the night. Una nibbles on a molasses cookie and scribbles a thank you note to Eva Stanton on a post card of the Kipling Hotel. Then, holding the sweet-smelling sachet to her chest, Una curls up under the covers and slips into a long-needed sleep.

Unsayable Absence

"Today's the day," Evelyn chirps. "My mouth is watering for some turkey and gravy, let me tell you."

"And pumpkin pie," Rosie adds while brushing her teeth and spitting into a cup.

"How can you be so noisy first thing in the morning?" Emily pulls the covers over her head and grumbles, "Can't a person sleep in at least one day a week?"

"Oh no you don't. Up and at 'em soldier-girl." Rosie tugs at her blankets.

"Rise and shine, sleepy head." Evelyn playfully joins in, pulls the blankets from the bottom of the cot, and tickles Emily's feet.

"Okay. Okay. You win." Emily reluctantly sits up. "Where's Una?"

"Gone for a walk, I think." Evelyn shivers as she puts on her cardigan.

"Where?" Emily rubs her hands together. "Good grief, when can we get some wood for the stove. They said it would be here by Thanksgiving. I'm freezing," she whines while looking out the window. "Speak of the devil. Quick open the door."

"Well, God helps those who help themselves ladies," puffs Una who drops an armful of firewood beside the stove. "There's more by the stoop. Mr. Henderson had some of last year's wood out back of his barn. He sold me a pile. It ought to keep us going until Mr. High and Mighty McPherson gets around to having it delivered."

It only takes a few minutes for Una to stack the kindling with bits of dried-up leaves and hay. The women huddle around and watch as the flame races up the mound. Una tosses one of the smaller pieces of wood on top. Then a larger one.

"We'll be warm in no time," says Una wiping bits of bark from her hands. "What time do we want to go to the village?"

"It's a nice enough day," Emily sniffs, "Why not go over mid-afternoon. We can take a walk along the beach."

"The IOED," Evelyn starts but then sees a puzzled look on Una's face. "The Imperial Order of the Daughters of the Empire. They are hosting a tea and bake sale." Evelyn sneezes. "Proceeds are going to the widow's relief fund. I think it starts at two this afternoon."

113

"Sounds good to me," Rosie says as she clears her throat. "Tea and treats, a walk on the beach, dinner at five and dance at eight."

Una holds her hands up to stop the conversation.

"Smoke. The smoke isn't going up the stack."

The women cough and wave their hands at the thick air wafting into the room from the belly of the stove.

"Damn it. It must be plugged. Bird nest or something." Una urgently dashes outside and sees that there is no smoke coming out of the chimney. She charges back inside.

"Open the windows."

Una frantically grabs the water bucket and sloshes it onto the smoldering pile. Immediately a black cloud billows into the room and tiny particles float through the air like dark gray snowflakes.

"Our clothes," Maisie shrieks. "Our outfits are going to be ruined. They'll reek of wood smoke."

In a matter of seconds all the women scramble outside of the building, their best clothes clutched to their breasts. Some of the gals are still in their pajamas and bathrobes. Others have come outside without their shoes, and several have their hair curled up with bobby pins.

In chaotic choreography they simultaneously turn their heads toward the oncoming sound of a horse's hooves. They spot McPherson approaching on his white horse. He draws up beside the dormitory.

"Charming sight," he bellows in his military-like voice, "and what, pray tell, is this commotion all about? Do I smell smoke?"

Una squeezes to the front of the crowd.

"Smoke? Do you girls smell smoke?" says Una. The women shrug their shoulders and look around while feigning expressions of innocence on their faces.

"It's probably someone burning off the fall leaves," says Una confidently.

"So, you've all come out to," he stops abruptly then, "Why in heaven's name would you come out looking like this?"

"It's a lovely day to air out our clothes for the Thanksgiving dinner, wouldn't you agree ladies?" says Una encouragingly.

"Yes," they chorus, "a perfect day. Couldn't be better."

"And we want to look our best for the dance." Una continues without taking a breath. "Are you and the missus going to be there? Of course, silly me, of course you will. Don't you just love turkey and gravy Mr. McPherson. Sure hope there is enough pie to go around. I'm a huge fan of raisin pie myself but most folks like pumpkin, especially on Thanksgiving. Will you be saying the grace? My father always says grace at our house." Una quickly changes the topic. "Oh, look at that," Una points toward the cornfield. "Geese, over there. Look Mr. McPherson. Look. Oh, golly, you missed them."

Una uses every possible tactic to draw McPherson's attention away from the wood that she had piled up beside the veranda. Meanwhile the women arrange themselves so that the evidence can't be seen by him, not even from the height of his horse.

"Right, well, I'll be making my rounds. Some of the women in Unit 10 say they aren't feeling well enough to work their shift this morning. Women's issues I imagine. And by the way, wood will be delivered on Tuesday but don't burn until the pipes are cleaned. Last thing we need is a fire out of control. We could be blown to sky heavens.

The women smile and hold their breath until McPherson disappears down the road. Finally, they exhale with gales of laughter.

"That was too close for comfort, if you ask me." Maisie holds out her emerald-green dress.

"I know," adds Emily, "I'd hate to see McPherson pop a cork. None of us would be having turkey tonight that's for sure."

"We fooled him." Una takes charge, "Come on girls, what are we waiting for? Let's get dressed to the nines."

12

October 1916

The trees boast an array of colors: maple red, oak orange, and poplar yellow. It is only a short mile from the dormitories to the New Village, and the season has gifted the women with sunlight, cool temperatures, and clean fresh air, a welcome relief from the stench of the factory buildings.

"I hear they are going to build a bowling alley," Evelyn shares the gossip.

"Really," Rosie wonders. "Will we be allowed to go there?"

"Maybe," Evelyn smirks, "maybe not. They built this place for the managers and their families. Not for us."

"I never liked bowling any way," Maisie adds acerbically.

Emily notices that Una has stopped by the roadside while everyone else has moved further toward the village. She saunters back to where Una leans over the side of the road.

"What are you looking for?" asks Emily.

"I love the last flowers of autumn. They are so beautiful. Look, Em.

Do you know the names of these?" Una points to a tall group of delicate purple flowers with yellow centers.

"I'm not sure. Is it a kind of daisy?"

"It's called a New England Aster and the tiny ones behind it are known as panicle asters. And look over here." Una steps into the meadow. "Oh, my goodness, I didn't think I'd see one of these so late in the season." Una crouches beside a yellow and orange cup-shaped blossom.

"I've never seen that one before." Emily kneels beside Una.

"Impatiens capensis."

"What?" Emily moves closer.

"Sorry Emily. I learned the Latin names from my friend. You know, Eva Stanton. Remember she's the herbalist I've told you about."

"Of course, but what should I call it?"

"Jewelweed. It's a touch-me-not."

Emily places her hand on Una's shoulder and comes to a standing position. "Well at least we can touch each other, if we want to."

Una doesn't seem to notice the intention of Emily's words. "Not only is it pretty to look at but it has medicinal benefits. Have you ever had a rash from poison ivy?"

"Thankfully, no."

"Rachel Little Feathers taught me about this plant. She taught me more than I ever learned at school."

"Have you mentioned her before," Emily says, her curiosity piqued.

"I believe I may have. I spent most of my growing up years with Rachel. I called her Nokomis. That's grandmother in Chippewa. One time, I guess I was about six, maybe seven years old, I wandered through a patch of poison ivy. I had this horrible rash all up and down my legs, on my hands and arms. Rachel collected these plants. She crushed the stems and rubbed the sticky sap on my skin so that the blisters would stop itching."

"Did it work?"

"Like a miracle cure." Una looks down the road. "I guess we should catch up to the others."

"Take my hand," Emily offers, "Don't trip. You don't want to stain you dress."

"Wait," Una reaches and picks several wild asters. She offers them to Emily. "Don't they make a lovely bouquet?"

As soon as Una opens the doors to the Recreation Hall the smell of apples and cinnamon makes her mouth water. "This is set up beautifully, Emily. You'd think it was someone's wedding."

Each table boasts a white linen cloth and lace-trimmed serviettes with potted ivy and purple chrysanthemums in the middle. Set around the perimeter is an assortment of bone china plates, cups and saucers, most likely borrowed from the women who live in the village.

"Welcome ladies," Doris Finnegan, donned in an apron with orange pumpkins on it, leads Una and Emily to the table where Rosie, Evelyn, and Maisie are seated.

"One of us will be coming around with cucumber or egg salad sandwiches shortly. I'll bring over the tea in a moment. Someone else will serve the sweets. It is the least we can do to thank you young people for your untiring efforts," she says in her usual unwavering tone of authority.

"We must find happy times while our boys are overseas fighting this wretched war. And if you care to donate to the widows' fund there is a basket by the door. I trust you will save room for the apple crisp. I made two this morning from this year's Macintosh apples."

"Thank you," says Una who sits tall trying her best to look like a polite young lady.

Rosie blurts out, "Do you have coffee?"

Evelyn kicks her under the table. "Don't be silly Rosie. This is a sit-down tea, not a corner cafe."

"If we could get coffee these days, we'd certainly have offered it but as you know some things are harder to come by." Doris fusses with her apron strings. Looking Rosie straight in the eye she points to a floral bowl with a tiny silver spoon in it and says sharply, "We do have sugar. I'll be back with the tea."

"Who wants to go to the beach afterward?" Emily looks expectantly at Una. "It's a perfect day for a walk."

"I've signed up for euchre," says Evelyn opting out. "Besides, I don't want to get sand in my shoes."

"Thanks Emily but I told Maisie I'd partner with her for the crokinole match," Rosie says as she reaches for the milk and pours a splash in her teacup."

"Una?" Emily says hopefully.

"I'd love to. I miss the lake back home. Yes, let's go to the beach."

"Won't this place look splendid once the veranda is finished," Emily says as they stroll past an unfinished bungalow. "It reminds me of our cottage near Kincardine. We go there very summer. You must come sometime. Does your family have a cottage?"

"Well, not exactly," Una answers awkwardly.

"What do you mean?"

"In the summer, my family lives on a scow. I guess one might consider it a floating cottage, of sorts. My father uses it to transport supplies across the Lake of Bays, near Huntsville."

"A scow? Now that is unusual."

"Not for me." Una winks. "I guess I'm a bit unusual too then?"

"I'd say so."

Una gives Emily a friendly push and scampers ahead. She calls back, "Come on slow poke. What's keeping you?"

They amble past two more cottages. One is painted yellow and boasts a white picket fence and a screened-in porch. The blue home adjacent to it is somewhat smaller and is nestled beneath a stand of poplar trees. A blonde cocker spaniel runs out to meet them.

"Oh, how adorable," Emily leans down to pet the pup. It rolls onto its back begging to be scratched.

"Do you hear that?" Una tilts her head to listen. "Music. I hear music. From around the curve. How very strange. Are you coming?"

"In a minute," Emily says cuddling her newfound friend.

The music grows louder as Una rounds the corner.

I know this song - 'By the Light of the Silvery Moon'. My father loves to sing it.

Una spots a gramophone set up on a table beside a workman's shack. A brawny man sits in a striped folding chair, the stub of a cigarette hanging from the corner of his mouth. He nods at Una.

"Beautiful day," he says flicking the ashes. "Haven't seen you around here before. You must be one of those gals working up at the munitions plant. Care for a smoke?"

"No, thank you." Una approaches the gramophone with curiosity.

"You like my arrangement here? I've got some other recordings, some Al Jolson. Maybe you'd care to stay and listen for while? I hear you gals are going to the dance tonight. Say, how about a taste of this apple cider. It's got a bit of a kick to it."

"There you are." Emily catches up to Una.

"Hello young lady," the man croons and tips his tweed cap. "Sure are a lot of bonny lasses here today. Why don't you join us?"

"I'm not staying," Una speaks up. "We're just passing by. Come on Emily." Una puts her arm though Emily's. "Good day sir."

Further down the road Una adds, "That man gave me the willies. Why isn't he in the army, I'd like to know."

They follow a narrow path that takes them from the road to the beach. Una stares at the waves in disbelief. "Oh my, this lake is enormous. I can't even see the far shore. Let's test the water."

Una sits on a rock, removes her shoes, and rolls her hose from her feet.

"In October?" Emily says with skepticism in her voice.

"Better now than in November."

Una hauls up her dress and skips toward the waves. Her toes sink into the dark, wet sand. Water swirls and pools around her ankles. She prances out and prances back in, again and again. Finally, she races out of the water toward Emily.

"I think my feet are going to drop off. Its freezing."

"Told you so," Emily jests. "Let's head back. Maybe we can take in a game of cribbage before the dinner."

"I'm so full can barely move," Una announces while pushing her chair toward the table. "Let's head out for some fresh air while the men set up for the dance. "I swear that dinner buffet had more food spread out than I've ever seen in her life. A whole lot more than at any church function back home. I had seconds of the roasted parsnips."

"I filled my plate twice," Evelyn says holding her stomach. "I feel more stuffed than a turkey."

"Not me. I saved room for dessert," Rosie says lighting up a cigarette.

"Good thing we're up here in farm country," Evelyn says. "Can't imagine what other folks are eating, especially in England."

"Quite the speech by that member of parliament, whatever his name is, telling us we need to do more to win the war. What more does he expect?" Una kicks a stone at the side of the road. "How many of our men have to die?"

"Let's not think about that tonight, Una. Let's just have a good time." Rosie takes a drag on her cigarette.

"Besides, we do more than most. Putting our own lives at risk." Evelyn speaks up, "Didn't you read the Toronto Daily Star? Last April there was a terrible explosion in a munitions factory in Kent, in England. Over sixty people were killed. Mostly women."

"Look, this is supposed to be a fun evening. Let's go back inside." Emily tries to bolster their spirits. "The band is going to start soon. Una, can you teach me the fox trot?"

"I suppose so. But don't step on my new shoes. They cost me nearly a week's pay." Una says.

"And if I do?"

"You'll be polishing them for a year."

The long tables have been stored away to make room for the dance floor while a few round tables with chairs have been set up off to the sides. Strung from the bare barn-like beams of the vaulted ceiling, several rows of lights twinkle like stars in the night sky.

"This is going to be wonderful," says Rosie as she twirls across the empty dance floor. She hoots at the musicians who are busy setting up their instruments on the small stage. "Let's hear some music fellas."

"Yes ma'am. Right away ma'am."

The saxophone player salutes Rosie from underneath the careful watch of a King George V portrait. Flanked on one side of the stage is the Union Jack. On the other side is a poster of a beaver chewing on a tree. The message reads: *Keep All Canadians Busy. Buy Victory Bonds.*

"Hit it boys!" The band breaks into "Bugle Hall Rag". Right away the floor fills up with dancers stepping to the lively rhythms. Una and Emily join a cluster of women gathered beside the punch bowl.

Rosie saunters over, hands on hips, "Slim pickings tonight ladies. Looks like we gals will be dancing with each other."

"That's fine with me," Emily jumps in. "Besides, who wants to dance with the likes of Mr. Stratton anyway. We'd be looking down at his bald spot the whole time."

Rosie points. "Oh, my dear Lord, if he isn't asking Doris Finnegan to dance. But who is that handsome bloke over by the door?"

"He's one of the construction crew," Una says.

"Really. And how do you know that?"

"He has a hut down by the beach, but I think," Una is cut short.

"Una Campbell, you little flirt." Rosie rolls her eyes.

"We ignored him, didn't we Una?" Emily says coming to Una's defense. "He offered us booze, but we just walked away."

"Hush up, he's coming over here," Rosie tosses her head back and wiggles her shoulders as she adjusts the bodice of her dress.

"Good evening ladies. And how are we all doing?" He notices Una. "Nice to see you again. Care to dance?"

"No, thank you." Una's mind races for an excuse. "I sprained my ankle down at the beach. I'm sure there are plenty of other woman you can dance with tonight."

"I'm sure there are," he says boldly.

Rosie fusses with her hair and looks at him flirtatiously out of the corner of her eye.

"Shall we?" he asks.

Una and Emily watch nervously as the man takes Rosie by the waist and leads her onto the dance floor.

"Sure hope she doesn't fall for him. He's got trouble written all over his face." Emily turns to Una. "So, does that mean we can't dance either?"

"Sorry Emily. I guess I put my foot in my mouth."

"Very cute.

Shortly after midnight the women arrive back at the dormitory still laughing and joking about the events of the day.

Una asks, "Has anyone seen Rosie?"

"Wasn't she dancing with one of the workers?" Evelyn snorts. "He had a flask under his jacket. Kept taking a tipple and offering it to Rosie."

Maisie pipes up, "I saw them earlier when I was having a smoke. They went behind the storage shed. Probably doing you know what."

"With that gongoozler?" Evelyn scoffs. "I hope not. Rosie ought to know better to keep her bloomers on."

"I could see right through that bloke," adds Una. "Hope she gets back soon. We have to be up for our shift before sunrise."

"No rest for the wicked," mutters Maisie.

As predicted morning comes far too early. With too few hours of sleep the women quietly prepare for another day at the plant. Una, who once again is the last to leave, notices Rosie curled up under her blankets. Una walks over and gives Rosie's shoulder a nudge.

Rosie moans.

Again, Una prods her friend's shoulder.

Another moan. "Go away. I'm not feeling well."

"You'll be docked your pay, Rosie. You've already missed too many days. They might even let you go."

No response.

"Too much booze last night? What time did you get in anyway?" Una waits a few moments, then pulls the covers down from Rosie's head.

"Jesus, Rosie. What the hell? Did he do this to you? You've got to report the bastard."

"I can't." Rosie tries to hide the bruises on her cheeks. "No one is going to believe me. They never do. They'll say I had it coming."

"No, Rosie. Men like that creep can't get away with this," Una pleads. "Look, I'll go with you. We'll report him."

"Report it, to who, McPherson?" Rosie throws the blanket aside and sits up. "He won't listen. They'll say I was drinking and that I asked for it. Just do me a favor. Don't do anything. Besides, I'm getting out of this hell hole anyway."

"But why Rosie? You're needed here. You'll never make this much money anywhere else. Why?" Una begs.

"Look Una, you don't understand. I can't go to work like this. People will talk. Don't tell them anything," Rosie pleads pitifully, "please."

"I don't understand."

"You're going to be late. Doris will be after you again and you don't want that." Rosie adds, her voice quivering, "I'll be fine. Don't worry, Una. It's for the best anyway. My uncle has a farm. I can help out there."

"You're sure?"

"Sure, I'm sure. Now skedaddle." Rosie walks Una to the door. "Please, Una, don't breathe a word of this to anyone."

Una quietly closes the door behind her, and steps into the first snow fall of the season. At the plant, several women ask after Rosie. Una just shakes her head. She doesn't want to lie, and she definitely doesn't want to tell them the truth. She made a promise to Rosie.

After a while folks stop fussing about Rosie. They have too many other things to worry about. There is a war going on. Bombs need to be made.

The factory workers have crammed into the cafeteria for the Friday night screening of a popular film and the war newsreels. Even though the reports on the war are sometimes weeks, if not a month late, everyone is anxious to get the news.

"May I?" Emily points to the chair beside Una. "I've been looking forward to seeing this ever since it was released. My cousin in Boston saw it last year. Mary Pickford is so beautiful. I can hardly wait to see her as Cinderella. She was born in Toronto you know. Even though she is America's Sweetheart, I don't hold that against her."

"She was born in Toronto?" Una asks, "I didn't realize that. Good, they are about to show the newsreel. Maybe we'll see what's really going on over there."

"They never show us that Una," Evelyn speaks up. "The government won't let the cameras go anywhere near the front lines. Believe you me they don't want us to know how bad it is."

Doris Finnegan shushes the crowd and turns the lights down. The whirling sound of the projector can be heard coming from the back of the room, and a stream of light cascades through the smoke-filled air. Images flicker on the large canvas sheet suspended on the far wall. A headline jiggles before their eyes: PATRICIA LIGHT INFANTRY ON PARADE. A silent moving image shows a long row of soldiers with rifles slung over their shoulders marching steadfastly across an open field.

Without hesitation Una, Emily, and Evelyn break into song and immediately everyone joins in.

And the man who's dressed in khaki
Is a man we're proud to know,
For he fights to guard the Empire
Our gallant soldier so.

"That'll be quite enough," Mr. Stratton's voice bellows out. "These are serious times."

Another headline with white lettering on a black background reads: ON THE WAY TO THE TRENCHES.

"It's not good over there. I've been listening to the wireless," says Evelyn.

Una calls out, "Look at them waving and smiling. Hey, that chap is twirling his rifle."

A firm hand grabs Una by the shoulder. Doris Finnegan stares down at her. Una looks up. Smiles. Doris just shakes her head and walks back to her chair beside the light switches where Stratton stands, arms folded across his chest.

"Guess I got told," giggles Una.

Images fade into another headline: BRITISH LINES ON THE CANADIAN FRONT.

Suddenly the room grows quiet as the film reveals the quagmire in the trenches at the front lines. Men in rain-drenched uniforms slosh though ankle-high streams of muddy water. The wasteland of the battlefield can be seen in the background. Not one single soldier smiles. Not one of them looks at the camera.

"Wish they'd hurry up and show the movie," Emily squirms impatiently. "What's this?" She reads out loud, WOMEN WORKING FOR THE CAUSE."

"It's us," Una stands up. "They filmed us working in the Gun Powder Plant. Oh, my gosh, there's Maisie winking and smiling at the cameraman." By this time everyone is on their feet pointing and making cat calls."

"If I'd known I would have worn my lipstick."

"Look at Stratton's bald spot."

"Isn't that Rosie? Whatever happened to her anyway?"

"Heard she got herself pregnant." A man's voice mockingly hollers above the din.

"Yeah, that's right," Una says sarcastically and equally as loud. "She did it to herself. By God, we ought to castrate the bastard like they do to horses." A noticeable gasp silences the room.

"I mean it," Una shouts. "Bloody bastard."

Una rushes from the cafeteria with Emily following on her heels.

"Wait Una. Wait. Don't you want to see Cinderella?" Emily catches up to Una who is visibly shaken. "It's a lovely movie."

"Em, it's only a fairy tale. It isn't real life, now is it? What are we thinking? There's a war going on. Who wants to wait around for Prince Charming to show up these days? There's no such thing as a Prince Charming. And now with Rosie. Damn it, Emily. I wasn't supposed to say anything to anyone. I promised."

"It's okay Una. We all figured out what happened to Rosie." Emily puts her hand on Una's arm, "You won't catch me holding my breath for Prince Charming. Other people are far more important to me than that."

"What do you mean?" Una asks still rattled by her own outburst.

Emily stutters, "It's just, that, well I don't like that kind of person you know, all full of themselves, thinking they're God's gift to women."

"Then why on earth do you want to see Cinderella?"

Emily hesitates, "I love Mary Pickford. I've seen every movie she's ever made. I adore her."

Emily wants to say more but holds back. She wants to say, *"And I adore you, Una."* Instead, she blurts, "Forget that chump in there. He's an unrefined, ill-mannered boor. What do you say? Are you coming in or just going to stand out here in the cold?"

"You're right. I need a good laugh anyway."

As they step into the cafeteria Emily leans into Una and whispers, "It's not a comedy. It's a romance."

13

July 1930 The Asylum

Una waits anxiously with the other patients seated in the auditorium. She twirls her hair with her fingers, while the hymns float up from the organ to the ceiling.

I'm a sinner. I shouldn't be here.

Everyone has been encouraged to attend the Sunday morning service whether they want to or not. Una, when given the option of being locked in her room, reluctantly gave in.

Sitting beside Una, a young woman with facial hair sprouting from her chin fixates her eyes on Una. "My dog, my dog, my dog," she repeats. "I've lost my dog. Where is my dog? I want my dog back."

I don't know where your blooming dog is, Una thinks without looking at the girl.

"I tied him to the car bumper," she says a bit louder. "I want my dog." Louder. "I want my dog."

Eventually, a nurse comes and takes the distressed woman away. Things like this keep happening to Una. Complete strangers want to tell her their stories, their troubles, their fantasies. One patient swore that Una was her reincarnated grandmother. But Una has no words to tell anyone about the pain that eats at her soul.

The minister's voice creeps into Una's drifting in and out of being there. She half hears his blessings, his prayers for the people, and his warbling vibrato for each hymn as it plays. Una thinks that he looks like an overstuffed penguin in his black suit and white priestly collar. He opens the bible and reads, "Turn to Psalm 71. Verses 1 to 24. In You, O Lord I put my trust; Let me never be put to shame."

Shame? How can this be happening? What sin did I commit? Why couldn't I stop him? I should have stopped him. I had a feeling something wasn't right. Why didn't I listen? Oh, God, why didn't I listen?

"Deliver me, O my God, out of the hand of the wicked."

I am a wicked, evil person. Una rocks herself forward and back, forward and back.

"O God, do not be far from me; O my God, make haste to help me!"

14

December 1916

The Parry Sound arena is packed with locals from miles around, plus a large contingent of women from the munitions plant. It is Una's first time attending a professional hockey game. When she was younger, she loved playing shinny with her brothers on the ice on the Lake of Bays. They used frozen horse-pucky. One time Robert got a black eye when Colin accidentally shot the icy dung smack onto the bridge of his nose. It bled like the dickens.

Tonight, the Northern Fusiliers are taking on the Ottawa Senators, a morale booster for the war. Una, who wears her wool scarf and matching hat, has picked a front row seat. She huddles with Emily, Evelyn, and Maisie to keep warm.

Both teams skate onto the ice and start warming up while the military band entertains the crowd with familiar marches and popular songs. The band plays "It's a Long, Long Way to Tipperary". Immediately, everyone sings and claps along.

The Senators wear red, white, and black striped sweaters and leggings. They pass the puck at one end. At the other end of the rink the Fusiliers, clad in khaki-colored uniforms, practice their skating maneuvers.

"The Fusiliers are in the 228th Battalion," Evelyn shares. "Look, it says so, right here in the program." She reads aloud, "These strong young men of the National Hockey Association are here to support our overseas troops." Evelyn folds the program and adds, "So far they're in first place."

Out of the blue one of the Fusilier players skates up to the boards where Una is seated.

"Aren't you Colin Campbell's little sister?"

Una's eyes open wide and before she can respond he says, "I must have made a mistake. Sorry for the confusion."

The referee blows the whistle and hollers, "Time to play hockey."

Tipping his hand to his brow the young hockey player salutes Una and her colleagues, "Enjoy the game. Keep your eye on the puck. It could come flying right at you."

Maisie leans into Una and drawls, "I'd rather keep my eyes on him."

The teams line up, face to face, while the band plays "The Maple Leaf Forever". Everyone in the bleachers stands up. Men remove their caps. Voices sing out enthusiastically:

> Our Emblem Dear, The Maple Leaf Forever,
> God save our King and heaven bless,
> The Maple Leaf Forever.

The crowd stays on their feet for "God Save the King", and again the cavernous arena echoes with their uplifted voices. Una waves her Union Jack in the air.

"Who was that player?" Emily asks.

"He knows your name," Evelyn states with confidence.

"Wish he knew my name," Maisie swoons. "So, who is he Una?"

"I think he came to our home for dinner with my brother once."

"Let's wait for him after the game, at the back door," Maisie suggests.

"At least that's what I'd do if I were you."

"Maybe," Una ducks. A puck whizzes over her head. "He was right. Keep your eye on the puck ladies."

Maisie lights up a cigarette and pulls the fox collar of her red wool coat tighter around her neck. Evelyn stamps her feet on the packed snow while Emily tugs her angora hat over her ears.

Una paces nervously back and forth. "It's cold enough to freeze the balls off a brass monkey. Whose idea was it to wait at the back door? Maybe we should forget the whole thing." Una starts to leave.

"Aren't you curious? Don't you want to know who he is? I know I do," Maisie blows cigarette smoke in little, circular rings.

Suddenly the door swings open. The women step aside as a steady stream of players boisterously leave the building. Maisie spots him first. "Hey you! Come over here. So, you think you know her?" Maisie waves her cigarette toward Una's face.

"Well, I thought I did, but then again I only met her once. Last year at her parent's place," he says looking at Una.

Una feels somewhat unnerved by his bright blue eyes and jet-black hair.

"You're Colin's little sister, aren't you? What are you doing up here? I thought you lived down near Huntsville."

"Now I remember," says Una a bit more at ease. "You worked with Colin at the lumber camp."

"Angus McFadden at your service." His eyes sparkle and his smile reveals a dimple on his left cheek. "It's Una, isn't it?"

"Yes." Una blushes. "Colin brought you to our place for New Year's dinner. I remember. You said you were going to take up a job with the Canadian National Railway. Where was that?"

"Capreol."

One of the Fusilier players hollers, "Come on Angus. They're giving us grub at the Presbyterian Church. I'm hungry enough to eat a moose."

Maisie steps forward, hands on her hips. "Will we be seeing you at the dance tonight. We'll be there. We gals from the munitions plant know it is our duty to keep you boys entertained."

"Sure thing. I'll see you all there." Angus runs to catch up to his teammates. "Save a dance for me Una."

"Wouldn't you know it, there's still more women than men," Maisie complains while looking into the Dance Hall's bathroom mirror. She dabs a bit of red rouge on her lips with her baby finger.

"You always get asked to dance," Evelyn say as she peers into the mirror and scrunches her forehead, "not like some of us who end up watching from the sidelines."

"Who cares who we dance with. I know I don't. I just like to dance. You don't care either, do you Una?" Emily stands in the doorway, about to leave the Ladies Room. "Una, you don't care, do you?"

"Care?" Una, whose mind is elsewhere, replies, "I guess not."

"Of course, she doesn't care. She was already asked to dance even before we got here." Maisie raises an eyebrow. "Nice looking fellow too, if you ask me."

Emily grabs Una by the arm, "The band's already playing. What do you say? Let's get things started. You and me Una."

"Why not." Una links arms with Emily. As they walk out of the Ladies Room Una glances out across the empty dance floor.

"Wait a minute, Emily. I hate being the first couple up. Besides it's a waltz."

Disappointed, Emily sits at a round table beside an ornately decorated Christmas tree. Una gestures that she is going to get some cider and fruit cake from the refreshment canteen when one of the hockey players approaches the table.

"Care to dance," he asks Emily.

Emily fidgets with her pearl necklace.

"Go on Em. Have some fun. I'll catch up with you later." Una turns to the young man, "She's shy, that's all."

Una slips around the perimeter of the dance floor toward the refreshment stand. She stops to admire the band, dressed smartly in black suits, white shirts. and red bowties.

To think that the Runnymede Orchestra has come all the way from Toronto for the dance. Don't they look elegant. Miss Stanton would love this evening. It must be like one of those ballroom affairs in England that she told me about. This tune is a fox trot. It seems like forever ago that she taught me the steps.

"There you are," Angus comes up behind Una who is in the middle of taking a bite of fruit cake. A crumb falls from the corner of her lips. "May I?" Angus offers Una his fresh handkerchief.

"No, I'm fine. Thank you." Una flushes with embarrassment. "This fruit cake is delicious," she mumbles while chewing.

"It certainly must be," he says while reaching for a slice.

"Great music tonight," he adds casually. "I've heard the orchestra before. They perform in other towns when we play, in Ontario anyway. There's another group for Montreal and Quebec." Angus hesitates then asks, "Would you care to dance?"

"Why not."

Angus leans and whispers into Una's ear, "I have two left feet. I hope we don't trip."

"That's okay. I have two right feet. We should be fine."

After several numbers, Una remarks to Angus that he is quite a fine dancer, to which he offers Una the same compliment. When the orchestra leader announces that the next number will be a tango Una stares blankly at Angus. Angus stares back equally stymied by the prospect of tackling the footwork. Instantly they both break out in laughter and quickly exit the dance floor.

Angus escorts Una to a table toward the back of the hall and pulls a chair out for her. "I've been wanting to ask you, have you heard from Colin? Did he enlist?"

"He's with the 162nd Battalion, you know, the Timber Wolves." Una sighs, "I've only heard from him once. On one of those whiz-bang cards. But I haven't heard from him otherwise. I don't even know if he's…" Una stops short.

"It's a bloody mess over there." Angus pulls his chair closer to Una's. "The letters get lost all the time. At least that's what I understand. Let's not give up hope. Right?"

Una smiles. "You're right. I would have heard by now if anything had happened to him. They'd let me know. The army. They'd let me know if he was wounded or, God forbid, worse."

"Say, tell me about yourself. How did you end up here? What do you do at the plant? I might get shoved against the boards now and again but that's not nearly as dangerous as what you do every day playing with explosives."

The evening slips away as Una tells Angus that she felt it was her duty to help somehow, especially since both of her brothers had enlisted. She tells him about what it was like growing up on a scow. Angus tells Una about his trip across the Atlantic when his family moved from Northern England to Northern Ontario. Una shares her fond memories of times with Rachel Little Feathers while Angus says he has learned how to hunt with bow and arrow and that he is fond of venison if it is cured the right way. They wonder how long the war will go on.

Angus says, "I've heard a rumor that our team might be sent overseas."

Una grows quiet.

"Look, we've got a game scheduled for up here in mid-January. Maybe we could see each other then?" Angus fiddles with the cuffs of his sweater.

"Maybe we could," Una teases.

"Maybe?"

"Maybe, yes, I'd like that."

Una is unaware that Emily is standing beside their table, her coat and hat in her arms.

"We're going now, Una. It's getting blustery. The hay wagon is ready to take us back to our dorm. Are you coming?"

Angus stands and pulls the chair out for Una.

"We've got an early start tomorrow," he says. "We're heading to London. With this weather I hope we make it in time for the evening game."

Angus escorts Una outside. "Better bundle up. It's a cold one tonight. I'll see you in the New Year. Happy Christmas. I'm sure you'll hear from Colin. It takes a while for the letters to get across the ocean."

The next morning is a clear, crisp day with the sun shining brightly, making blue, pink and yellow colors shimmer like tiny crystals on the freshly fallen snow. As usual Una is the last to leave the dorm. She mindlessly traces the footsteps of the other women who, like sheep, had left earlier for the factory building. Even now the cacophony of the machinery spills into the air. But Una hardly notices. She knows she is walking to work but her mind is reliving the previous night. Angus McFadden made her body tingle in ways she had never felt before, and when he looked into her eyes, it was as if they had known each other forever.

Inside the change room as she tucks her hair under her bonnet Emily asks, "Are you going home for Christmas Una? Only three more shifts. I can hardly wait to give my ears a rest."

Distracted by her thoughts, Una kicks off her winter boots and changes her clothes for another day of working on the line. *That old man Hudson, always bossing me around. As if I don't know the ropes by now.*

"Alright ladies, put a move on. We don't want to let our boys down now do we." Doris Finnegan stands hands behind her back. "Bombs don't make themselves."

Emily asks again, "Are you going home?"

"Yes," Una seems unsettled. "I'll be staying with Eva Stanton, but I will drop in on my family."

She sees wrinkles of concern on Emily's face.

"It's complicated. My mother and I, well, we don't always agree on things, and I'd rather not have a miserable time trying to explain myself when it never does any good anyway. Besides, I adore Eva Stanton. She has always been so supportive. So yes, I will be going home."

"I'm glad that we chose to work over New Years," Emily says. "It's awfully swell of the other gals to sacrifice their Christmas. I sure will be glad to get away from this stench." Emily opens the door to the factory floor. She shouts above the din, "See you for our tea break. I have a little something for you."

"Do you like it?" Emily drapes the necklace around Una's neck and closes the clasp.

Una fingers the tiny gold heart. "It's lovely Em, but I didn't know we were exchanging gifts. I'm so sorry Em. I don't have a gift for you. Really, I feel terrible. How about I treat you to lunch in town when we get back."

"Don't worry Una. I just wanted…" Emily stammers and looks at the floor. "I just wanted to let you know what a dear friend you are to me. And in any case, there's no expectations with love."

Una stops sipping her tea, then places her teacup on the table. "Love?"

Emily reddens profusely, "Well, yes, there are all sorts of love, like how sisters love each other."

Una gives her head a shake. "Emily, you've never had a sister. Some sisters don't even like each other much. My older sister Martha, let's just say, we have taken different paths in our lives, and I barely know my little sister Beth."

"If I could have had a sister, I would have liked it to be you."

"Enough chit chat ladies." Doris rings the warning bell to drink up and leave the cafeteria. "Remember to pick up your Christmas boxes on your way out this afternoon. A little something for everyone."

"One of the gals on the other shift said there are candy canes, humbugs and tickets to the next hockey game," says Maisie as she catches up to Una and Emily. "Guess you'll be wanting to be there, won't you Una? Say, maybe he's got a friend you'd like to introduce me to?"

"Oh Maisie, you don't need me to help you find a man. You'll do just fine on your own. I'm sure of it." Una heads over to her station where Mr. Hudson waits, a grim expression on his face.

Hudson points to Una's station on the line. "You should have been here sooner than this, yakking away like a chicken with that bunch of biddies. Keep your eyes on your work Miss Campbell. Remember what happened to the last girl who took her mind off the job."

Una mutters sarcastically under her breath, "Why Mr. Hudson I do believe you are in fine spirits for the Christmas season."

"What's that," he snaps back.

"I hope you have a lovely Christmas Mr. Hudson."

15

December 1916

The first night on the brass bed in Eva Stanton's home provides Una with the most restful sleep that she has experienced in months. In the morning she slowly awakens to the delectable aroma of fried bacon and cinnamon pancakes, a breakfast Eva had promised when Una arrived late the previous evening. They had little time for a visit, and it was evident that Una was quite exhausted. They agreed to get caught up the next day.

"Make yourself comfortable my dear," Eva calls from the kitchen, "Breakfast will be ready in no time."

In the living room Una leans on the piano, still draped with the same silk embroidered shawl, and the floral Tiffany lamp on top. In some ways it looks as if time has stood still, as if war had never broken out, as if Una had never left for the munitions factory.

The ferns in the window seem a bit bigger than she remembers, and a pile of newspapers and books take up most of the space on the chaise lounge, the usual place where Eva likes to keep up on the affairs of the world.

A tall fragrant spruce, fully decorated with colorful glass ornaments, takes up the far corner of the living room. The Victrola has been moved to beside the marble statue of Gaia, the Greek Goddess of nature, now adorned in a garland of holly.

Over breakfast Una shares her experiences at the munitions plant. She offers an animated description of Doris Finnegan's abrupt manners which amuses Eva greatly.

"She does have a kind heart," adds Una.

"I do like the way you have bobbed your hair. Suits you," says Eva tucking her own loose curl around her ear. I must consider that myself one day."

"And then there's Maisie. She is a flirt beyond words, but easy to get along with, most times. My best chum is Emily. We met on the train to Parry Sound even before our first day."

"I am so pleased for you Una," Eva says passing her the maple syrup.

"I certainly have missed your delicious pancakes."

For a while, Eva and Una discuss the changing roles and responsibilities that women are taking on the home front and overseas, and yet, somehow, men still treat women as property. Eventually, Una's boisterous impersonation of Mr. Hudson breaks the solemn mood.

Eva shares the neighborhood comings and goings. "There are fewer men in the village these days. Our university women's group meets weekly to knit socks for the soldiers. I suppose you've noticed that the newspaper has stopped printing the names of the young men who have succumbed to the ravages of war. There are far too many now."

I hope to God my brothers are okay.

"Any word from your brothers?"

"I did get a cheery note from Robert. He's stationed in England, somewhere. He couldn't say in the letter of course. A while back I received a notification card came from Colin stating he had arrived safely and would write soon. No, letter yet."

"These things take a while," Eva says encouragingly.

As the morning unfolds, they reminisce about their times together, how Una learned piano, and helped with the herb gardens, and how Rachel Little Feathers had reluctantly come to live in the shed behind the house.

On Christmas Eve, Una and Eva attend the candlelight service at the Anglican church. Una wears her bright red cloche with a silver pin of holly and ivy, an early Christmas gift from Eva. Afterwards they toddle home to enjoy Eva's fruitcake and rum-tinged eggnog.

Christmas Day passes peaceful. Eva invites Una to put together a puzzle with a picture of an old English thatched cottage surrounded by pink, yellow, and white flowers. They knit, read, and play a rousing round of Loo, Eva taking most of the tricks.

That evening they dine on stuffed guinea fowl, apple squash casserole, cranberry preserve, and mashed potatoes. Eva opens a bottle of her own elderberry wine, and they toast one another repeatedly until the bottle is empty and they are quite ready to call it a day.

"I promised my parents I'd visit them tomorrow," Una says as she climbs the stairs. "This has been the most memorable Christmas ever, Miss Stanton. I can't thank you enough."

"No thanks needed, my dear girl. You have given me such a joyful Christmas."

As soon as he sees her coming toward the house, Duncan Campbell, wearing neither coat nor hat, barrels through the snow to give his daughter a jovial bear hug. Una detects the odor of stale whiskey lingering on his breath from the night before.

"Come in before you freeze yourself," he guffaws, "Ah, but it is good to see you. Your mother, she's been busy making a special meal for us, though her back, it gives her such pain."

Una steps into the warmth of her parent's home, and the smell of dinner simmering on top of the wood stove fills Una with a rush of memories.

I wish my brothers were here. I can't imagine what it must be like for them.

"Good to have you finally here Una," her mother says without looking away from stirring the pot of venison stew. "Glad you could find some time to come and see your family, especially at this holy time of year," she adds acidly.

"Now Maudie, let's not get our knickers in a knot. Not today my love." Duncan stands behind Maud and gives her a peck on the neck.

Una turns to her younger sister, "My goodness Beth, you've grown so much taller than when I last saw you."

Beth looks away and runs to the corner of the room where, despite her age, still plays with the dolls handed down from Una and Martha.

"She's terrible shy that one," Duncan explains. "Not like you Una, not like you at all."

"Is Martha coming over?" Una asks.

"You missed her. She was here yesterday. Christmas Day," snaps Maud. "Most families spend Christmas Day together."

"I'm sorry," Una begins.

"Being sorry won't change a thing," Maud says with bitterness like bile rising in her voice. "Lord knows I've been sorry for most things in my life. I wish my mother had never brought me up here when I was a girl. But she did. I'm only sorry I didn't move back south when I had a chance."

Una doesn't respond. Over the years she has learned it is better to let her mother rattle on about her discontented life.

"Being sorry that I married your father who spends more time at the pub than at home won't change a thing, now will it?" Maud unabashedly directs her stare at Duncan.

"Mother," Una comes to her father's defense.

"It's fine Una." Duncan speaks up, "Leave your mother alone. It's Christmas. We just want to have a nice family time. Don't we Maud?"

"A nice family time," Maud scoffs.

Duncan tries to smooth over the fragile mood by telling one of his favorite tall tales. Maud gripes about having heard it before.

"I caught a lovely trout while ice fishing last week," he boasts. "I nearly fell into the damn hole."

"Now that would be a shame," Maud says mockingly.

During the meal Una makes every effort to cheer her mother up. She tells her about the pranks the women play on each other, like the time they stole Maisie's rouge and hid it in her own shoes. She gives a detailed account of her work at the munitions plant and assures them it is safe. She relates a play-by-play description of the Fusilier's hockey games, but she does not tell them about Angus McFadden. Not yet.

A knock on the door disturbs the uneasy atmosphere.

"That must be my ride back to Miss Stanton's," says Una.

"So soon? Haven't seen hide nor hair of you for months. You've barely arrived and had your supper, and now you're leaving without so much as a please or thank you." Maud says her jaw fixed with anger.

"I promised Miss Stanton not to be too late," Una says struggling for an excuse. "Thank you for the lovely dinner. There's nothing in our cafeteria that is as good as your cooking Mama, believe me."

Maud starts to clear the table.

"Wish I could stay longer and help with the clean-up," Una says even though she is much relieved to be leaving.

"This is for you." Una says as she reaches into her satchel. She hands her mother a blue silk scarf with daisies, "I know how much you love flowers."

Una pulls out a book, 'Thirty Folk Songs from the British Isles'. "Thought you'd enjoy this Papa. It even has the Skye Boat Song in it. You already know that one. The illustrations are beautiful.

"And here are some bonbons for you Beth," Una offers them to her sister who quietly takes them.

"Thank you, Una," she says in a meek voice. "I miss you."

"I miss you too Beth." Una says.

I wish I could take you away with me. Away from Mama's moods and Papa's drinking bouts. Oh Beth, I hope you can get away, like I've done. Get away. As far as you can.

"Come again my bana-phrionnsa," Duncan slurs as he gives Una a hug. "I'll have learned every ballad by heart by the next time we see you."

"Be careful Una," Maud says fingering the delicate sheen of the scarf in her chafed fingers.

"I will Mama. I will. I'll be home in the Spring. I promise."

16

January 1917

Una fusses with her hair, dabs rouge on her lips, and looks for a fashionable scarf to wear. She has waited weeks for this day. Angus is back for an exhibition game against the Quebec Bulldogs.

She received his Christmas card shortly after New Year's. He had written that he was looking forward to seeing her at the game and taking her to the dance afterward. Una didn't share her card with anyone, not even Emily. Instead, she placed a sprig of lavender in the envelope and slept on it under her pillow for that past three weeks.

"Almost ready gals." Una applies a touch of the tuberose oil behind her ears, another gift that Eva Stanton had given to her during her Christmas visit. Her palms perspire in anticipation of holding hands with Angus on the dance floor this evening.

"What a divine essence," Maisie swoons as she swaggers past Una. "Wearing it for that Mr. Somebody Special?"

"Of course, she is." Evelyn holds the door of the dormitory open. "Quick. Let's go before the cold gets in."

"A woman has the right to wear a perfume regardless of her intentions." Emily briskly pushes past the other women.

Una barely hears their comments, so lost in her own thoughts about seeing Angus again.

I hope I haven't put too much rouge on. I really like Angus. He must have plenty of women wanting to go out with him. What if he doesn't feel the same way I do.

She takes one last look in the mirror, grabs her scarf and gloves, and closes the dorm door behind her. Just as the hay wagon starts to pull away several women, already seated in the wagon, holler for the driver to wait.

"We almost left you behind young lady." The driver looks at Una over his shoulder. "Hop up. We can squeeze you in."

By the time they arrive at the arena, the game is already in motion. Una spots Angus leading with the puck. He darts around one of the opposing players who tries unsuccessfully to check him with his stick. Angus twirls around, recovers, and picks up the puck once more. He raises his stick. He shoots. Cheering wildly the crowd jumps to their feet. Angus makes the first goal of the competition.

"He's quite the athlete," teases Maisie elbowing Una in the arm.

Suddenly the referee skates to center ice and blows his whistle. "No goal," he shouts. "Number 14, offside."

Boos and hisses echo throughout the smoke-filled arena. Some spectators call the referee unthinkable names. Then all the players from both teams jump from their benches and start yelling obscenities in each other's faces.

In the end, after much coaxing and separating of the players by the referee and the linesmen, each team returns to their respective benches. Just as the crowd simmers down the referee once again makes the announcement.

"No goal."

In a flash the Fusilier manager races straight for the referee, his fists flying in the air.

Una watches in horror. She's never witnessed anything quite like this in her entire life. Then she notices that Angus has come back on the ice.

Oh no, what is he doing?

Angus skates directly toward the manager, pulls him away from the referee, and escorts him back to the bench. Una looks up at the score board. Still no goal.

Una waits anxiously for Angus to emerge with the other players from the back door of the arena. She had told her friends to go ahead without her. She'd see them at the dance. A light snow starts to fall. Una sticks out her tongue to catch the flakes when, unexpectedly, Angus walks up to her.

"I used to do that as a kid," he says catching her unaware.

Una cringes. *Why did I have to stick my tongue out? Why did he have to see me doing such an idiotic thing?*

"One time, on a dare," Angus begins, "I put my tongue on a frosted glass windowpane outside of my school. It got stuck. The teacher had to come with warm water and pour it over my tongue."

"You're just saying that." Una tilts her head suspiciously.

"No, honestly. It really happened."

"How old were you?"

"Seven, or maybe eight. Not sure." Angus offers his arm to Una. "I was wondering if maybe you might like to have dinner with me tonight before going to the dance. I hear they have a nice selection in the hotel dining room."

"That sounds lovely," Una agrees. "We go there for lunch whenever we have a chance to come to town." Una pauses then asks, "By the way, what did you say to the manager that got him to stop fighting with the referee?"

"I just reminded him of the game we played against the Toronto

Blueshirts. He was hit with a twenty-five-dollar fine because he got into fisticuffs with that referee."

While having dinner their conversation flows like water burbling over pebbles in a brook. *He's so easy to talk with. We have so much in common.*

Una says, "I play piano and mandolin."

"I play guitar and fiddle."

"My father plays fiddle."

"My father fought in the Boer War. After the war he sent my mother, my sister, and me to Canada while he stayed behind to work on the docks in Newcastle upon Tyne."

"I wish we weren't at war," says Una changing her tone to a more concerned nature. "Is it true, do you think, that a million men have died in the past three months?"

"From what I hear the carnage to the Newfoundland Regiment is horrific. Nearly every one of their men as been wiped from the face of the earth."

"It really has to end Angus. This can't go on forever. Not like this." Night has fallen. Una stares out the window and into the darkness. All that can be seen is a streetlamp and the snow swirling in circles about its cascading light.

Angus reaches across the table and places his hand on top of Una's hand. "We've been called up."

"What?"

"The order came down last night. We have one more game against Toronto and then we leave for St. John, New Brunswick. We won't even get to play the Bulldogs in Quebec."

"But I thought you told me you wouldn't have to go, that your team was supposed to promote the war, not fight in it." Una looks directly into Angus' eyes.

"That's what we all thought. The truth is we are employed by the army.

That's what they told us when we joined up, we'd never have to go. They want us to be the railway troops, to build a railroad to the front lines. The supplies have to get there somehow, and God knows, there are so many wounded soldiers that..." He stops short. "I'm going to be fine. I don't have to fight. I just have to lay the rails. I'll be alright. Look, we're late for the dance. You still want to go?"

"Of course. I've been waiting weeks for this." Una tries to make light of the news. "You better write to me Angus McFadden. And if you don't, I won't send you smokes and socks."

"It's a deal."

Angus goes behind Una and pulls the chair out so that she can stand.

"I really think you're something Miss Campbell. I really do." And he kisses her lightly on the cheek.

At midnight, the Runnymede Orchestra plays a waltz for its final number. When the last note fades away, Una and Angus remain on the dance floor, holding hands.

"I don't want this night to end," Una whispers. She looks around as all the other couples leave the dance floor.

"It doesn't have to," Angus offers. "We could go for a walk in the park. It's not that cold."

"And how do you propose I get back to Nobel."

"Well, I have this friend Aladdin, and he has a magic carpet."

"Now I would love to do that," Una smiles broadly. "I really have to go back with the others. I wish I could stay longer with you Angus, what with you going overseas. And I don't know when I'll see you again."

Without saying a word Angus escorts Una to the cloak room. He holds her coat for her as she slips her arms into the sleeves. Outside they stand close, gazing up at the night sky.

"Do you think you might be able to get some time off from the plant?" Angus continues, "Maybe you can meet me in Toronto to see our last game. And we can spend a few days together."

I want to go. I want to spend more time with Angus, but I've never been to a city like Toronto.

"Where would I stay?"

"I know of this rooming house. It's quite decent," says Angus. "My sister Edith often stays there. I'm sure you will be comfortable. And don't worry about the cost. I'll pay for your train fare. You won't be out a penny."

"I can afford it," Una says defensively. "I make a decent wage,"

"Then you agree to come?"

"Yes, I do."

"Then let me treat you to a wonderful vacation in a fantastic city."

Una turns abruptly. It's Emily tugging at Una's coat sleeve. "The wagon is leaving Una. Are you coming?"

Looking to Angus she says, "When do I meet you in Toronto and where?"

"Our last game is on February 6th. I'll get a ticket for you to arrive on the 5th." Angus rushes his words, "I'll meet you at the train station. Don't worry. I'll have it all arranged."

Together they walk briskly across the snow toward the wagon. Angus pulls Una close and gives her a passionate kiss.

"Una's got a beau." The women call out teasing barbs and point their fingers. "Oo-la-la."

The wagon pulls away with Una seated at the rear. Angus tries to keep pace with the wagon.

"You're going to trip Angus McFadden. You're not on skates," Una shouts gleefully.

At last Angus stops to catch his breath. Una watches until he disappears into the depths of the snowy evening, but not from her heart.

17

July 1930   **The Asylum**

"We had to bring her inside," the head nurse complains to her young assistant. "You'd think she'd at least have come in when it started to rain. Drenched to the bone."

"Some of these people are so disturbed. Lord knows what's going in their heads," the assistant says as she gathers up Una's wet clothes. "Maybe if they treat her with electroshock therapy she'll start eating again. She didn't touch her breakfast this morning. And it took me over an hour to convince her to get out of bed."

Numb, Una sits motionless, a towel draped over her shoulder.

"I'll set her dry clothes out. Hopefully, she'll dress herself," offers the assistant. "Here you go Mrs. McFadden, a nice clean dress."

That's not my dress. I don't like that dress.

The nurse speaks to Una in a slow, loud voice, each word distinctly enunciated, "You can come to the sewing class this afternoon Mrs.

McFadden. You'd like that now wouldn't you."

I'm not deaf. I'm not stupid. Leave me alone.

Una scratches her scalp vigorously.

"Now, now Mrs. McFadden," the head nurse scolds, "You shouldn't be doing that. You could cause bleeding and infection. Is that a good idea? No. We don't want to have to put mittens on you." The nurse reaches to take Una's hands down. Una jerks suddenly away and crawls into a fetal position in the far corner of the room.

"Not again," the nurse says exasperated, "We'd better leave her for now. I'll make a report to the doctors. This can't go on."

This can't go on. This can't go on. This can't go on.

"Very well Mrs. McFadden," the nurse condescends, "If this is how you want to be." She leads the assistant from her room. "I really don't know what else to do with that woman."

Una drops into a whirlpool of haunting memories of things that happened when she was a little girl.

It wasn't my fault that I got lost in the woods. Nokomis found me. I was okay. Why did Mama yell at me? Why does the nurse scold me? Stupid, stupid, stupid, no good, no good, no good.

A flash of lightning and instantaneous crack of thunder strikes a tree outside the room. Una trembles in the corner.

My God, I'll never see him again. I'll never kiss him again, hold him in my arms. Angus, Angus, my darling Angus. My sweet, my love, I can't go on without you.

18

February 1917

Wringing her hands, Una stands beneath the towering clock inside the Toronto Union Station. The bell chimes. *Six o'clock. Angus promised to meet me here. He paid for my fare. He'll come. I know he will.* She scans the crowd hoping to find his face among the horde of people.

Last week Doris Finnegan spoke with the plant manager and convinced him that Una was well deserving of this special time away from her duties. He had agreed on the condition that she knew she would not be paid for the days she was absent.

Delicately, Una adjusts her new wide brimmed hat, a gift from the women in her dormitory. Again, she anxiously searches for Angus. Her friends who have been to Toronto told her that she had nothing to worry about, but right now Una feels more lost and alone than ever before.

The station swarms with hundreds of people, soldiers in uniform, women wearing fashions that Una has only seen in newspapers and in the movies, businessmen in bowler hats, children in pinafores darting around their mothers' ankles.

Unreasonable notions swim in her head. *Did I come on the wrong day? Did Angus forget? He said six o'clock. It's already ten past. Maybe he's hurt somehow.*

Suddenly Una hears her name being called out from the other end of the station. *At last.* Angus waves his military cap in the air and like a fish swimming upstream, he weaves his way through the mob.

"You are a sight for sore eyes." Angus leans over and kisses Una on her cheek. "Were you waiting long? Sometimes the streetcars are quite unreliable especially after a snowfall. It can take hours for the tracks to be cleared. But never mind. Are you well? Hungry? Have you had dinner?"

Una's eyes open wide with delight at his barrage of questions. "Yes, actually. Other than a biscuit and cheese I have not eaten since I left this morning."

"Then we shall get you fed and settled in at the Avalon Guest House. There's a cafe not far from here. Shall we?"

"Yes, let's." Una reaches for her travel bag which Angus quickly picks up. He holds his other arm out for Una.

"I can hardly wait to show you the town," he says cheerfully. "Have you heard of orchids growing in the winter? Well, they do in Toronto. Tomorrow I will take you to see for yourself."

The Queen Street trolley jostles along the road making a straight line past cars that dart in and out of traffic. When pedestrians cut across the street the driver frantically rings the bell and bellows, "What a bunch of old saddle-geese. Don't they know I can't swerve this thing?"

Una grips tightly to Angus' arm.

"I take this route every day and no accidents have happened, so far." He squeezes Una's arm closer to his body and gives her a reassuring smile.

Angus points out different landmarks, The Dominion Bank, the

Unsayable Absence

Eaton Department Store, and in the distance, the towering fifteen storey Trader's Bank Building. As they cross University Avenue he points to a large poster of a little girl sitting on a sofa with her father. "Daddy, what did you do in the Great War?"

He tells Una that the day before he is to leave there will be a military parade running down University Avenue from the Ontario Legislature to the fairgrounds of the Canadian National Exposition. He asks, "I hope you can be there with the other soldiers' wives." When Una blushes he quickly adds, "soldier's sisters, mothers, grandmothers, Adam and Eve, and all the animals on Noah's Ark."

Una laughs softly, then asks, "Where will you be staying?"

"At the Exhibition Fairgrounds. They've been converted into accommodations for us soldiers. It's a bit rough but it beats sleeping in a tent in the rain and snow."

Further along, the streetcar stops to pick up passengers at Spadina Avenue. Angus leans over Una and points to a marquee on the right-hand side.

Una reads, "Popular Vaudeville. Pictures Change Daily."

"This is the Pickford Theatre. You know, Mary Pickford. A few of us boys have been there."

"I've never been to a vaudeville theatre." Una stares at the building as the streetcar pulls away.

"When you go back you can tell all the women that you, Una Campbell, attended the one and only Pickford Theatre."

"Angus, really? I would love to go. Emily will be so envious. She simply adores Mary Pickford."

Angus reaches up and pulls the cord to alert the driver to stop at the next street.

"The Guest House is a short block north of here. These days it's hard to find a place that isn't housing the new recruits." Angus explains, "I asked around and my commanding officer told me where his mother often stays, and I think I mentioned that my sister Edith has stayed there as well."

Angus stands up and steadies Una as the streetcar jerks to a stop.

157

"Quite the balancing act, isn't it?" Una says holding onto Angus for dear life.

The newly constructed Edwardian house boasts a wraparound veranda and stained-glass windows. Angus turns the bell on the oak door. In a split second they hear the excited yapping of a dog and voice reprimanding it to behave.

"It's Nathaniel, the owner's terrier," Angus tells Una. "Its bark is all show."

"Nathaniel?" Una shakes her head, "That's quite the name."

"He answers to Natty. By the way, the owner is a retired elementary schoolteacher. Mrs. Johnson lost her husband in the Boer War. She'll talk your ear off if you're not careful."

The door opens. "Mr. McFadden," Mrs. Johnson beams while holding the dog back with her foot. "Do come in."

"So, this is the young lady you've been telling me about. Sit Natty. Sit. Let the good people in. Do I have to put you in the kitchen? Silly dog." She grabs the collar and leads it to the back of the house while calling, "Take your boots off. Just hang your coats on the rack. Natty, Natty, behave." And again, to her guests, "Sit by the fire. I'll be right back."

Una is overwhelmed by the lavishness of the house. To her eyes the interior is far more ornate than any home she has ever seen, and a far cry from her humble upbringing. Even the eclectic furnishings of Eva Stanton's home in Baysville pale by comparison. Every inch of one wall is covered with watercolors and oils in elaborate gilded frames. What really catches her eye is a boar's head over the mantle.

"Oh that." Mrs. Johnson returns with a tray holding two cups of hot cider. "I call him Frederick, after Frederick Foster, a good friend to my husband. God rest his soul. He was a bully of a man. He and my darling husband caught the beast in Africa.

She hands the cider to Una and Angus. "I had this simmering for you.

It's just what we need on a cold winter night like this. But just wait until tomorrow. I assume you've mentioned this to, what is your name my dear?"

"This is Una Campbell, Mrs. Johnson," Angus says before Una can speak. "She's come all the way from Nobel where she is employed at the munitions plant. It has been a long day." Angus hints that Una would like to go to her room sooner than later.

"Yes, where was I? Oh, yes, tomorrow is going to be cold. We are not allowed to burn coal on Mondays. Strict rules. These times are exceptionally difficult as you know. I couldn't buy chicken at the market on Saturday. But don't worry you can always come down here and sit by the fire. At least I have a pile of logs. They took down a rotting elm tree last summer. Good thing too. And I have a hot water bottle. Thank God they haven't cut the electricity. At least I am lucky to have an electric cooker. Not everyone has one of those. There are extra blankets and besides it's only one day and it'll be over before you know it. At any rate, this house holds the heat quite well. Oh, my goodness, I should let you two have a quiet moment. I remember my darling Reginald and I when we were courting." She pauses. "Did you hear that whimpering? It's Natty. Whatever would I do without Natty. Now I'll be in the kitchen when you are ready to go up to your room Miss Campbell."

Angus stands as she leaves, then whispers to Una, "I told you."

Una covers her mouth and muffles her laughter.

"I won't stay long. Curfew is at midnight. At least I was able to secure day leave to be with you tomorrow Una."

"Can I not pay for the cost of staying here?" Una offers.

"Do you wish to insult a gentleman?" Angus jests.

"I do earn wages and I don't want you to have to…" Una hesitates.

"It is my pleasure to have your company, Una, before I leave for Europe. I have it all arranged." Angus looks at his pocket watch. "I really do have to leave. I'll pick you up at nine. I promise to prove to you that orchids grow in January."

"A promise is a promise," Una says as she walks to the front door with Angus. Without another word Angus kisses her fully on the lips. They smile at one another, and Una kisses him.

Turning his collar up Angus slips out into the cold night. Large soft snowflakes fall gently upon his uniform. Una waves. She slowly closes the door, leans her back against it, and holds her hands to her heart.

So, this is the feeling of feeling in love.

With her hat, coat and gloves on, Una waits impatiently in the vestibule. Just as Mrs. Johnson had warned, the heat is not on in the house and Una awoke shivering under the covers. The hot tea and porridge did little to take the chill away.

The clock in the hallway chimes nine. Una peers through the lace curtain on the front door just as Angus walks up the stairs. A sudden surge of excitement that seems to have lingered since they kissed the previous evening races up her spine.

"Good day to you Mr. McFadden."

"Why Miss Campbell what a pleasure to see you this bright winter morning. Are you ready for an adventure in the city?"

"Yes, indeed, I am."

Angus offers his hand to assist her down the snow-covered steps.

"I can manage. Thank you, Angus." Una takes one step, loses her balance, and slips forward toward Angus who catches her in his arms.

"Looks like we are off to a good start," he beams.

Slightly embarrassed Una straightens her hat and coat. "Where are we going?"

"You'll see soon enough. Trust me."

They ride the streetcar for several miles. Una shares more stories about her adventures as a child growing up with Rachel Little Feathers, and how Eva Stanton taught her to play piano. Angus explains that his father had worked on the coal docks in England before coming to Canada. Nothing had prepared him for the black flies of Northern Ontario.

"Bear fat," says Una. "They don't like it. Nokomis and I used it to keep those nasty insects away."

"I've heard of that, but never tried it myself," Angus says, "I don't suppose there will be much need of it in Europe."

"No, I suppose not," Una muses. "Angus, does it ever get quiet here? I had no idea that Toronto was so... so..."

"Wonderful?" suggests Angus.

"Yes, I do find it extraordinary. But have you noticed, how people don't even say good morning to one another? I find that very strange."

The streetcar stops outside the Eaton Department Store.

"Oh my, Angus. Look at all the mannequins in the window. I've never seen so many, and the outfits, oh my. Do you think I might be able to go shopping later? I would so love to buy myself a little something. We gals at the plant rarely get time to go to town, and even when we do there's nothing like the fashions they have here."

"I don't see why not," Angus agrees. "Shall we go there after our lunch?"

"Oh, yes, Angus. Please. Let's do that."

"We're here," Angus exuberantly announces.

Through the streetcar doors Una glances at what appears to be a glass palace.

"This is Allen Gardens. They keep it heated throughout the winter." Angus leads Una from the streetcar. "Let's go inside and warm up."

The air in the Palm House is so warm and humid that Una immediately removes her winter outerwear and sits on a stone bench to take in the lush atmosphere. She deeply inhales the rich aroma of damp earth and flourishing plant life.

"To think that one can preserve summer under a glass dome. This is magical, absolutely magical. If only Miss Stanton could be here to enjoy these specimens. There must be hundreds of orchids from every corner of the world. Unbelievable."

"It is my understanding that people risk their lives to collect these rare plants. Look, there's a Lady's Slipper." Angus leans to read the label, "These bright yellow ones are called Dancing Ladies. Just like you my fine dancing lady."

Una blushes. "Oh my, this is an unusual one. Isn't it splendid Angus? Star of Bethlehem or Darwin Orchard from Madagascar. Where is Madagascar?"

"It's an island off the east coast of Africa if I'm not mistaken," Angus says while looking at more plants.

"How on earth did they ever manage to bring it all this way?" Una wonders.

"Not by carrier pigeon, that's for sure."

The rest of the day unfolds as if in a dream. Angus insists they have tea at the newly constructed King Edward Hotel where, fortunately, they keep the heat on for their guests. Una is most impressed by the tiered display of sweets - miniature cream puffs, lemon tarts, coconut squares.

Afterward they ride the streetcars from one end of the city to the other. They sit arm in arm and share hopes for the war to end soon and thoughts for what life will be like after the war. As promised Una visits the Eaton Department Store. She wanders through the fashion departments for more than two hours while Angus sips coffee and reads a newspaper in the store's cafeteria.

"You have had a spending spree, haven't you," Angus says upon seeing Una proudly prance up to him with four bags, two on each arm. "And you smell like the flowers at the Gardens. Lovely fragrance. My, what do you have there?"

"Just a few things," Una says coyly. "A woman can never have enough shoes."

Unsayable Absence

Una sits in a noisy crowd of spectators at the hockey game between the Northern Fusiliers and the Toronto Blueshirts. She feels so small, so very, very small, and lost in a sea of faces.

There are more people here than there are people in all of Huntsville or Parry Sound put together.

As soon as the game is over Una waits for Angus by the front door of the arena. She squeezes into a corner as the throng of fans spill out onto the street. When Angus finally arrives, he sees that she is noticeably shaken.

"Are you not well, Una?" Angus asks with sincere concern.

"I need to go back to the guesthouse Angus. Do you think we could do that? I'm feeling a little tired, I suppose. There has been a lot to take in," Una hesitates, "but, I have enjoyed every moment with you Angus. It's just that I'm not used to the crowds and all."

"I understand."

He does understand me so. And I do believe he loves me. I know I love him. I've never felt this way before. And he's going to leave me. I won't let on that it troubles me. I promise I won't. Oh God, please help me smile. I feel as if he knows my every thought and feeling. I don't want him to see that I am scared. Scared of losing what I have just found.

As they enter the guesthouse, they discover that Mrs. Johnson has retired for the evening, but not before leaving biscuits and sherry on a table by the fireplace. The burning logs cast a soft glow over the room. Angus and Una tiptoe to the sofa. There is a comfort in the silences between them, and Una feels as if she has known Angus for longer than forever.

"Will you wait for me Una?"

Una looks puzzled.

"I mean, will you wait for me to come back. Will you be my girl, Una?" Angus holds Una's hands in his hands.

"I am already your girl." Una flashes a smile. "I'll wait until the ends of the earth for you Angus McFadden. I will."

It is a raw and bitter day as Una prepares to leave from Toronto's Union Station. She stares blankly at her blurred reflection in the train window while in the distance the snow-white fields slip by like a film falling off the reel. The rhythmic sound of steel wheels on steel rails lulls Una in and out of her sensual memories. Ecstasy fills her whole being as she relives every moment spent with Angus.

If only I could have had more time with you. I have no idea when I will see you again and I pray to God that you come back to me. You must come back.

She holds fast to the last words he said to her that very morning when she went with him to the station. *"You're my forever girl Una. Keep the home-fires burning. I'll be back before you know it."* And then he held her close and kissed her. When his train pulled away Una tried to get a glimpse of Angus waving from an open window. So many soldiers, all cramming for a window. *Did he see me? The platform was so crowded. I took off my hat and waved it above their heads. Oh, I do hope he saw me.*

And now as her train slices through the rural landscape more thoughts flood Una's mind. *My darling Angus, can you read my mind right now? I am so proud of you, making those goals. Remember how the fans of the Fusiliers stood up and cheered. And thank you for taking me to the Pickford Theatre. The trapeze artist really scared me. I said, "My God, Angus, what if she falls." And you said, "Don't worry. There's a net to catch her."*

The black faced minstrels sang beautifully, and I got a kick out of the Russian midgets playing their harmonicas. Remember what you said about the female impersonator? You said, "If I met him on the street, I wouldn't know that the mimic was a man."

I've never laughed so much in my life as I have with you, my darling. It was so easy to forget that there is a war raging in Europe and that you would be leaving me so soon.

Thank you for introducing me to some of the soldiers' wives and mothers. I almost froze waiting on that corner. Where was that again? Oh, yes, the corner of University and King. I waited and watched all the different regiments march south from the Provincial Legislature. And then, I saw you looking so handsome in your uniform. You saluted and winked at me; you devil.

Una reminisces on their last night together when he kissed her just before he left and she went up to her room. She had pondered over what to give him as a love token. Before switching off the lamp she sat on the edge of the bed, bowed her head, and prayed that he would come home. *Come home to me, wherever home might be one day.*

In the morning she clipped a lock of her hair and tied it in a red ribbon that Mrs. Johnson had kept in her sewing basket. Red for courage. Red for passion. She placed the love token into a white envelope and wrote a note on the outside, "I love you more than there are stars in the heavens".

Before he boarded his train, she stood close to him and slipped the packet into his top left pocket. "Open it when you get to England, promise me you will," she emphasized. Angus placed his right hand over her hand and held it against his heart. Looking deeply into her soul he whispered, "I promise."

Una's train rumbles across the countryside. She presses her hands on her beating heart, imagining the warmth of his touch and the sensation of his lips on her lips. She closes her eyes and sighs.

I will wait for you, my love. I will. As long as it takes, I will be here for you.

19

March 1917

"There's a fortune teller in town." Maisie folds the newspaper and reads the advertisement to the other women in the change room. "Madame Florence Knows All, Sees All, Tells All". "This sounds like just the thing to do ladies. She reads palms, tea leaves, and Tarot. I've always wanted to have my palm read." She looks at her hands. "Which line is the love line? Una, you want to have your love line looked at, don't you?" Maisie teases.

Una, who has her back turned, seems lost in her own world.

"I'd say you're head-over-heels in love with that hockey player," Maisie taunts.

"No, I mean yes," Una sputters. "What I mean, is I need to get to my place on the assembly line. Mr. Hudson will be cracking the whip like a deranged lion tamer."

"Let me see that," Evelyn takes the newspaper from Maisie. "A fortune teller. That could be entertaining if nothing else. None of it is true, you know. It's just a game."

"Some people do have psychic abilities," Emily offers. "I'm up for it. Una? Let's go. What harm can it do anyway?"

"Sure, okay," Una says halfheartedly. She tucks her hair under her cap. and thinks of the lock of hair she gave to Angus.

I wonder if he kept his promise, not to look at it until he gets overseas.

"Where did you say this Madam, whoever, is going to be?" Una asks.

Maisie scans the advertisement. "It's this Saturday in the tearoom at the hotel. What fun!"

"You're next Una. She's very good," Maisie enthuses, "and so are these scones. Madam Florence told me that I am going to meet a man who has already been married. And he is going to be very wealthy. Do you believe it? What good fortune is that? She knew all this just from looking at my palms." Maisie stares at her hands. "I've always dreamed of marrying an older man?"

"Who says he's going to be older?" Evelyn looks sideways at Maisie. "Maybe he's a womanizer or a no-good bum."

"Come on Evie, don't be such a wet rag." Emily tries to make light of their outing. She speaks to Una, "Maybe you'll find out you are going on a great trip or something like that."

"Maybe, maybe not," Una says skeptically as she walks toward the rear of the tearoom.

Behind the blue velvet curtain a tiny woman of dark complexion sits at the far side of a small round table. She wears a red floral scarf wrapped around her head, and a matching brocade vest over a silky white blouse. There are gold rings on her fingers, and jangling bangles on each wrist. She holds out her arthritic hands for Una to take a seat across from her.

"Fifty cents for a reading of your choice." Her voice cracks as she points to a brass saucer. Una drops her coins onto it. "What will it be for you, young lady? Palms? Cards? You do not bring your teacup with you so I do not read the leaves, but I can tell by looking at you that you are very lonely. So, what shall we do today?"

"Cards, please."

"Shall we do love?"

Una hesitantly nods yes, and watches as the woman slowly places three cards face down in front of Una and points to them. "This card is for love in the past, this one is love right now, and this one is for what will come in the future. Let us look at your past." The fortune-teller turns over the card for the past. Una sees that it has three women facing each other in a circle.

"It is the women in your life but not your family. You have always had the love of women friends since you were a very little girl. Am I right?" The woman's piercing gray-blue eyes look directly at Una. *She's right but I'm not going to give her any clues to go by. This is just a gimmick and even if there is bad news would she tell me?*

"That's okay my darling girl. You no have to say anything. The cards tell me all. Madam Florence can see." She turns over the next card. "Now we look at the love that is in your heart right now." The illustration reveals a nude woman floating among the clouds.

"So, so beautiful. You are in love, so very much in love. That's why you look so sad. He is not with you right now. But look. See how she dances through the air. You should be very happy my dear for this is true love and you see she is surrounded by a wreath of victory. He has won your heart and you have won his. This is good news, no?"

Una cannot stop the blush from rising to her face.

"You can tell me his name."

"Angus."

"I am so happy for you and your Angus. Now we see where your love goes in the future." The woman turns the card over, and slowly draws back from it.

"What does it say? Is it good news?" Una asks anxiously looking at the image of a tower perched on top of a rocky mountain. A bolt of lightning strikes the tower, and two people leap headfirst toward the ground. Una feels a tightening in her gut. "What is going to happen? Tell me. I need to know. Is Angus going to die? Is he going die in the war?"

"No. I do not see this. What I can tell you is that life will have its challenges but what life does not have to overcome such things. Your love is true. Trust this. Remember the power of your love. It is far greater than anything else in the universe."

April 1917

The psychic reading haunts Una for weeks. When the other women in her dormitory receive letters from overseas, but none for her, Una fears the worst. Each night, as she waits for sleep to come, the disturbing image of the lightning bolt hitting the tower increases her longing to get news from Angus. The lights go out. Una prays.

I hope to God he is okay. I have to believe that he is. I have to. Please God. Please.

In the morning Una wakes with a start. She hears the door slam and one of the women calls out that the mail has arrived. *Please let there be something from Angus.*

Emily shuffles through the letters. "Una, here it is. A letter from England."

With eager anticipation, Una grabs the envelope. The post mark indicates that it has taken over a month to get to her.

March 4, 1917

My Darling Girl,

Everything is fine here in England, and I am glad to be on solid ground once again. During the crossing we experienced some high seas, and many of the men were overcome with sea sickness, but not yours truly. I am unable to write any details to my location but just let it be said that England is damp at this time of year, and a good shot of brandy warms one right up.

The towns are very different here, narrow streets and old stone buildings with slate roofs. There is little time for recreation, although a group of us did venture into a nearby town the other day. There are little bakeries, and I confess I have eaten more than my share of pastries. Saw a wonderful haberdashery with lovely hats displayed in the window. I immediately thought of you proudly wearing one of them.

I miss you deeply and pray that you are keeping a smile in your heart. It will be wonderful to be with you again. When I come home, I hope to get out my guitar and play some songs with you.

As always,

Angus

PS: Our Battalion has been changed to the 6th Battalion Railway Troops. Same boys, different name.

That evening immediately following dinner, Una chooses not to attend the film night. Instead, she remains in the quiet stillness of the dormitory, and rereads his letter: "I miss you deeply".
And though Una has been worried sick, she will not let on in her letter. It will be all good news.

April 3, 1917

Dearest Angus,

I have done nothing but think about you each and every

day since our time in Toronto. It was so wonderful to get your letter, and I am happy that you did not get sick while crossing the ocean. I read in the papers that President Wilson has declared war on Germany. Our American allies are rallying. And hopefully, we will see an end to this war, the sooner the better.

You will be glad to know that I have formed an all-women's band. The plant manager's wife donated an upright piano and a few weeks ago a group of us gals got together in the cafeteria. I play the piano and I hope to bring my mandolin back with me after Easter. We have a guitar, banjo, trumpet, and even drums! It really keeps our spirits up.

You may not get this package until after Easter. I made the socks from an old sweater that I unraveled. Hope they fit. And don't eat all the chocolate at once.

Be safe. You mean the world to me.

Love Una

20

Easter 1917

Eva Stanton's gardens are just starting to show signs of spring, the green hosta leaves barely protruding out of the dark, damp earth. Una sees Eva in front of her home raking the autumn leaves that have been left on the garden beds over the winter.

"There you are." Eva dusts the dirt from her work-gloves. "Come in, come in. Tell me your news. Mint, chamomile, rose-hip?"

"Rose-hip sounds divine. The tea at the plant has enough tannin in it to rust a kettle."

"What news, my dear?" Eva asks.

"I've formed a band. We rehearse after our shift and on our day off. Last week we played for a tea in the factory village. The ladies seemed to enjoy it. Remember teaching me to play piano?"

"You took to it naturally, Una. You have a very good ear for music. If only you had spent more time learning how to read the notes." Eva pours the tea. "Honey?"

Una places a dab of honey in her cup and stirs thoughtfully. "And I met someone."

"Yes?"

"He's overseas now. With the Railway Troops. I met him some time ago at my parents' place, but then he showed up in Parry Sound as a hockey player with the Northern Fusiliers. You've heard of them? The Northern Fusiliers? Anyway, we went to few dances, and I spent a weekend in Toronto in February, and I..."

Eva smiles, "So you are in love with this young man? What is his name?"

"Angus McFadden."

"Tell me more."

"He took me to this wonderful glass green houses at a place called Allen Gardens. You would absolutely love it there. They have hundreds of flowers, even an orchid brought in all the way from Africa." Una prattles on about the Pickford Theatre, the parade of soldiers, and her shopping spree at the Eaton Department Store.

"I wish you could meet Angus. He looks so handsome in his uniform," brags Una, "and, yes, he is every part a gentleman."

"Say, that is all good news my dear girl." Eva hesitates, "Have you seen Colin yet?"

Una stares in shock. "No. Where is he? Is he home? I've been waiting and worrying for months. Please Eva, tell me he is alright."

Eva says cautiously, "You mean you don't know?"

"Of course, I don't know. Eva, tell me. Where is Colin?"

"I thought that your mother or your sister would have written to you. He's been in the Whitby Convalescent Hospital since January."

"What happened Eva? Is he going to be alright?" Una stands up from the table.

"I understand he was badly wounded Una. Shrapnel, I believe, and gas. But it's the shock. He won't talk about it. At least your father told me that when I saw him the other day. Colin's visiting your family." Eva walks over to Una and places a hand on her shoulder. "You will go and see him, won't you?"

First thing the next morning Una borrows Eva's bicycle. The route to the scow seems so familiar. In some ways it is as if she had never left, the smell of the pine trees filling her lungs. She pedals down the grassy slope from the dirt road toward the scow. Una can clearly see Colin's back. He sits at the far end, facing out toward the lake, the morning sun shining down upon him.

Una lets the bicycle fall to the ground, and races onto the scow, "Colin, Colin, my God, you're home."

Her brother seems not to hear Una. She crouches down to look him in the eye, but he does not look back, his eyes fixed upon the water.

"It's me Colin. Una."

Colin slowly raises his left arm and points. "Loon."

Una glances at the ripples on the lake as the loon swims under the water and then surfaces only a few feet from the edge of the scow.

"There's another one. Wait. There it is." Colin watches motionlessly.

What has happened to my brother? Something horrific, and my God, the burns. They've scarred half his face.

Una swallows her revulsion. "When did you get here?"

No answer.

Una tries again, "How long will you stay here Colin?"

She waits, confused.

What do I say? What can I do?

"They mate for life." Colin finally looks directly at Una. "Una? I thought you were working up near Parry Sound. Are you home to stay?"

"Only for Easter. My God Colin, it is so good to see you." Una wraps her arms about her brother.

Colin winces.

"I'm so sorry Colin. I didn't mean to; are you hurt terribly?"

Colin reaches for his cane, and awkwardly comes to a standing position.

"I've got three legs now. Right, left and this wretched cane." He points to his right leg. "This one's only half a leg. It got sick of me and decide to run off. God-dam leg."

Una is relieved that Colin still has a sense of humor. She teases, "Suppose you'll have to become a pirate. Maybe we can call you Short-pegged Pete. Why we could even get you a parrot."

"If I could, I would toss you right into this lake for that."

"You'd like that, wouldn't you?" Una takes a breath. "Colin, you remember Angus McFadden, don't you?"

"Angus?" Colin shakes his head."

"You brought him here one time, remember? Tall, black hair, blue eyes."

Colin slowly replies, "Yes, yes, the hockey player. He could skate circles around me back then."

"We are friends Colin. Very serious friends. In fact, I think I love him."

A loud, sharp noise of someone dropping a hammer causes Colin to swing his cane violently at an invisible force behind him. "Jesus Christ. What the hell was that?"

Una cautiously approaches Colin. She places her hand on his arm, but he shrugs it off. He reaches under his coat and pulls out a flask. "Brandy. It steadies my nerves."

Duncan comes from behind the shed, hammer in his hand.

"Una, my shining ray of sunshine. Your mother and Beth have gone to town to do some errands, but I think I can manage to make you a cup of coffee." He sees Colin putting the cap on his flask. "A bit early to be having a tipple, my son."

"You're one to talk old man. You're one to talk." Colin turns his back and limps to the edge of the scow.

"He's not quite right in the brain Una. Not quite right at all." Duncan leads Una into the shack. "He won't talk about it. I've tried. Think it might do him some good but, no, he clams right up and sometimes he gets downright belligerent. He's not the brother you once had Una. The war has killed his spirit."

"What's going to happen to him? He can't do physical labor anymore."

"He's only home for the weekend, then back to the hospital in Whitby." Duncan passes the sugar to Una. "But he's a smart lad. Always wanted to go on in school. Maybe there is a way for him to improve his education. Maybe he can get a desk job in an office somewhere. God only knows if he keeps drinking like that. I don't know where he got it. They don't allow it at the hospital."

For a while Una and her father sit together without any words.

"Any news from Robert?" Una asks.

"His name hasn't come up on the list of killed soldiers, thank God." Duncan downs his coffee. "We last heard that his battalion had moved to the front lines. It was in the paper."

"I worry about him Papa."

"We all do my love. We all do."

"Papa, is my mandolin here or up at the house?"

"Right where you left it. Under your cot. Will you be joining us for Easter supper tomorrow?"

"Sorry Papa, but I've already made plans to spend the day with Miss Stanton." Una stands to leave. "Give my love to Mama and Beth? I suppose Martha will be coming over?"

"I suppose."

"I must be going. It's good to see you. What's this you're doing?" Una points to what looks to be a pile of scrap wood.

"Just some old shutters that need fixing. I've brought them here from the house. I need to be down here on the scow in case a job comes along. Lots of folks still building cottages across the bay, and they'll be looking to take supplies over, so it's best I be here."

Una retrieves her mandolin then affectionately kisses her father's forehead. "I'm in a little music ensemble at the munitions factory."

"Now that does not surprise me, my princess. You were born singing." Duncan asks, "Will we be seeing you again sometime soon?"

"Sometime this summer, I hope," Una offers.

As she steps outside, she notices that Colin has returned to the chair, and is still staring at the lake. Una stands beside him. "I'll write Angus. He's been asking after you." Una waits for a response. Nothing. "I'll tell him I saw you. He's with the 6th Battalion, the Railroad Troops, in Europe somewhere. I know he'd like to know how you are."

"Tell him to keep his head down and get the hell out of there as fast as he can."

Una closes her eyes for a moment, then says, "Cheer up Colin. I'm so glad you're home." Una slings the mandolin over her shoulder and walks up the slope away from the scow. She takes one last look back, hoping her brother will wave good-bye but Colin sits facing the lake as if frozen in time, and Una pedals away.

The Methodist Church Hall is filled with women, many of them dressed in their Easter finery. The Women's University Society, to which Eva belongs, had invited a guest speaker from Hamilton and her only available time was the afternoon of Easter Sunday.

"Meredith McCain is quite outspoken on the rights of women. She comes highly recommended." Eva gestures for Una to take a seat. "Looks like we got here just in time."

A matronly-looking woman dressed in gray approaches the podium. Everyone applauds. When the orator begins her speech, Una is unable to settle her mind. She can't stop thinking about Colin and what might have happened to Robert. This just makes her even more fearful for Angus. She pinches the tips of her fingers to help her pay attention, and only catches fragments of the speaker's delivery.

"Let our thoughts dwell for a few moments on the sacrifice of our noble manhood and the effect of such a sacrifice on the future of our country. The cleverest men have answered the call from all our universities, divinity colleges, medical schools, technical schools, and schools of practical science. The majority of these men have paid the extreme sacrifice. They will come back mauled, crippled and disabled in many ways."

Colin is one of these men. Uncomfortable with her thoughts, Una adjusts the way she is seated and sits tall.

"The casualty list for Canada is already far over two thousand. Our country will receive a serious setback. Is not the taking of life contrary to the period of advanced civilization? Does war not belong to the dark ages with millions of men butchering each other over petty National disputes? War is an unspeakably disgraceful."

Eva notices Una's restlessness. She places her hand on Una's knee.

"It is the heart of Rachel crying for the children. In the present war whole towns, villages, and hamlets have been laid to the ground. Our factories have been changed to munitions plants and what is to happen after the war? Have I not convinced you that war is too injurious to mankind to be allowed to continue?"

Una stands up. "I have to go."

When they arrive at Eva Stanton's home Una is still furious.

"I just don't understand," Una paces across the parlor rug. "This is a war that must be fought. Is it not? But at what cost? Honestly, Miss Stanton, what Miss McCain had to say is true. Too many men will never come home. And those who do come home, crippled and maimed, will have to live a life of what? A life of pain and disillusion, like Colin. God forbid if Angus comes back wounded, or worse."

Eva wisely listens.

"Everything we have been told, the posters, the films, the rallying for troops. Why? What is it for? And the bombs of destruction. Lord help me, I make bombs, Eva. How many more people have to die before this war ends?"

After a few seconds of silence Eva begins, "I am terribly sorry Una."

"I wish I had never gone. How can I erase those words?"

"I truly had not expected an anti-war cry this afternoon. My associates told me that Miss McCain is an historian, and I thought it would have shed some light on the history of the events. But did you not notice how many other women left once you stood up and boldly did so?"

"They did? They followed me out?" Una hesitates, "I didn't see the other women leaving."

"Yes, Una, a great number of the women have sons, brothers, and husbands who are fighting in this horrendous war." Eva puts it in plain words. "Still, I do believe that no one should be forced to engage in warfare. Nor should they be shunned by the pinning of a white feather. You, Una, have chosen to work at the munitions plant. You should never feel badly about that."

"I thought it was my duty. At least until this afternoon." Una looks down at her hands folded on her lap. "Maybe it will make a difference. We have to protect our men, don't we? We have to help them win this war. I would give anything for it to be over. Anything."

"This is our last day together before you go back," says Eva. "The sun is shining, and I would dearly love to collect some pussy willows down by Watson's Mill. Shall we?" she suggests, hoping to lift their spirits.

"Yes, let's," Una agrees. "It will help clear my head. Good idea."

On the train back to Nobel Una picks up a newspaper left behind on one of the seats and reads the headline in The Toronto Globe.

"April 10, 1917. CANADIANS LEAD IN TRIUMPH. Canadians Put in Front to Capture Vimy. Strongly Supported by Some of the Most Famous Regiments in General Haig's Army."

Una lets the paper drop on the empty seat beside her. She stares out the window toward the sun setting over a farmer's field. Peaceful. Serene. Colors of crimson, turquoise, and rose radiate toward the darkening sky.

Maybe this is the beginning of the end. I pray my darling Angus will come home soon.

21

May 1917

April 10, 1917

My dearest Una,

    There is little time to write but I want you to know that I am alive and kicking, and even doing a little jig now and again. A terrible battle has been fought and we are kept busy building and repairing the tracks. It seems we no sooner have them mended and the whole thing gets blasted apart.
    It has been snowing and cold enough to make me homesick for the winters back home. We do our best to keep our spirits up. Our boys really gave it to the Germans on Easter

weekend. The shelling was as if a hundred claps of thunder were all going off at the same time.

By the time you get my letter you likely will have read about how our Canadian Infantry stormed and captured Vimy. Our rails were not far from the trenches, and it was all we could do to keep them open. As soon as one car delivered supplies to the front it was filled again with the wounded soldiers.

Here's a little ditty I heard, and I've added your name my love.

"I'm laying the track while under attack, and the mud it is up to my knees,
But there's still one thing, that makes me sing, it's knowing I'll give my sweet Una a squeeze.
When I get home, when I get home, I'll give my sweet Una a squeeze.
The food here is rotten, it tastes just like cotton, and I'm itchy from scratching these fleas,
But there's still one thing that makes me sing, it's knowing I'll give my sweet Una a squeeze.
When I get home, when I get home, I'll give my sweet Una a squeeze.
We'll eat turkey for dinner, for you know I'm much thinner, and apple pie if you please.
Yes, there's still one thing that makes me sing, it's knowing I'll give my sweet Una a squeeze.
When I get home, when I get home, I'll give my sweet Una a squeeze."

Your always, Angus

Una bursts out laughing.

Unsayable Absence

"What's so funny?" Emily sits beside Una on her cot.

"It's Angus. He just wrote the silliest poem to me. 'The food here is rotten and it taste just like cotton.' He'll never be a Shakespeare." And she laughs again.

"I've got some cookies from the bakery in town, oatmeal raisin. Want one?" Emily offers.

"Sure, Em." Una takes a bite. "Oh my, there's real butter in these cookies. What a treat. This rationing is making our meals in the cafeteria pretty boring. One more night of hash and beans and I might as well eat the hay when its mowed."

"Want to go for a walk down to the lake before it gets dark?" Emily asks hopefully. "We could use some fresh air."

"I really want to write back to Angus tonight before lights out. But thanks anyway Em."

"That's all you think about these days, Angus this and Angus that." Emily whines, "We never do anything together anymore. What is it with you?"

Una feels perplexed. "What is it with you Emily? What is it with you?"

"Nothing. Nothing at all. Nothing that you will ever understand."

Una watches as her friend storms out of the dormitory and slams the door with so much force it rattles the windows.

"Don't you get it?" Maisie saunters over. "She's in love with you Una and has been ever since you two arrived by train."

"No, she's not."

"Yes, she is." Maisie shrugs. "It happens to girls like Emily. Her wiring is all screwed up if you know what I mean."

"My God, I had no idea. I should talk to her. She's my best friend." Una grabs her duffle coat and runs out the door. "Emily, wait up."

"Thought you had a letter to write?" Emily looks straight ahead and continues to march along the path.

Following in her footsteps Una replies, "I do, but, jeepers Em, slow down."

Emily comes to a full stop, her back to Una.

"Can't we talk about this? I really didn't mean to hurt your feelings?" Una says.

Emily swiftly faces Una, tears streaming down her cheeks, "But you always do."

"Look let's just go down to the shore before it gets too cold." Una gestures for Emily to keep going.

At the beach, the sun is already sinking behind a bank of gray clouds that hug the distant horizon. "Let's sit here, on this log," Una suggests. "We can watch the sunset."

Emily, still not speaking a word, plops down beside Una and kicks the sand with her boots.

"You're my best chum Emily. I hope you know that. I would never mean to hurt you. Not as long as the birds fly north for the summer."

Emily gives a half smile, "What's that supposed to mean?

"I don't know but it sounds right. I mean you are my forever friend," Una pauses slightly, "but I can't love you the way that you would like me to. Oh, my God, what I mean is, I love Angus. I want to make love to Angus. And you Emily, you want to make love to me, I think, but I am not like that Emily. It doesn't mean I don't like you or even love you for being such a good friend. I am making a mess of this. Emily, it is okay with me if you like women. I won't tell a soul, but I can't be that way. The way you want me to be."

A few returning gulls cry out as they head for shelter for the night.

"Am I right?" asks Una.

Emily nods. Tears well up in her eyes. "I thought you would hate me if you knew."

"Are you kidding? I'd never hate you, Emily. Even if you are a bit of an oddball." Una nudges Emily with her elbow.

"Oddball? Emily perks up. "You're calling me an oddball? You're the oddball, going and getting your hair bobbed, telling Mr. Hudson off behind his back." She gives Una a little shove back. "Una don't tell anybody. I'm begging you. My parents don't know. They think I'm going to get married after the war and have babies. Swear Una. Swear. Promise you won't tell a soul."

"Promise. Now can we go back while we can still see the path?"

Suddenly, a thunderous explosion rips through the air. Shocked, Una and Emily grab onto one another. They look up. Flames and smoke shoot skyward over the munitions plant.

May 27, 1917

My darling Angus

How relieved I am at hearing of your good spirits and my what a jaunty poem. I can almost imagine you singing it. At least it seems like a song to me.

I have terrible news to share with you. There was a terrific explosion two nights ago at the munitions plant. Fortunately, I was not on shift when it happened. Several people were seriously hurt, and seven people died. I don't know the people in that crew. They work in a different building. It seems some sparks from the chimney may have ignited a pile of empty TNT bags behind the wooden structure. But don't worry about me. I'm fine.

It has been raining a lot this Spring and the fields are ever so green with wildflowers starting to bloom. If only you were here to go for a long walk with me. And the ice is finally gone from the shoreline. Plenty of birds have come back too.

Did you get my socks?

Colin has come home. Wounded. I saw him over Easter. He was visiting our parents but had to return to the convalescent hospital in Whitby. Sure hope he can make a go of it. No word yet from my brother Robert.

Every day I think of you. Every day I dream of you coming home to me. I am here for you. You mean the world to me.

Love Una. Xoxoxo

June 06, 1917

My darling Angus,

Today the most remarkable thing happened. I went for a walk on the beach after the dinner hour. The sun stays up longer and the sunsets on the lake are so beautiful. I only wish you could have been by my side. I did however have a companion. A young red fox came out of the woods and sat no more than twenty feet from me. Can you imagine that? Neither one of us afraid of the another.

I think it was trying to tell me something. Courage? I sure do need it these days. Rachel Little Feathers would tell me that my frisky friend was trying to tell me that I need to prepare for a change.

When you come home do you know what you want to do? I often think about what will happen after the war. The munitions plant will likely lay us women off since the men will need jobs when they come back.

At night when I look to the stars, I think that you too are under the very same stars. I pray that you are safe my dear Angus. I do miss you ever so much.

Love Una

July 12, 1917

My dear sweet Angus,

I have not heard from you in such a long time, and I try not to fear the worst. I pray this letter finds its way to you and that you are well, and God help us, not wounded. We have not heard from my other brother Robert in quite some time either. I received a cheery note from Colin last week. He was able to further his studies while at the hospital. I am so happy for him.

There have been picnics for the workers now and again, and the band I am in plays most Sunday afternoons at the Recreation Hall in the Village. You should hear us. We are really quite splendid. One of the gals is great at yodeling. It usually brings the house down.

I look forward to the day you and I can be together again. We can play music, something we have yet to do. And there are many more things I hope we can do together, my darling.

You mean the world to me.

Love Una.

August 12, 1917

My lovely girl,

Your letters are worth more than treasures of gold to me. There has been little time to write. I hope you can forgive me. I keep your lock of hair close to my heart and I want you to know that I yearn to hold you in my arms and tell you just how much you mean to me my dear girl. You are one of a kind. Precious in so many ways.

We have been under attack more than I can tell you, but I remain safe. Sometimes I think I have an angel watching over me. Everywhere I look it is a sea of mud. And by God if we can lay tracks here, we might as well lay a track across the ocean.

I have befriended a mongrel I found near an abandoned village. He is a good little buddy and stays by my side at night. Probably because I give him a bit of my grub. I call him Lucky.

I too think about what to do when I get home and I hope that whatever it is, it will be with you, my love. Chin up my darling. I will see you one day soon.

Love Angus

September 21, 1917

My darling Angus,

You cannot imagine how overjoyed I am to get you note. I have been following the battles in Europe and while I don't know where you are, I know it is one hell of a time by all accounts.

I am learning to play the banjo which is a bit different from mandolin and much louder which I like. There is a barbershop in Parry Sound that sells sheet music and instrument strings. Last month I bought a used four-string long-neck banjo from the owner. I am driving the gals in my dormitory mad. They say if I play "Old Susannah" one more time they are going to burn my banjo!

My best friend Emily left the plant last week. Her mother passed away and she has gone home to care for her father. I will miss her very much.

There will be a full moon soon. When our little band plays this song, I think of you, my love.

By the light of the silvery moon
I want to spoon,
To my honey I'll croon love's tune.
Honeymoon, keep a-shinin' in June,
Your silvery beams will bring love's dreams,
We'll be cuddlin' soon,
By the silvery moon.

You mean the world to me,

Love Una

October 31, 1917

Dearest Angus,

It is Halloween. Some of the gals are going to a dance in Parry Sound but I have decided to have a quiet night. I am knitting you a pair of socks which I am sure you will need if the war goes on through the winter.

I spent Thanksgiving with my dear friend Eva Stanton who has taken to rescuing stray cats. Only two are allowed inside, Hayden and Mozart. The rest are welcome to take shelter in an old shed at the back of the property.

My parents are much the same and are getting ready to move off the scow for the winter. Colin didn't make it home this time, but I hear he is doing well. He has been given a position as an office manager with a forestry company near

Timmins. My brother Robert is still somewhere in France.

I miss you more than you can imagine. I cherish the memories of our time together in Toronto and maybe one day we can go there again?

Love you to the ends of the earth.

Una

November 10, 1917

Dearest Angus,

Merry Christmas my darling and even though it is still weeks away I want to make certain you get this before December 25. I do hope you like the photograph. A group of us gals had our pictures taken by a woman photographer in town last week. Do you like my new dress? It shows off my ankles just so.

I embroidered our initials and linking hearts on the cotton handkerchief. And one can never have enough chocolate, and of course some humbugs. I have decided to stay on at the plant over the holidays and give some of the others a chance to get away.

How is your little buddy Lucky? We have a mascot here at the plant who is usually seen scrounging behind the cafeteria. We call him Duffer. He looks part shepherd and part collie, and he's a real softy. One of the guards thought he'd make a good guard dog, but Duffer would befriend anyone willing to pat his head.

Do stay safe my love. I miss your smile, and your wit ever

so much. And I miss your kisses even more. I can hardly wait to welcome you back home. Happy Christmas!

Love you to the ends of the earth,

Una

December 2, 1917

Dearest Una,

You have no idea how thankful I am to get your lovely socks even if they are pink! They are warm and that is all that matters. It has been snowing for days and the ground is starting to freeze. We have been repairing miles and miles of destroyed rail lines. I have muscles where I never knew I had them.

We make up songs to help us work the rails. Here is a ditty one of the American boys wrote.

One day our Uncle Sammy, he had a war with Spain,
Not all the boys in blue were in that battle slain.
They were not killed by bullets, Oh! not by any means,
For most of them that died, they were killed by pork
and beans.
Oh! when the war is over and once again, I'm free,
There'll be no more trips around the world for me.

Lucky is still my buddy. He keeps me warm at night but by God I'd give anything to have you snuggling up with me. I'd wrap my arms round you and hold you so close. And when I get home that's just what I want to do.

All my love, Angus

December 31, 1917

My darling Una

    Your Christmas packet arrived on Boxing Day and cheered me up to no end. You look ever so charming in your photograph. Thank you, my dear girl. But what touches me the most are the two hearts on the handkerchief.
    I received a package from my mother and a letter from my sister Edith saying that Capreol is buried under two feet of snow. They are having a jolly old time with our horse and cutter. One day I hope to take you to meet my family. I know they will adore you the way that I do.
    Christmas was unusually quiet, save for the occasional gun shot. Dinner was pork, potatoes, and cabbage, but at least we had an extra ration of rum. Our crew gathered in a stone barn and built a fire to keep warm. We told stories of Christmas at home which made us all feel terribly homesick.
    Who knows when the war will be over, but I am hoping my next Christmas will be with you.

From my heart to your heart

Love Angus

Unsayable Absence

February 9, 1918

Happy New Year My Dear Angus,

One year ago, on this very day I stood on the train platform as you left for the war. My, but it feels like an eternity since those wonderful days, but if I close my eyes, I can still see us sitting together under a palm tree in the conservatory at Allen Gardens.

Our band played for the New Year's Eve Dance. It was a masquerade theme, and everyone seemed to have a jolly, old time. The gals in the band decided to be gypsies but there were clowns and pirates, and some even dressed as animals. At midnight confetti fell from the ceiling and the apple cider was poured, no champagne unfortunately. But my darling there was one thing missing. You. I do hope we get to spend next New Year's Eve together.

Colin writes now and again. He sent some wonderful news. He is engaged to a young woman from Quebec.

Tonight, the coyotes are putting up a real fuss. They must be very hungry as winter has been extremely harsh. I bet they spotted a rabbit. A soft snow is falling, and it is almost time to call it a day, but not before I kiss this page with my rouged lips. Hold then to your lips my love and let us dream of our life together.

It will be lovely to meet your family as you have already met mine so many years ago.

Much love, Una

March 28, 1918

Dearest Una,

I dream of my lips kissing your lips every morning and every night. And how they long to kiss so much more of you.

Our crew was given a very special order this week. We were charged with transporting the piano, props and costume crates for an entertainment troupe known over here as the Dumbbells. We carried all these items over to a makeshift theatre of old crates, and a tarp set up as a backdrop. We collected a bunch of biscuit tins and put candles in them to light up the stage.

They sang, danced and told jokes. Several of them dressed as women and made farces of the officers. All the while we could hear gunfire off in the distance. We joined in with "It's Canada, The Land for Me." Their show had us filled with gales of laughter.

Una, my love, I am beginning to think it is time for you and me to make plans for my return. It is my one desire to spend time with you as often as humanly possible. I have a few more skills now that I can apply to working with the Canadian National Railroad. Edith writes that there are plans for expansion of the railroads in Northern Ontario, and I am hoping that after the war is over, you will join me in Capreol.

Must sign off now. My midnight shift is about to begin. You are my one and only love.

Angus xoxo

Unsayable Absence

May 3, 1918

My Dearest Angus,

    As I write this letter, I am overlooking the lake. It is such a refreshing afternoon and we gals have come down here for a picnic. How wonderful to get away from the clatter and stench of the plant. Of course, it is far too cold to consider swimming, but I may go and test the water with my toes.
    Our lake at home was not as huge, and the waters warmed up sooner. By mid-May I was already swimming like a fish. We have yet to spend spring or summer together my love and I can hardly wait to do so.
    Yes, let's make plans for your return. Do you think it would be best for me to go to Capreol sooner than later? I am up for the change, and more than ready to find work that will get me away from the plant. What shall we do my love?
    I pray you have a guardian angel who will keep you safe from harm until you come back home. We will have such fun. I long to look into your eyes, to hear your voice, and to feel the warmth of your embrace.
    With all my heart I remain yours always.

Love Una

June 16, 1918

My darling Una,

    Your letters fill me with such hope and desire. I would give anything to be sitting on a blanket with you by the

Vermilion River in Capreol. We'd indulge in ham sandwiches, sweet pickles, lemonade, and sugary butter tarts.

We've been working from sunup to sundown, and some of us take the midnight shift. Most often I am assigned to repairing the bridges. Several men on our crew have fallen ill with fever and chills. The Spanish Flu. But don't worry my dear. I have been chewing green garlic. My mother told me she used it as a cold remedy growing up in England. At least it stinks like hell.

I have written to my sister Edith to see if she is willing to let you stay with her in Capreol until I come to be with you, my dear. I have asked her to write directly to you. She is a wonderful gal. I know you two will get along quite well.

Sad news, my love. My little companion, Lucky, wandered off and was killed by a bomb last week. I buried him below the bridge that I've been working on. But never fear I do have a guardian angel on my shoulder, and I have you in my heart.

Forever yours,

Love Angus

22

July 1918

"I don't care if we do get caught." Una strips off her clothes and piles them beside the lantern on the rock. "Last one in is a horse's ass."

Maisie, also as naked as she was on the day she was born, yelps with joy as she skips past Una and into the lake. Evelyn looks on in disbelief.

"I'll stay here and guard your things," she says. "What if someone sees you two?"

"Oh, come on Evie. It's dark out. We won't peek. Promise." Una splashes water at Evelyn. "Don't be such a sissy. It's divine, absolutely divine."

Evelyn grabs Una's skirt from the rock, shakes it in the air. "Do that again and I will come in and I'll take all of your clothes with me. Then you'll be sorry."

Una ignores her friend and falls gently backward against the water. All that she hears is the swirling motion of the waves, and the swishing of her hands and feet as she paddles about. She looks up at the full moon as it sails behind a bank of clouds, then out again.

One day I am going to swim naked with Angus. I will kiss him under the water, then come ashore and make sweet love beneath the stars.

On their way back to the dormitory the three women laugh and tease each other about the playful escapade.

"Next time," says Una, "you have to try it, Evie."

"Not on your life," states Evelyn. "I'm calling it a night. It's so hot we won't need our blankets. Hope we can get some sleep."

Una and Maisie stay outside in the lingering humidity. "It's unbearable," Una starts, "I think I will absolutely lose my mind if I have to keep working in this wretched heat. My clothes are dripping wet with sweat by mid-morning." Una sits on the stoop by the front door. "We women are nothing but slaves in this place. Yesterday, the new girl, what's her name, Alice? She fainted. They took her to the sick room but I'm telling you, she could have fallen into that machine, and who knows what would have happened. But old man McPherson, he doesn't give a damn."

"Don't get your knickers in a knot Una." Maisie hangs her towel on the line outside the building. "There's no point. You'll just get yourself fired. Then what?"

"I don't know what." Una swats at a mosquito. "But I know that once this war is over, I'm heading north."

"North? What's up there? Black flies and more mosquitoes? It's back to Toronto for me." Maisie lights up a cigarette.

"Angus. His family lives outside of Sudbury. He's asked me to join him there when he comes home."

"So, he's proposed, has he?" Maisie takes a drag.

"No, not exactly but I know he loves me. He says so in every letter."

"You're taking your chances if you ask me."

"Well, that's just it, Maisie, I'm not asking you."

The seeds of doubt are firmly planted in Una's head. She tries to sleep, first on one side, then on the other, and finally on her back. Still awake she stares into the darkness of the room. A slender shaft of moonlight creeps across the ceiling. Try as she may, she cannot chase the angst away.

What if Angus is lonely like so many other soldiers? Maybe his words are just flattery and lies? What if he has no intention of marrying me?

Una rolls over again.

What if he dies? What is going to happen to me after the war? But he does love me. Maisie is just jealous. I don't like Maisie. I don't like anything about her. Why am I so stupid? Why did I ever come here? I hate this place. I hate this bed. I hate my life.

Then she hears it, an owl calling to her. *Come outside. Come outside.*

Una sits up. The owl calls again. *I have a message for you.*

Una rises from her bed, and quietly steps out of the dormitory into the haze of the hot summer night. She spots it. A magnificent great horned owl on an outstretched branch of the maple tree. The majestic bird swivels its head to look at Una.

Una whispers, "What are you trying to tell me?"

Someone is going to die.

Una collapses on the ground sobbing. "No, no. Angus cannot die. He can't. He has to come home."

She remembers what Rachel Little Feathers had told her when one early evening they saw an owl swooping over a field. "Gookooko'oo has bad news. Someone going to die." The next day her friend drowned in the river up at Indian Village.

Una cries out, "No. The gypsy woman's cards are wrong. Owl is tricking me."

"Una, what are you doing out here?" Evelyn and a couple of the other women reach down to help Una stand back on her feet. "It's well past midnight. We heard you calling out."

Una wipes her tears with the back of her hand. "Owl. I heard the owl. Someone is going to die."

"Oh, Una, that's not true," Evelyn tries to reassure Una. "You're just imagining things. Come on. Let's go inside. You're having a bad dream, that's all."

"I'm not dreaming. Owl called to me. This is not a good omen." Una knows there is no way of explaining this to Evelyn, or anyone else for that matter. She curls up in her bed, clutches her hands beneath her breasts, and silently calls out to Rachel Little Feathers' spirit.

Nokomis, I need you. Come and help me Nokomis. Help me.

A week later to the day that the owl had visited Una, she receives two letters. One is from her sister Martha. A distant cousin of theirs, whom Una has never met, died on the Battlefields of France. She will send a note of condolences to her aunt and uncle. And Una thanks God it is not Angus.

The other letter is post marked from Sudbury.

August 2, 1918

Dear Una,

    Angus has asked me to write to you to let you know that you are most welcome to come to Capreol whenever it suits you. While we have not yet met, I am sure we will get along fine as I know Angus thinks the world of you.

    My husband Charlie and I live in a modest dwelling. Like many of the railroaders we have been given a boxcar to adapt into our living quarters. It really is quite cozy, and Charlie has added an additional room to the rear, so we now have two bedrooms. Our first baby is due in the New Year.

    You will like it here, I am sure. There are always plenty of fresh fish from the river and wild blueberries as far as the eye can see. Charlie and the boys are off hunting for deer, and I make a delicious venison stew.

Please drop a line to let me know your plans.

Best regards, Edith Wainio

September 8, 1918

The train is late.

Una joins a handful of people waiting to go north. At one end of the platform an older couple leans against the wall of the station house, a small scruffy dog at their feet. Every time it lifts its leg to urinate the woman pulls on its collar and scolds it.

Further along the platform a young woman stands with a baby in her arms, and a toddler at her side. Her eyes dark and sullen.

I wonder if she's a widow. I hope her husband hasn't been killed somewhere in France.

Noticeable is the absence of any young men. Even the station master shows his age. He pulls on his gray moustache, and repeatedly checks his pocket watch.

Una has packed her few possessions in a second-hand suitcase that she purchased at a church bazaar. Her mandolin case is strapped to it, and her banjo is slung over her shoulder. She brushes her hair back from her face and leans over the train tracks to look for any sign of a locomotive.

None.

Her doubts rise to the surface.

Is this the right thing to do? Should I go to Capreol before Angus returns?

But it's too late. Una gave her notice to McPherson a week ago, and last Friday she picked up her final pay. A group of women from her dormitory gave her a splendid send-off. They took her to lunch at the Kipling Hotel in Parry Sound and gave her a pair of red kid gloves. Una proudly wears them with her new navy-blue trench coat.

Still, she wonders, *Will I like Edith? Will I fit in? What if Angus never returns. What if, what if, what if…*

A blast of smoke can be seen in the distance and Una hears the rumble on the rails. There is no turning back.

PART THREE

All water has a perfect memory and is forever
trying to get back to where it was.

Toni Morrison

23

August 1930   **The Asylum**

Wolf, deer, rabbit.

    Shivering, Una sits on the one bare wooden chair in her room, her hair still damp from another morning in the shower rooms. She stares at the distorted imperfections on the plastered wall, letting the shapes shift into being creatures of the woods. Una recalls the things Rachel Little Feathers taught her.

    Watch them. The birds, the animals. They teach us things.

    Una traces a crack with her finger. *Snake. I remember the first time I found the skin of a large water snake.*

    "Did the snake die?" I asked.

    "No, big snake is growing too big for old skin. Big snake needs new skin."

    It terrified Una then in the same way that each moment does now. She thought she would lose her skin when she got bigger. Rachel had smiled and simply pointed to Una's feet.

"*No, but soon you will need new shoes.*"

Una wishes she could be on the Lake of Bays with Rachel Little Feathers.

Nokomis help me. Nokomis is dead. Remember. She died with her people at Indian Village. You took her there.

Una closes her eyes and rocks herself gently back and forth.

Why am I still alive? Why am I still here? Nokomis, please. Get me out of here.

A flock of geese honk as they pass over the cornfields of the Asylum farm. Una looks up at them through the barred window.

Footsteps. Someone is coming. I hear a woman's voice.

Even though the door to her room opens, Una remains transfixed by the world outside her window.

The woman speaks to Una. "It looks like they are going down to the river. The geese."

A soft voice. Not one of the nurses barking at me.

"I'm Dr. Harrington. I thought we might have a little chat today, if you are up for it, Una. Perhaps we could go for a walk. It's a beautiful day. Not too hot and we can sit under the trees if you like." Dr. Harrington waits for a few moments. "We can do this another day when you feel more like it, Una."

Una listens as the footsteps fade away down the hollow corridor. After a while, she spots another flock of geese and thinks she hears Rachel Little Feather's voice.

Ninniijaanis, Ninniijaanis, My Little Goose. One day you going to spread your wings and fly.

But Una cannot fly away from the Asylum. And even if she could, she has no idea of where to go.

24

September 10, 1918

My darling Angus,

It is my second day in Capreol and how I long to have you here with me. Edith met me at the train station. She is so lovely and ever so helpful. She assures me that I will like it here. Next week we are going on a little shopping trip to Sudbury.

Charlie is up north at his hunting camp and is due back in a few days. The train drops the men off in the bush and picks them up a week later. I have been invited for Sunday dinner at your parents' place. I hope to make a good impression.

The boxcar is quite comfortable. Just inside the front door

is the living area complete with a sofa and dining table. Behind one partition is a kitchenette with a coal oil stove, sink, cupboards, and tin counter. At the other end, a partition has been added to create a bedroom big enough for a bed and night table. The walls are tongue and groove and painted white making it very cheery and bright. The ceilings are pale blue, and Edith has adorned her boxcar home with family portraits, porcelain vases, and framed dried flower arrangements that she has done herself. Charlie added a new room through the back door. I am staying there, at least until the baby comes. I am hoping you will be home by then.

Yesterday I walked about the village. There certainly are a lot of trains.

Every day I think about your smile. I long to be held in your arms once again. I miss you so, so much. Be safe my darling.

Yours forever, Love Una

Una jerks awake. Again.

Throughout the night she has been startled repeatedly by the grinding sound of shunting boxcars slamming into one another. Just as she is about to nod off the train whistle blows and the whole room shakes as if it is going to fall to pieces.

My God, this is hell on earth.

Una clutches the sheets over her head and holds her breath until the rumbling subsides. Then, when the sun begins to rise, a murder of crows congregating on the nearby dome of the railroad water tower break into a cacophony of caws and croaks. The final straw.

This is enough to wake the dead.

Bleary eyed Una stumbles into the parlor.

"Coffee?" Edith, still in her night robe, greets Una with a wide smile, "You'll get used to it."

"Coffee. Oh, yes please, the darker the better." Una slumps onto the sofa. "Is it always like this?"

"Most times. But don't worry, the crows will move on in a few weeks."

"Well at least that is one good thing."

Edith hands Una a fine bone china teacup. "It's hard to come by sugar these days but we do have honey, and I've skimmed the cream off the top of the milk."

"What a delicate china cup," Una says admiring the floral pattern. "Lovely yellow roses. That means friendship, doesn't it?"

"I never really thought about that, but I suppose you're right," says Edith topping up her own china cup. "We gals have to do our best to keep up a sense of etiquette in these parts. Charlie would never dream of having his coffee this way. It's either in a tin cup or mason jar for him."

Edith pulls back the curtain on the tiny window and peers outside.

"It's warm enough for a swim. I thought we'd pack a picnic and go with a couple of other ladies to Lake Wanapitae. It has a glorious sandy beach, and the lake is so shallow it never gets too cold. We can wade in for miles."

"I could use a swim. I haven't had a bath in a few days and I'm beginning to not like being followed around by this disgusting aroma." Una waves at her armpits. In a fit of giggles, Edith nearly chokes on a mouthful of coffee.

"Now I know why Angus likes you. You are so refreshing Una; I can tell you that. There aren't too many women up here who would be so bold as to admit to the smell of their perspiration. They'd probably blame it on someone else. Mind you I hadn't noticed. I stink too much myself."

"Speaking of manners, " Edith continues, "It's fine for you and me to joke around about these personal matters but not everyone is so, shall we say, relaxed about such things. Especially Judith Emerson. And Judith will be picking us up in her father's new Oldsmobile Roadster. Her father is the CNR Superintendent. He owns the biggest house in town, the white one across the tracks."

"I was wondering who lived there," Una says, her interest piqued. "So, mind my Ps and Qs around Judith. Anything else I should know?"

"Well," Edith hesitates, "She had a crush on Angus, but he certainly did not have a crush on her. And Sarah Albright is coming. She's the minister's daughter. Need I say more."

"So, Edith tells me you were working in a munitions plant." Judith nibbles delicately on her cucumber sandwich. "I couldn't imagine working in a place like that. I hear those factories are extremely filthy not to mention dangerous. But then again someone has to do the job, now don't they."

Suddenly Judith stands up, "Oh, dear God, look at all these ants. I told you we should have sat on the rocks."

Una is lost for words. Fortunately, Edith retorts, "Actually Judith you were the one to suggest that we sit on the grass."

"Maybe so, but at any rate I do not like ants." Judith shakes her skirt. "They can bite you know. Remember the time I got bitten by a wasp and Angus, such a darling man, put wet mud on my arm."

Sarah interrupts, "I thought you were supposed to use ice."

"But there wasn't any ice," Judith snaps. "So, he used mud."

"Vinegar. It takes the sting away." Una adds to the discussion.

"I doubt that." Judith declares sharply.

"Well, I don't." Una is up for the challenge. "I've used it myself. Several times."

Judith, who is seldom confronted by anyone, displays a childish pout. "Angus and I spent a lot of time together. I'm sure Edith has told you. I went to all of his hockey games whenever they played in Sudbury."

"Is that so?" Una says. She feels the heat of her ill feelings for Judith rising in her chest.

"What? He didn't mention my name? That's odd." Judith stamps her foot on an anthill. "Pesky ants."

Unsayable Absence

"So, Una, I hope you will be joining us for the church service on Sunday." Sarah desperately tries to quell the discomfort.

"I don't know yet, I mean, I suppose so." Una is noticeably unnerved. "If you're going. Are you Edith?"

"We all do, Una." Edith hands her a glass of lemonade. "There's really nothing else to do on Sunday unless you want to join the old men at the train station who sit and gossip until the next train pulls in. You should hear their chins wag."

Edith passes her homemade sweet pickles. "Let's stop by the Trading Post on our way back. They always have some interesting things. I am looking for a new pair of moccasins for the winter."

"Who are they, Edith?" Una asks.

"Chippewa. They live all around this lake. Sometimes they come to the station to sell the porcupine quill baskets and hair clips, that sort of thing." Edith adds, "But not too often anymore."

Sarah speaks quietly, "That's because Judith's father has them chased away."

"I heard that." Judith adjusts her sun hat. "Someone has to keep those heathens in line. They'll rob you blind if you're not looking. Besides they're vulgar."

Una stands face to face with Judith. "I'd love to go to their Trading Post. Miigwech."

"What did you say?" Judith says thinking she has just been insulted by Una.

"Miigwech. It's what you say when someone does something nice for you. Miigwech is thank you in Chippewa Judith. You should know that. It might come in handy someday."

That evening Edith goes to bed early, leaving Una alone with her thoughts, her worries, and her deepening loneliness. At the Munitions Plant she had often craved time to be alone but tonight Una feels the isolation like a rock stuck in her throat.

The visit to the Trading Post earlier that afternoon brought back a flood of memories. In many ways, it reminded Una of her time at the Indian Village. And today when Una bought a porcupine clip and put it in her hair Judith chastised her immediately. Una mimics Judith's words.

None of us would be caught dead wearing one of those things. But then again you probably wouldn't know about that.

Una undresses, sits on the edge of the bed brushing her hair.

How can I possibly tell them about Rachel Little Feathers? How can I get them to appreciate the ways of the Chippewa people? Judith would be the first to use this against me. I met women like Judith in Nobel. I had nothing to do with them. But up here? It's just not possible to avoid people. In a place like this everybody knows everybody, or at least they think they do.

Reaching under her folded clothes in the top drawer of the bureau, Una pulls out a small deer skin bag. Her fingers slip into the opening. She feels for the bear claw and feather talisman given to her by Rachel many years ago. She softly cradles it in the palm of her hands.

Ninniijaanis, Bear will protect you now and goose gives you strength to fly, to go where you must go.

Una places the talisman beside her pillow and turns down the oil lamp on the side table. The full moon cascades its light across her blankets.

I wonder if I should have waited for Angus to come to Capreol before making this move up north. Ah, well, one day at a time grandmother moon. One day at a time.

25

September 1918

Una walks down the road with Edith. She had long ago stopped attending church with her family and had only gone once or twice in recent years. Try as she might, Una cannot think of an easy excuse not to go this Sunday morning.

As they approach the Canadian National Dining Hall, Edith explains, "We don't have a church yet, so our services are being held here. Anglicans at nine, Baptists at eleven."

When they walk inside the building the clatter of the pots and pans being washed in the kitchen echoes throughout and the smell of bacon permeates the air.

"I feel like having breakfast all over again," jests Una.

She takes in every detail of her surroundings. The dining tables have been pushed aside, except for one which serves as an altar. Orange potted chrysanthemums and a wooden crucifix sit atop a freshly ironed, white linen tablecloth that has been draped over a rough wooden table. On one side someone lights the tall brass memorial candle. On the other side, a large crate has been upturned to act as a pulpit, complete with a brass eagle lectern. Several locals have already taken their seats at the rear of the semicircular rows. Una's eyes are drawn to the upright piano in the far corner.

I wonder if I'll know the hymns. I hope so. I don't want to be noticed because I can't find the tune.

When Edith quietly introduces Una as a friend of the family she is taken aback by the shallow warmth of their smiles.

Not a friendly bunch here. Act properly, Una Campbell. Why did I wear this hat? You don't want rumors flying about, now do you? Or do I?

"Let's sit here," Edith whispers. "I always do. Heaven forbid we should sit in someone else's place."

During the sermon, Una floats away with her dreams.

I wonder if Angus will want to come here on Sundays. We haven't really talked about going to church or about God or anything like that. I wonder what he believes in. I don't feel God here in this place. But I know that God exists somehow, doesn't he? He? Who says God is he? God is in the trees, in the earth, and in the water. God is in all things. Please God be with my Angus. Bring him home soon.

Una's head falls to her chin. She jerks up with a start as the Anglican priest, his bulging neck rolling over his clerical collar, calls out in a thunderous voice, "He reached down from on high and took hold of me; he drew me out of deep waters." Una's insides crumble beneath his cold stare. "And now for Hymn 231: Onward Christian Soldiers".

The chairs scrape on the floor as everyone stands. Una is thankful for this familiar song, and she sings with such commitment that her voice sails above the others. Perhaps the minister will be pleased, but the one person who seems to be most pleased is the music director, a middle-aged man with a noticeable curve in his spine. After the service, he catches up with Una outside the building.

"You have a remarkable voice," he says enthusiastically. "We can always use a strong alto. You will join our choir, won't you? Rehearsals are Thursday evenings around seven-thirty," he says rubbing his hands together like an eager chipmunk.

"Oh, you'd be a wonderful asset," Edith adds encouragingly. "You do have a lovely voice, Una."

"Very well, I'll give it a try, but no promises," Una offers. *What else is there to do in this railroad town?*

September 14, 1918

My darling Angus,

Last night I finally met your parents and your little brother Andrew who was born only six months ago. What an adorable baby. His eyes are just like yours my love, full of light and laughter.

Your father told me about his hunting camp in Cartier and how he took you there when you were a boy. Maybe we can go there sometime. Or is it just for the men?

You are a rascal. Your birthday was yesterday. You didn't even mention that it was coming up. Your mother made a lovely vanilla cake, and we sang happy birthday to you. Happy 21st my love. Kisses all over. Hope you like the socks and scarf that I knit for you. At least they are in a more masculine color this time.

I am waiting on some sheet music that I requested from a mail-order catalogue. They have banjo chords so I will have a few new tunes to play for you when you come back. Mostly old folk songs like "Hand Me Down My Walking Cane".

Every night I hold you in my heart. Every day I wake up wishing you were here by my side. I am counting the minutes until I see you again.

Yours forever and ever

Love Una

PS: I've decided to join the church choir.

"Goodness Charlie, look at that beard of yours and for heaven's sake take your boots off. Oh, but it's great to have you home, even if you do smell like the outhouse." Edith takes his jacket. "I'll just hang this outside for a bit."

"Give us a hug."

Charlie is a bear of a man. He picks up Edith in a single swoop and spins her around until he notices Una looking in from the kitchen doorway. "And who do we have here?"

"This is Una, Angus's friend. Remember, I told you she'd be staying with us for a while." Edith gestures for Una to come forward.

"Una, now that's a pretty name. So, something smells good. What's cooking in there? I'm starved for anything other than a tin of beans."

"Blueberry pancakes and sausage. You're just in time," says Una who warms to Charlie right away. Straightforward and bigger than life.

Over breakfast, Charlie brags about the buck they brought back on the train and how he'll cook up some venison steaks for them. When they talk about the war Charlie explains to Una that he had tried to enlist but he has flat feet. He was turned down.

"That's not the only reason," brags Edith, "the Canadian National needs men to work the rails. He's a foreman on a line going up north of Capreol."

Charlie downs his mug of coffee. "It's good to have you here Una. I'll be away most of next week and Edith sure can use your company.

Especially now that she has a bun in the oven."

"Oh, Charlie, we don't go around talking about being pregnant, now do we." Edith stands and gives Charlie a kiss on his cheek.

"I'm one hell of a lucky man. By the way, I picked up the mail from the station." Reading the names on envelopes Charlie says, "Looks like there is one for you, Una. From overseas."

"Thank you, Charlie." Una takes the envelope. "It's from Angus."

"Wonderful, let us know how he's doing Una. I'll just clean up here, and then Charlie and me, we have some catching up to do." Edith raises her eyebrows in a flirtatious manner.

"Of course. Lovely to meet you, Charlie. Think I'll read this in my room and then practice some banjo or go for a walk."

"Don't go off into the woods," Charlie warns. "It's been a dry summer and the bears are hungry. There was one in town a few weeks ago. They shot it before it could hurt anybody. Stick to the roads and take this with you in case." Charlie reaches into a bowl on the table by the door. It's a bell. Bears don't like jingly things and if you do meet one, use this."

"Walk away backward, slowly, and don't make eye contact." Una finishes Charlie's advice.

"How did you know that? Aren't you from Toronto or some town down south?" Charlie scratches his armpit.

"I grew up in the woods around Muskoka. We have bears there from time to time."

Una closes the door to the bedroom and stands by the window in her room. Carefully, she opens the letter so that the pages do not get torn. Right away she sees the date. It has taken nearly a month to get to her.

August 20, 1918

My sweet girl,

    Tonight, some of us boys are taking shelter in a bombed-out farmhouse. I found some preserved peaches left behind in a root cellar. So tasty. Better than anything the army gives us. I am writing by candlelight. Don't worry. The Germans won't see me. I am huddled up against a stone wall and far enough from the front lines. Sorry for the scribbles. My pencil is worn down to the nub.

    More than once I have seen women in the fields. They do the back-breaking work that the men would do. I've even seen women pulling plows. Their horses have been taken by the military. Yesterday we passed a woman carrying a load of wheat on her back.

    There are times the trains pass through fields stacked with hay and it seems that there is no war at all. But soon enough the dream of peace is shattered by planes dropping bombs, or bullets flying over our heads.

    I hope to hear from you soon my love and to know how things are with you. I miss you so, so much. Let us look forward to happier times together.

Yours lovingly, Angus.

Una rereads the date, August 20. Once again, their letters have crisscrossed over the ocean.

He won't get my letter from last night until the beginning of October. And when was the last one I wrote? What if he hasn't received it? He'll think I don't care. Oh, but I do, I do care.

Her fearful thoughts end abruptly. Thumping. Edith and Charlie's headboard rhythmically strikes against the thin wall of their room.

There must be some place to go. But where? The train station. I'll check the timetable for trains to Sudbury.

Una grabs her sweater and purse, and dashes through the front door. She passes by three more boxcar homes that lie next to each other only a few yards back from the tracks. Like Edith's place, Una sees that they still have the Canadian Northern letters and numbers on the outside, and elevated wooden planks that lead up to the doors.

A car horn honks. Una jumps to the side of the road. Right away she recognizes the red roadster that pulls over. Judith is at the wheel.

"Where are you off to?" Judith asks suspiciously.

"I'm just going for a walk," Una says fiddling nervously with her purse.

"I wouldn't be out here on my own if I were you. It's not safe. Hop in." Judith taps the seat beside her.

"No thank you. I need to stretch my legs. I'm not afraid of bears." Una starts to walk away.

"Suit yourself. But there's more trouble than bears around here. Don't say I didn't warn you. See you at choir practice on Thursday. I heard you're joining the choir. Don't be late. Mr. Brentwood can be prickly about such things. I'm always on time." Judith grinds the gears of the car, and it pulls away with a jolt. Dust blows into Una's face.

When the grit finally settles Una looks around at the gray rugged rocks in the distance. The train yard ahead appears solemn and still. The roundhouse, pits, car shop, and yard swallow up most of the nearby land. Further along, Una is disappointed to discover that there is a closed sign on the train station door.

"Good day young lady." A man's voice calls out.

Una swings around to find three men standing side by side, one with his hands jingling coins in his pockets.

"Looks like we got ourselves some company, boys." An unshaven man tips his bowler hat back on his head and takes a swig from a brown bottle.

The third man wipes his hands through his greasy hair. "Suppose we take her for a walk along the tracks down by the river."

Una steps to the right but is blocked by the man in the bowler hat.

When she tries to go left the man with his hands in his pockets steps in her way.

"I just want to be left alone, if you don't mind." Una's voice quivers.

"You don't need to be afraid of us. Give us a kiss." The greasy-haired man lunges toward Una.

Una ducks out of the way. The drunken man stumbles forward. In that split second Una makes a run for it. She races down the road, their hoots and hollers disappearing behind the station. Finally, she reaches Edith and Charlie's boxcar home, breathless, her lungs aching, and her heart beating like a drum.

What kind of hell hole is this?

Una goes straight to her room, shuts the door, and bursts into tears. She has never felt so lost, so abandoned and alone in her life.

I wish Angus were here. He'd take care of those boors. How long do I have to wait? I know, I know. It was my choice to come to this horrible place. Where else am I supposed to be? Angus made these plans. For us. I know he did.

Fully dressed, Una crawls under the covers and curls up in a fetal position. She feels dirty and ashamed, angry and resentful.

"It's Thursday, Una." Edith looks at the wall calendar next to the icebox. "This afternoon I saw Mr. Brentwood, the church choir director. He was asking if you are going to come out for rehearsal this evening."

"I'm not sure. It gets dark early."

"You can take Charlie's coal oil lantern," Edith suggests. "You've barely gone out all week. It'll do you good. Get to know a few more people. What do you say?"

What if I run into those men again? What if the lamp doesn't work?

Edith continues, "You have such a lovely voice, and God knows that warble choir needs all the help they can get to stay in tune. Now put on your coat. You don't want to be late."

"Okay," Una reluctantly agrees, "I'll go. But leave the lights on so I can

Unsayable Absence

see them in the windows for when I'm on my way home."

Una steps out onto the road and looks to the west. A thin line of pink clouds hugs the horizon. The stark black trees sway like dancing silhouettes against the last of the day's light. Una hears the call of the jays but longs for the mating song of the loons at night.

I'm going to be fine. This is a good thing to be doing. Going to join the choir, I hope. I'll smash those bastards over the head with this lantern if they come anywhere near me. So help me God, I will.

Una looks up at Mr. Brentwood's apartment which is situated above Plexman's General Store. *Is this really what I want to be doing. Oh, well, here goes nothing.* She enters through the side door and mounts the creaking staircase toward an open door at the top. She hears Brentwood's voice.

"Turn to 146 in your hymnal."

Peering inside, Una sees that he is seated at a shiny Heintzman upright.

"We want to be prepared for a melodious Thanksgiving Service," Brentwood says cheerfully. "Let's make a joyful, joyful sound."

Judith, who is strategically seated beside the piano so that she faces the rest of the women, and in turn demands that she be acknowledged as the self-proclaimed leader of the choir, stands up when Una enters the room.

"Ladies, this is our newest member, Una Campbell. She's an alto I believe. We already have enough sopranos. Do make her feel welcome." In a tone that denotes arrogance and disdain for tardy choir members, she coos, "Ready when you are Mr. Brentwood."

"Thank you, Judith. We will rehearse a hymn with words by the great poet Rudyard Kipling, 'God of Our Fathers Known of Old'".

"Before we start," again Judith interrupts, "Una, I hear you play piano, do you not? Perhaps you can entertain us with a song later?"

Una feels put on the spot by Judith and a rush of blood reddens her cheeks.

Judith is quick to add, "Wouldn't that be lovely ladies? I'm sure we'd all enjoy hearing you play something. Good then, let's get started. We don't want to be here all evening. Need I remind you to be on time." Judith flashes Una a haughty smile. Then leaning over the piano, she whispers to

Brentwood just loud enough for the others to hear, "My father says he'll pay you on Sunday."

What have I got myself into? Okay. I know this hymn. I can do this. Just ignore Judith.

> God of our fathers, known of old,
> Lord of our far-flung battle line
> Beneath whose awful hand we hold
> Dominion over palm and pine
> Lord God of Hosts be with us yet,
> Lest we forget, lest we forget.

For five more hymns, the choir weaves in and out of tune. At the end of the rehearsal, Una, prodded on by Judith and the other members of the choir, finds herself facing the piano, her fingers placed above the ivories.

"This is a song that I did with my band in Nobel. We women at the munitions plant often played it for dances. I'd be happy if you'd like to join in. Una takes a deep breath and begins.

> Some of these days
> You'll miss your honey
> Some of these days
> You'll feel so lonely.
> You'll miss my hugging
> You'll miss my kisses
> You'll miss me, honey
> When you go away.

A saxophone. Brentwood is playing it. Una gives the song more gusto.

> I feel so lonely
> Just for you only
> For you know, honey

You've had your way.
And when you leave me
I know you'll grieve me
You'll miss your little honey
Some of these days.

Much to Judith's chagrin the women have been singing along and are responding with a rousing round of applause.

"Brilliant! " Brentwood beams from ear to ear, "You must come out on Saturday afternoons. We have a little ensemble, nothing much, a guitar, two banjos, and a fellow who plays trumpet."

"You know, Mr. Brentwood, I would really like that." Una is thrilled. "I also play banjo and mandolin. Where do I go?"

"Call me Archie. We play from two to four most Saturdays. In the same place where we hold church, at least until the theatre gets built?"

"Theatre?" Una asks.

"Yes, a theatre," Judith interjects. "Everyone knows that. My father held a meeting last month and introduced the investors." Judith faces the other women, "Well that's all for tonight ladies. See you at church on Sunday."

The women hesitate to leave. Finally, one of them asks Una to play another song.

"Stay if you like," Judith barks acerbically, "Some of us have more responsibilities to attend to."

No response from the women.

"Goodnight then." Judith walks out, head held high.

"Goodnight," the women chorus, happy to see her leave.

26

October 1918

"What on earth is that stench?" Una scans the landscape from her seat in the passenger car.

"Smelters." Edith points to the smokestacks and the sprawling industrial acres. "It's one of the less attractive aspects of living near a mining town."

"I'd say." Una is quick to agree. She pulls out a handkerchief and holds it to her nose. "Does all of Sudbury smell like this?"

"Not if the wind is blowing away from the town center," Edith says gaily. "I thought we'd start at Goodfellow's Department Store. They have three floors. I'm sure you'll find what you are looking for there." Edith pauses. "What are you hoping to find?"

"Something for when Angus comes home. A new hat, maybe. Shoes. I've saved a bit from my pay at the munitions plant. It's been ages since I treated myself to a new outfit. I could do with a new trench coat. Who knows? I need a dress for Saturday. I want to look my best when I play in Archie's band. You are coming, aren't you?"

"Archie?" Edith tips her head slightly.

"Archie Brentwood. He said I could call him Archie." Una is unaware of any disrespect that this might entail.

"We only know him as Mr. Brentwood." Edith cautions, "It's not proper to call him by his first name. It's too personal. People might think that…"

"No, it's not like that. Edith, you know I love your brother. I would never dream of doing anything inappropriate."

"I know Una, but people will talk if you seem too familiar with Mr. Brentwood." Edith advises Una, "I know you mean well Una, but please be careful."

The train lets off a blast of steam, lurches slightly, and grinds the brakes to halt as it enters the station.

"It's just a few blocks to Silverman's," Edith says as they step onto the platform. "This way."

"My word, Edith. So many beautiful hats. Look at this one." Una picks up a mint green poke bonnet with an ostrich feather and puts it on her head. "What do you think?"

"It's stunning. Judith will be jealous, that's for certain." Edith notices the price tag. "My word Una, that's more money than we have for a week's worth of groceries."

Una looks at herself in the mirror. "And I'm worth every penny. Now you pick out one."

"I can't."

"Yes, you can."

"No, Una, I can't," Edith says firmly. "We don't have that kind of money. Besides every extra little bit has to be put aside for our baby."

"Then let me buy one for you. Try this one." Una hands Edith a broad-brimmed hat with fabric flowers and a satin yellow ribbon.

"No, Una, no." Edith starts to walk away.

"Wait, why not? I'll pay for it?"

"Charlie would think it's frivolous. Me, wearing this sort of thing. Look, Una, he's a good man. And the last thing I want to do is upset him over a stupid hat."

"You're right Edith. I guess I got a little excited." Una quietly places the hat back on its stand. "You look tired. Is there a cafe where we can have soup or tea or something? My treat. What do you say?"

"That sounds like a good idea. My ankles are more swollen than usual." Edith places her hands on her midriff. "I'll be happy when the baby comes. There's a little spot across from the Opera House."

"Splendid. Maybe there's a show we can take in some time. That would be wonderful if we could do that Edith." Una gives Edith a hug. "I am so thankful to have you as a friend Edith. So thankful."

Snow. Huge soft snowflakes. The first of the season. Una watches them swirl outside the bedroom window.

I wonder if it will stay on the ground or are these flakes merely fleeting by on the wind. But either way, winter is coming. I pray Angus will be alright. I should send him more socks. Tonight. I will start a pair right away.

Una picks up the new fountain pen that she bought in Sudbury and begins yet another letter to Angus. What Una does not know is that on this very night Angus is writing to her, a letter that will not make its way across the ocean until the war is over.

October 20, 1918

My darling Angus,

I hope you are well my love. Every night I pray that you

are safe and that soon you will come to be by my side. Edith and Charlie are so kind and generous. Edith is really starting to show. You will be an uncle in a couple of months from now.

We went to your parents' house for Thanksgiving dinner. Turkey, potatoes, beets, the works. Edith made two pies, raisin, and pumpkin. So much food I could hardly move. You should have seen the mess we had to clean up afterward. It took hours.

Our band plays on the weekends at the CN Dining Hall. We have even been invited out of town next weekend. I play the piano most nights as they already have two banjo players. But I am afraid I may have upset your parents. They were not pleased that the band played a special Thanksgiving dance on a Sunday afternoon. I didn't mean to offend them, but I love playing music, and I made a little money to give to Edith and Charlie for my rent.

I am planning a trip to see my family over Christmas. I am sure I will stay with my dear friend Eva Stanton. My brother Colin expects to come with his wife and new baby. It troubles me that we have not heard any news from Robert for quite some time.

You are the one and only reason I stay here in Capreol. I can't imagine what it would be like if you did not return. So, my darling, keep dodging those bullets. And don't go strolling in an open field.

love you love you love you, Una

PS: How do you like this photo? I had it taken at a studio in Sudbury just for you, my love. xoxoxo

November 11, 1918

"It's over! By God, the bloody war is over." Charlie barges in. Stands in the open doorway. "Don't just sit there staring like two groundhogs about to get shot. It's over. It's finally over. Everyone is meeting on the main street. By Jesus, I thought we'd never see this day. Come on Edith. Grab your coat. You too Una."

Tears flood Una's eyes. "Are you sure? How do you know? You're not playing a joke now are you, Charlie? You're not pulling my leg?" She grabs Edith by the arm, Edith who is too shocked to utter a single word.

"It came by wire. To the train station. Just now." Charlie gives the details, "I'd just arrived from up the line. I was on my way home. I heard everyone shouting. I thought maybe there was a fire like we had last year when the hotel burned down, but no. Are you listening to me? The war is over. Done. Finished. What are we waiting for? Let's go."

Outside they join the throng of people flooding in from every direction. Cheers. Shouts. Exuberant joy fills Una with a storm of emotions. People she has never met before give her hugs. An older man kisses her on the cheek. Children race past and she is nearly thrown off balance. The clatter of horses' hooves and rattle of farmers' wagons pass by. Car horns honk. Women wave their scarves in the air.

Suddenly Una feels her head spin, and in slow motion, her body falls to the ground.

Edith shouts, "It's Una. Quick Charlie. Quick. She's collapsed."

"I'll take her back to our place." Charlie bends down and lifts Una's limp body up into his arms.

When they arrive at the boxcar Charlie lays Una down on her bed.

"I'll stay with her Charlie," Edith offers. "You go on ahead. You can tell us all about it when you get back."

Edith places a damp cloth on Una's forehead and waits until she slowly opens her eyes.

"Angus is coming home, isn't he Edith? Angus is coming home."

"In time. Yes, Una. Angus can come home now."

November 30, 1918

The longing for a letter from Angus eats away at Una's heart. In the morning when she ventures out to pick up the mail her wish comes true. A letter from France has arrived.

Please tell me you are coming home. I don't think I can bear another moment without you. Some days I think I am losing my mind in this place. Oh, please, oh please oh...

Una rips open the envelope, pulls the notepaper out, and she sees that it has taken some time to get to her.

October 20, 1918

My dearest Una,

How I miss you, my love. Your letters mean the world to me.

I am surprised to learn that Mother had a baby. Andrew. She named him after her older brother, my uncle Andrew.

The battle scars are everywhere. There is no way to describe the vast devastation to the land, the towns, and the innocent people. At times I fall into such deep despair to see the number of our soldiers wounded and maimed, or worse, the bodies of those who have sacrificed their lives on the battlefields. We are charged with transporting them to safe burial grounds.

News is spreading among the troops that this dreadful war will soon come to an end. Many towns have been liberated. We attended a Thanksgiving service and celebration in one of the towns. The cheers for our Canadian troops were splendid. I caught a glimpse of his Royal Highness, Edward, The Prince of Wales, and several other dignitaries.

My darling, I take comfort in knowing you are well

and that you are in Capreol with my sister and my family. One day we will be together again, God willing. Chin up, my girl.

Love Angus

PS: I do miss our Thanksgiving dinners. Nothing like turkey and the fixings. What I wouldn't do for a slice of pumpkin pie. And a hug and a kiss from you.

Una rereads his words, 'How I miss you, my love'. She slumps down on the bench outside the train station and whispers to the air. *And I miss you, Angus. More than you can ever know.*

27

December 23, 1918

"My dear girl, you look like you just stepped out of an Eaton's catalogue. What a charming hat. Burgundy. My favorite color." Eva Stanton welcomes Una inside. "You certainly have become a handsome young woman."

"I've missed you terribly," Una says stomping the snow from her boots on the rug. "How are you?"

"As well as can be expected," Eva says as she closes the oak door. "But tell me about yourself. How is Capreol? I hear it is a booming little place. Are you hungry?"

"Eva, I am so happy to be out of that place." Una hangs her new navy-blue trench coat on the rack in the foyer and slips off her boots. "It's dreadfully dull most days although I am playing piano in a small ensemble. If I weren't doing that, I think I would go absolutely crackers."

Eva leads Una over to the wing-backed chairs by the fireplace. "Well, music is your passion, my dear. I've always known that about you. Have you heard from Angus? I suppose you must be very excited to see him now that the war is over."

"I've been counting the days. I've only received one letter since the Armistice, just last week. He says it may take a while before his unit can even leave France. But honestly Eva I am so, so tired of waiting."

Eva is noticeably silent.

"What is it, Eva? Did I say something wrong?"

"No, not at all. I've been meaning to tell you," Eva says quietly as she adjusts her position in her chair. "I think it would be better for you to hear it now before you go to see your family."

"Hear what Eva?"

"Last week a list of soldiers missing in action and presumed dead was posted at the local churches." Eva takes a deep breath. "Your brother Robert is one of the boys."

Una immediately doubles over in tears and whimpers. "No, no, not Robert, not my brother. My God. No."

Eva moves closer. "I am ever so sorry Una. Let me get you a cup of chamomile tea and we'll call it an early night. Perhaps you'd like to go see your family first thing in the morning. I can arrange for my neighbor to take you there."

Una wipes a tear, "Yes. I must go. I must."

On the way to Una's family home Eva's neighbor, Mr. Higgins, an amateur arboriculturist, decides to tell Una everything he knows about his latest obsession, the oak tree.

"The oak is a fascinating species. There are many varieties, as many as ninety I believe, and some can grow to heights of over forty-five meters. The oldest known oak is over one thousand years old, and in an average lifespan an oak can produce close to ten million acorns, which," he guffaws, "keeps the squirrels busy."

Una politely nods and manages to say, "Is that so," and "I didn't realize that." When they finally arrive at Newholm, Una thanks him and asks him to come back in three hours.

"My pleasure. Perhaps we can talk about the maple."

Una wades through the knee-high drifts that cover the pathway to the house. It seems that no one has attempted to shovel it for some time.

Do I knock? Do I just walk in? I used to live here.

Una turns the knob and opens the door to the kitchen. Una's mother sits by the wood stove darning the elbow of an old wool sweater. Doesn't look up.

"We weren't expecting you until tomorrow."

"Now Maudie, we've not seen our girl for some time." Duncan slowly rises from his chair at the kitchen table and limps toward Una. "Come here my bana-phrionnsa. Give your old Da a hug."

Una embraces her father and smells the familiar yet stale odor of pipe tobacco on his clothes and the pungent trace of whiskey oozing from her father's skin.

"I heard. About Robert. It's terrible news. I see you're both wearing the purple armband. I must get one," Una says.

"Yes, you must. It is the least you can do for the sacrifice your brother has made." Maud still refuses to look up at Una. Silence. Unbearable silence.

"Damn it, mother. I know Robert is never coming home. You think I don't feel anything? You think I haven't been worried sick every day. And look what the war has done to Colin. Jesus mother."

"Don't you dare take the Lord's name in vain. Not in this house." Maud slams her hands on the arms of the rocker.

"Why do I even bother to come and see you? I never do anything right, do I? Just a stupid girl. That's what you think. That's what you have always thought." Una flushes with anger.

"Now, now, settle down. The two of you." Duncan tries to quash the situation. "Your mother here, she loves you, Una. She does. She's just dealing with the news. We all are." Duncan speaks to Maud, "And the least you can do is be civil. She's come all this way from that place. What's it called?"

"Capreol." Una quietly replies.

More silence.

"Tea?" Maud reluctantly offers.

"Yes. Thank you."

On the sideboard, Una notices the framed colorized photograph of her brother in his military uniform. The death penny, the medal no mother wants to receive, has been put to one side. Thousands of the commemorative awards have arrived in Canada this past year, along with a signed letter from King George. It too is on display.

"That's been sent to us all the way from Buckingham Palace," Maud says proudly. "Your brother is a hero."

"He was such a tease," Una says as she takes off her coat and drapes it over a kitchen chair. "He loved to sneak up behind me on those hot days on the scow." Una laughs slightly. "He'd sneak up and push me into the water, the devil. Remember the time he had all those chickens. And he and Colin got into that scuffle with the Anderson Twins. Robert had a shiner for the longest time. But they won. Remember?"

"That's in the past Una. That's all gone. And so is your brother." Maud's chin sets hard.

"But we can still talk about him, can't we?" Una's hands shake with agitation.

I have every right to remember my brother any way I want to.

"Here's your tea. You'll be wanting it before you leave." Maud pushes the teapot toward Una. "Help yourself to the milk, but easy on the sugar. It's hard to come by nowadays and your father's not working as he used to, not now with the gout."

I am so sick and tired of this. Why can't I even come home to see my own family without my mother acting like such a bitch.

Una forces back the tears as she picks up her coat. "I really don't feel like having any tea. I'd hate to waste your precious sugar. Sorry, Papa. I promised to lend Miss Stanton a hand with, oh I don't know, something."

"But you just got here my girl. You will be back for Christmas dinner, to see Colin and the wee bairn, won't you?" Duncan's voice quivers, a sound Una has never heard coming from her father. "And your little sister, she's a nanny now for the doctor in Huntsville. She'll be here," he adds plaintively.

"I don't know Da. Can you give me a ride to the village in the sleigh?"

Duncan nods, grabs his worn winter coat and tweed cap. "I'll be but a minute. You stay in here and keep warm."

"No, I'm coming with you."

Una refuses to look at her mother. Without a word, she steps outside and shuts the door behind her.

28

December 30, 1918

"It was a difficult delivery for Edith what with the baby coming early," Angus' mother whispers to Una. "She's quite exhausted. Lost a lot of blood. But don't worry, she and the baby are going to be fine. And it was Christmas Day of all days. They are thinking of calling her Carol. She's my first grandchild, no bigger than a loaf of bread."

"You must be so proud," Una smiles.

"I'm thankful that you've come back early. How was your Christmas?"

Una hesitates slightly, "It's never what I expect it to be. I had a feeling that I really should be coming back sooner than later." Una peers around the corner of the bedroom where Edith rests soundly, the baby in a wicker cradle tucked close to the side of the bed.

"Charlie is expected home soon. Do you think you could make some supper? I really need to get home. Little Andrew has a terrible croup cough, and he can't keep anything down."

"Yes, go ahead Mrs. McFadden. I can manage."

"Goodness Una. You're practically family now. Call me Agnes."

"Very well," Una adds awkwardly, "Agnes."

"Before I forget there's a letter that came in just after you left. It's on your dresser."

Una slumps on the side of her bed, her brain in a whirlwind. Exhausted from the trip back to Capreol, excited about the birth of the baby, disappointed by her visit with her family. And she desperately misses Angus.

Picking up the envelope from beside the lamp she immediately recognizes the return address. It's from Emily. Eager to hear from her friend Una quickly rips it open. The Christmas card displays a church with bows of evergreens surrounding it. The greeting reads, "Blessings of Christmas and Happy New Year. May it be filled with strength and charity." On the inside flap, Emily has scrawled a quick note.

December 18, 1918

Dear Una,

So sorry for this late greeting card. I hope you get it soon. My father slipped on the ice and broke his ankle in early December, so I have been looking after him more these days. From your last letter, it sounds as if Capreol is quite a change for you. Keep busy. It will take your mind off things. I volunteer for the Red Cross and help at the church. Too many families have been hit by this dreadful flu. When will it all be over? As we used to say, keep on the sunny side of life.

Stay well, Emily.

Una hears Charlie stomping the ice from his boots onto the carpet at the front door. Immediately she steps out of her bedroom and holds her fingers to her lips. "They're sleeping. You must be so happy Charlie, to have a baby girl."

Charlie beams from cheek to cheek. "It wasn't easy on Edith, that's for sure."

"I just got back a few minutes ago. Is there something I can make us for supper?"

"There's some leftover chicken stew and pineapple upside-down cake that the women from church brought over."

"Wonderful. I'll get that ready for us. But let's leave Edith sleeping for now."

In the dim light of her bedside lamp, Una rereads the card from Emily. She throws a blanket around her shoulders and jots a message to her friend.

December 30, 1918

Dear Emily,

> Your card was a welcome sight. I read it as soon as I arrived back this evening. I spent Christmas with Miss Stanton and paid a visit to my family.
> I am so sorry to hear about your father's accident. Families can be worrisome sometimes.
> Exciting news here. Angus' sister Edith gave birth to a baby girl on Christmas Day. I only wish Angus were here.
> Just a short note dear friend. We really must find a way to visit one another. Do you ever hear from the other gals from the plant?
> Cute card, isn't it? I love the kittens lapping up milk. I

bought it at the department store in Sudbury.

Fondly, Una

January 1919

Una stands with her back leaning against the closed door of the bedroom. Exhausted. For over two weeks she has been taking care of things. Cooking for Charlie and Edith, washing diapers, and hanging them outside until they are frozen stiff. Then, she brings them in and hangs them on a line strung across the living room ceiling near the stove. Edith put together a list of chores for Una to do if, as Edith puts it, she doesn't mind. Even though Edith apologizes for not being able to be more helpful, Una is beginning to feel resentful.

Why does the baby have to be colicky? Crying day and night. Lord knows Edith and I take turns rocking and holding the baby. Nothing soothes her. It works for a while and then the poor thing wails again and again. Is this all there is to my life?

No word from Angus. No hint. Nothing. When will he return and why does Mrs. McFadden, I mean Agnes, she says I can call her Agnes, why does she say I am almost part of the family? Am I? Will Angus finally propose?

Una sprawls on her bed, her feet dangling over the edge.

I hope to God Robert didn't suffer when he died; lose his legs or worse. Will they ever find his body and if they do where will they bury him? Where? I don't ever want to go home again. I'm sick and tired of feeling like I'm walking on eggshells whenever I see my mother. And I'm fed up with this backward place. I won't stay here if Angus doesn't come soon. Maybe I should write to Emily again. No. She has her own life now. And Eva is selling her house and moving in with a cousin in Goderich this Spring. Eva is getting older. The cane. She needs a cane now. 'Oh, it's nothing that a bit balm can't make better.' That's what she said. Just like Eva. But if she moves from the Lake of Bays there's no reason for me to ever go back there. No reason at all. It's just not home anymore. But where is home?

Una sits up and reaches for a folded poster on the nightstand. It has a photograph of Una sitting at a piano, surrounded by the other musicians, and below is a caption: "Bobby Burns Dance at the Warren Hotel - Sellwood".

I haven't touched a piano in weeks. My hands are chapped from all the scrubbing. I'm going to be awful. I just know it. What if I forget the songs? Maybe Archie will let me use the piano he has in his apartment. I hope he doesn't mind my asking. Should I still call him Archie? Why the hell not.

"The anthem is coming along nicely." Archie Brentwood collects his music from his piano and addresses the choir members who have come out for the Thursday evening rehearsal. "Remember there's a rest at the end of the verse before the chorus. Some of us are speeding right past it. Don't forget to bring your music with you on Sunday. And please be on time."

"Yes, ladies. Let's do as Mr. Brentwood asks. White blouses this time," says Judith who always makes certain she has the last word at choir practice. She looks directly at Una. "Some of us are going snowshoeing this afternoon. Care to join us?"

"I'd love to but I'm staying here."

Judith's forehead ripples into a frown of curious condescension.

"Archie, I mean Mr. Brentwood, is kind enough to let me practice for the Bobby Burn's dance. I don't own my own piano."

"I see," she says flicking her eyebrow judgmentally. "Well, then. Another time."

Judith and the other women disappear down the stairwell toward the street. Archie watches as the door shuts behind them.

"You do realize rumors are going to spread like wildfire thanks to our lovely soprano. But never mind Una. I hear that I'm secretly in love with the store clerk, the freckled red-haired girl who works downstairs. All because I gave her a ride to Sudbury one Saturday afternoon. I was going there anyway. My Lord," Archie puts one hand on his hip and flaps his other hand in a rather effeminate manner. "If they only knew."

"If they only knew, what?" Una asks quite innocently.

"Never mind. Let's get started. Here's a new one, "Rock-A-Bye Your Baby". I think you'll like it. It's slinky if you know what I mean."

While Archie soaks the reed for his saxophone, Una slides onto the piano bench, opens the sheet music, and quickly scans the notes.

"Ready when you are," Archie pipes up.

"Here goes nothing." Una rubs her hands together. To her delight, the notes dance beneath her fingers. And as they do her mood grows lighter and lighter until this is the only moment that exists.

"They must have pretty deep pockets." Una looks around the Ballroom. "I mean, they brought us up here to Sellwood by rail and we didn't have to pay a cent. A passenger car just for us Archie. I feel like royalty." Una takes a fashion magazine pose. "Do you like my new dress?"

"You're as lovely as a blossom on an apple tree. Pretty as a picture, my dear." Archie sets up his music stand. "Looks like a good crowd already. We need to tune up. Come on boys, step to it. Downbeat any minute now."

"They've given us rooms for the night. I guess I get my own room, seeing as I'm the only woman. And I am so looking forward to a good night's rest. Baby Carol has been crying non-stop. Poor thing. But honestly Archie, I've got to get out of there. I've overstayed my welcome."

"About the rooms." Archie lays his saxophone across his lap.

"What about the rooms?" Una swivels from the piano to face Archie.

"We've only got two."

"Two." Una's eyes open wide.

"They thought we were all men," says Archie tightening his suspenders.

"Jeepers Archie. I can't be sharing with a bunch of men. You fellas are going to have to chip in and get me my own room." Una defiantly folds her arms across her chest.

"I tried but the hotel is full up. Completely booked. Look, we don't have much of a choice. There are two double beds in each room. I'll share a room with you and the boys can squeeze into the other room."

"I can't do that. People will say things." Una's lips start to quiver.

"We'll talk about it later. It's eight o'clock. Time to make some music."

By midnight most of the clientele have left except for a few inebriated miners who remain seated at the bar, downing more whiskey than wisdom. Just as Una and the other musicians make their way past the stools, a burly man in a kilt, his legs splayed wide, grabs at Una's arm.

"What's a beautiful lassie like you doing with a bunch of fairies like this lot," he slurs. "You need a real man. Not some limp-wrist fag."

"Leave her alone," Archie says firmly.

"I'm going to take her home with me. Going to put her in my bunk, that's what I'm going to do," he says teetering off his stool. His rugged hands forcefully clutch Una around her waist."

"Let go of me." Una tries to pull away.

"Come here and give us a kiss," he blubbers into her face.

"You no-good lout." Lights out.

The next thing that Una knows, she is lying on a bed in one of the hotel rooms. Archie sits beside her, holding a bag of ice to her swollen eye.

"What happened?" Una moans with pain.

"You don't remember?" Archie removes the ice bag.

"You kicked that drunken Scotsman in the shins and then all hell broke loose. You punched him right in the gut. My word woman where did you learn to fight like that."

"When you grow up with two brothers you learn a few tricks," Una admits.

"There was no stopping you." Archie adds incredulously, "The air was blue with swearing."

"Really?" Una feels her swollen eye.

"You were as fierce as a junkyard dog," teases Archie.

"Well, he was an ignorant lout," Una says defensively.

"I tried stepping between the two of you. It was obvious you were going to do some serious damage to the man. He threw a punch at me. Of course, I ducked. And he plowed you smack on your proboscis."

"You ducked? My what?"

"Your nose. What else was I supposed to do?" Archie continues, "It took the bartender, the band, and two other miners to hold you back."

"He had it coming," Una mumbles defensively.

"Just remind me never to get on your wrong side," Archie says with a wink.

Una walks over to the mirror above the dresser, "Oh, my God. What am I going to do? A black eye. And I'm sharing a room with a man who's not my husband. Oh, this is bad, this is very, very bad."

Archie quietly walks up behind Una and glances over her shoulder and into the mirror. "You look just like a cat I had as a boy. It had a black patch over its one eye. I called him Morgan like Henry Morgan the pirate."

"Archie this is not funny," Una says, tears trickle down her cheeks.

"Look Sweet Pea, I won't tell anyone about you and I sharing this room tonight. I can keep a secret." Archie walks away, "But can you? Can you keep a secret?"

"Yes, I suppose I can." Una hesitates, "Still, you know how people find out about these things."

"I like men," Angus says bluntly.

Una is speechless.

"It's something I've never told anyone within a two-hundred-mile radius. I have a special friend in Toronto. He's married and we're very, very careful. We don't want to end up like Oscar Wilde, you know, the British playwright?"

"Oscar Wilde?" Una appears to be confused.

"Never mind. You are as safe as a free-flying bird in my presence." Archie leads Una back to her bed. "May I suggest you get some shut-eye, and in the morning, we'll see if we can find some sort of powder to cover up that shiner. And if you dare tell a soul what I just told you, I'll say you slept with every man in the band."

"You wouldn't."

"Of course not." Archie switches off the bedside lamp. "Goodnight Sweet Pea. You played divinely this evening."

In the darkness, Una takes off her dress. Instead of completely undressing and putting on her nightgown Una keeps her slip on and crawls under the covers.

She whispers, "Archie, are you asleep yet?"

"Not anymore," Archie answers sardonically. "Why?"

"I had a friend at the munitions factory. She was like you, you know, but not like you."

"Yes?"

"She fell in love with me. She likes women the way you like men. I liked her well enough but not the way she liked me." Una stops short. "What I'm trying to say is you're alright by me Archie. I had a swell time tonight."

Archie waits, "Is that all Sweet Pea?"

"Yup."

"Good. Now go to sleep. We're leaving first thing in the morning. Don't let the bed bugs bite."

"You too."

As Una drifts into her dreamtime her thoughts ramble on. *This is mad. Sleeping in the same room as Archie. I know he's harmless, but words can cause more harm than actions, especially if someone like Judith gets wind of this. How will I ever tell Angus? What if the boys in the band tell someone? Hell, I don't care. I'm sick of what people think of me.*

29

February 1919

"Charlie and I have been thinking things over Una," Edith says sitting at the kitchen table breastfeeding baby Carol. "We think it's time you got a place of your own, a place where you can come and go as you like."

Una listens, tugs the sleeves of her sweater.

"You've been coming in at all hours. After your engagements. Like last night. And it disturbs the baby. It seems any little sound wakes her up and she's off crying again. That, and the time you came back from Sellwood with that black eye." Edith adjusts the baby in her arms. "I know you explained how it happened but really Una, we have to consider things like this, especially now that we have a child."

"I see." Una shifts uncomfortably in the chair.

Edith continues, "And Charlie wants to make a nursery out of the room you've been in."

"You're right Edith. It's time. I'll move out. Besides, I need to find some work somewhere. My savings are about to run out."

"Oh, by the way, there's a letter for you from Angus. It arrived before you got up. I put it on top of the icebox." Edith tries to sound more cheerful, "Maybe he'll be coming home soon. That would be good, wouldn't it?"

Una doesn't answer.

"Wouldn't it Una? Wouldn't it be good if Angus came home sooner than later?"

Yes," Una sighs, "yes, that would be very good. I'm going over to Archie's apartment this afternoon. For a rehearsal."

"You seem to spend an awful amount of time over there. What would Angus think?" Edith cautions, "It won't do well when he gets back you know."

Una feels her temper rising, "I've told you before Edith, there is absolutely nothing going on between Archie, and me. Nothing. We rehearse. That's all."

"I was talking with Judith the other day after church. She says you are always the last to leave the choir rehearsals. Why is that?"

"She's just jealous, that's all. There is no reason for you to ever believe a single word that comes out of her mouth." Una grabs the letter and heads toward her room. "You and Charlie have been very good to me, and I don't want you to get upset because of what people might be saying or thinking of me. Don't worry. I'll pack my things and be out of here as soon as I can."

Una closes the door to her room and eagerly opens the letter from Angus.

January 12, 1919

My dearest Una,

>Happy New Year my love. I hope you had a smashing good time with Edith, Charlie, and the other folks who went out to celebrate. You did celebrate, I hope. A bunch of the boys in our unit bought some champagne and got a

bit tipsy ourselves. I even recited my favorite Robert Service poem, The Cremation of Sam McGee.

There are strange things done in the midnight sun.
By the men who moil for gold,
The Arctic trails have their secret tales,
That would make your blood run cold.

It is hard to believe that the war ended nearly two months ago. But the destruction is unimaginable my love. Whole towns lie in ruins. Our crew has been kept busy repairing trestles and broken lines so that we can get our guns and tanks out. It might be well into the Spring before we can even leave for England. But never fear my dear, my heart is always with you, every hour, every day.
  Give my greetings to Mom and Dad, Edith and Charlie.

Love you always, Angus.

Una folds the letter, slips it back into the envelope, and places it into a shoebox along with all the other letters from Angus.
  Spring? My God, I can't wait that long. For all I know, it could be next summer. I must tell Angus about Archie. I am so sick and tired of this town and its petty rumors. But what the hell am I supposed to do? Sit and stare at the wall? Where am I going to find work in this one-horse town? Where?

Una grabs her coat, hat, and boots and heads for the front door.
  "Where are you going?" Edith asks while patting baby Carol on the back. "You can't see two feet in front of you with all this snow. Look there are no hard feelings between us, are there? I mean, you do understand, don't you?"

"I'm going over to Archie's," Una says. "I need to practice piano."

"Be careful out there," Edith calls as she closes the door behind Una.

"This is a surprise." Archie opens his apartment to Una. "It's a wonder you didn't get blown halfway to Sudbury with this storm. It's really coming down. You must be freezing."

"My nose is numb." Una touches it with her fingers. "So are my fingers."

"I can see that. Well, come in then. Sit by the fire." Archie offers Una a chair. "What's up, Sweet Pea?"

"I hate it here Archie, and I don't know if and when Angus will ever come home. Edith and Charlie have told me I have to move out. I don't have a job. I don't have a place to live. I can't go back to my parents' place. That's the last place I want to go. My mother and I, we just don't get along, Archie, and you're my one and only friend in the world. Then, this morning Edith says I shouldn't be spending so much time with you because it will ruin my reputation. What am I supposed to do?"

"Well now, this is a conundrum."

"A what? You sure do use the strangest words sometimes."

"A kettle of fish?" Archie waits. "A problem. But nothing we can't deal with. First off, I don't give a tiddly-damn what people say or think and neither should you. When I was hired to be the music director for the church two years ago, I thought I'd go right off the deep end, but after a while, I found ways to cope."

"How?" Una holds her hands closer to the fireplace.

"I don't know really. I read a lot. And I go to the theatre in Sudbury as often as I can. And of course, there is my music. When I'm feeling lonely, I play "Songs Without Words" by Mendelssohn and when I am really angry I play "Golliwog's Cakewalk". Do you know it? It's by Debussy." Cheers me up right away.

"Would you play it for me now?" Una asks.

"My pleasure."

Archie lifts the lid to the piano, and his fingers glide across the keys. Una feels her shoulders relax. She imagines herself to be the little golliwog doll dancing about the room. And she is. She tip-toes over to the piano, twirls and spins, skips and prances. When it is over, Una makes an elegant curtsy much like what she had seen at the vaudeville show when Angus took her to the Mary Pickford Theatre.

Archie claps his hands, "See my dear, music is the best medicine."

"Yes, Archie it really is. You truly are a dear friend." Una looks out the window. "Do you mind if I wait until the storm passes?"

"If you don't mind warmed-up chicken stew for lunch," offers Archie.

"You are a dear," Una beams.

"I know," teases Archie.

"But the thing is Archie, I still need a place to live, at least until Angus comes back." Una shares her concern, "I'm afraid my funds are running low. I do need to find some employment, somewhere, anywhere. The thing is, I have no idea where to even begin to look for work."

"I have something that might interest you," Archie says moving to his kitchenette and donning his apron. "Have you met Mrs. Barton? She always comes to the church service late and sits in the back row. She usually has on her black coat with the red fox fur collar," then aside he says, "which I find quite striking."

"I think so." Una asks, "Is she the one who sometimes laughs during the sermons?"

"Precisely." Archie continues, "Last Sunday, I overheard her saying to one of the women that she needs a housekeeper. Her husband is an operations foreman for CN. They own that lovely three-storey brick home over by the livery stable. It's a big house, probably four bedrooms anyway. Their last housekeeper had to leave for some unexplained reason." Archie's voice rises suggestively, "I am sure you can figure that out my dear. You could approach her about an arrangement where you work in exchange for room and board, and some spending money."

"Archie, that sounds very good, very, very good. I kept house for Eva Stanton back home in Baysville. Could you speak to her this Sunday?"

"That I can. However, there are a few things you should know about our Mrs. Barton." Archie looks over his wire rimmed-glasses and whispers, "Not that I'm spreading rumors or anything. God forbid. She seems to host gentlemen callers whenever Mr. Barton is away. And he is often away for weeks at a time."

"Oh, really?" Una ponders the notion.

"So it seems." Archie nods.

"Don't worry Arch," Una perks up. "When I came home with a black eye people said, 'Look at Una Campbell, she's been into fisticuffs.' I hang out with you, an unmarried man, God knows what they say about us. 'Think of the hanky-panky those two are up to in that apartment.' What have I got to lose? Let the tongues wag. Frankly, I don't give a rat's ass what people say."

"That's the spirit. Let's have some lunch and play a few tunes before you leave. That is if you want to leave?" suggests Archie.

"I could use the storm as an excuse to stay," hints Una.

"Yes, you could."

March 2, 1919

My dear Angus,

    How are you, my love? It seems so long since your last letter. I am sure you must be very busy with all the post-war efforts. We can thank God that no more bullets are flying in the air.

    I have good news. Last week I started a new job. I am a housekeeper for Mrs. Barton. You must remember her because she has told me all sorts of things about you when you were a kid. Remember the time you locked yourself in her back shed by accident? Hee! Hee!

    Mrs. Barton is very kind to me and not too strict about my coming in late from playing for the dances. She has given me some of her hand-me-down clothes, a beautiful blue dress, a silk blouse, and a delightful jacket. They are hardy worn at all. She does like to buy new things.

I wrote some time ago that I am in the church choir and in a little band. You know how much music means to me. Mr. Brentwood is the music director and the bandleader. I often practice piano at his place, and he has become a dear friend. I've told him all about you my love, and how I long to have you here with me.

We are all snowed in. No one is going anywhere. I had no idea that winters could be so cold up here. I've taken to wearing two pairs of pants under my skirts. If only I could show you.

Yesterday I saw the oddest thing pulling a sleigh. Two moose. I thought I was seeing things, but no, there they were, as plain as the nose on my face. I'm told they were raised from when they were calves and couldn't be set free in the wild. Life is full of surprises up here.

I miss you dearly. Have you any word as to when you will set sail for Canada?

Yours as ever,

Love Una

Una tries to be patient. Weeks pass and still no letter from overseas. It isn't until late April that Una finally receives news from Angus. She reads his letter several times that night, and in the morning, she devours each word again.

Deborah G. Dunleavy

March 31, 1919

My darling Una,

How happy I am to read your letter with all the news of things back home. Mr. Brentwood had better keep his hands to his music my darling. All kidding aside, I am pleased that you have found ways to keep busy with your music. And it is good news that you have some work to keep you occupied until I come home. Mrs. Barton is quite eccentric, very theatrical in many ways, as I am sure you are discovering.

I've just been to Paris for the first time. It is an astonishing city and slowly coming back to life. I saw the magnificent Eiffel Tower. The small street cafes are open, and the coffee is stronger than anything I've ever had before. If only you were with me to see these things.

Our troop has been working close to Versailles Palace. It was built in the 1600s by Louis the 14th. It defies description. The ornate architecture is unlike anything I could ever have imagined. Visualize a cathedral-sized room with mirrors on both sides. The estate itself is likely bigger than all of Capreol. We had our photograph taken in front of the palace. That is me, yours truly, on the far right.

Has the flu made it to Capreol? We are witnessing a rapid increase in deaths among civilians and soldiers. Our unit has been spared for the most part. But don't worry, I'm fit as a fiddle and we have been issued masks to wear.

No word yet when we will leave France. But know that as soon as I can, I will be the first to leave. And when I do come back, I will give you the biggest hug that you have ever had in your life. And plenty of kisses too. All over.

Love Angus

Una lets the letter fall to her lap. The weight of not knowing when Angus will return fills her with deep despondency.

I know today is my day off. I know I should go out, but I just don't feel like it. Why do I have to wait so long? Why?

There is a sudden rap on the door to her room.

"Una, I'm going to Sudbury this morning," Mrs. Barton announces from the hallway. "The train leaves in twenty minutes."

No answer from Una.

"It's your day off. Do you want to come?"

Again, Una does not respond.

"Very well then. I was going to pay your way and take you to lunch, but if you'd rather sulk all day in bed, I guess that's your business."

Una peers through the door and says, "That sounds lovely Mrs. Barton. Yes. I'd like that very much."

"I know my dear. This town can be dreadfully dreary. We ladies need to treat ourselves now and again. Don't dilly dally. Get dressed and meet me downstairs."

April 28, 1919

My sweet Angus,

It is nine o'clock and I've just returned from another lovely day in Sudbury with Mrs. Barton. We went once in March and another time earlier this month to see a double bill with Lillian Gish in "Hearts of The World", and Charlie Chaplin in "Shoulder Arms". He is deliriously funny.

Delirious, that's a new word for me. Mrs. Barton uses it all the time.

I had been rather down in the dumps lately, so it was a real pick me up. I know some people say miserable things about

Mrs. Barton, but she is so thoughtful. She paid for the train fare and took me to a fine restaurant for lunch. I felt rather sophisticated for a change.

I am so sorry about little Andrew my love. Your mother told me that she had written to you to tell you that he lost his battle with the flu. There have already been several deaths in Capreol. No one knows how long it will go on. We do wear masks whenever we go out. Mrs. Barton joked that we looked like bank robbers. She has a wicked sense of humor.

The trees are starting to bud and most of the ice has melted in the river. There was a jam, miles upstream that caused some flooding, but no one was hurt. Did I mention that one of the ice cutter's draft horses died last month? Poor thing fell through the melting ice.

No other news really. I'm told the black flies will be biting any day now. I'm sure you really miss them, don't you?

Come back soon,

Love Una.

30

Summer 1919

Mr. Barton stands shirtless in front of the bathroom mirror, waxing his handlebar moustache. Una tries not to look through the open door as she carries a load of clean linen to the bedroom.

"Una," his voice bellows even though he knows she is right there. "Bring me my undershirt and the blue striped shirt with the white fiberloid collar. I have a meeting at the bank this morning."

"Yes, Mr. Barton, right away sir." Una much prefers the days when Mr. Barton is away. Why Mrs. Barton ever married him is beyond Una's comprehension. She's always short with Una when he's home.

"Do as he says, Una," Mrs. Barton snaps, "It is never a good idea to keep a man waiting."

And it's never a good idea to have him around the house. I can hardly wait for you two to go out this morning and leave me to my own peace and quiet, thank you very much.

As soon as they are out of the house, Una finishes her morning chores and prepares lunch for when they return. She is about to set the table when there is a sudden knock at the screen door to the kitchen. Standing on the other side is the store owner, Mr. Silverman, dressed in a suit and brandishing a bouquet of pink roses from his garden.

"Oh dear, Mr. Silverman, you really shouldn't be here today," Una says from inside the kitchen.

"But it's Saturday. I always call on Saturday," Silverman lisps, "when it is arranged to do so."

"I know, but Mr. Barton returned unexpectedly last night," Una explains hurriedly. "You're just lucky he's not home right now."

"But I thought..." Silverman wears the look of a scolded puppy.

"You'd better go now. Use the lane-way," Una urges. "He's due back any minute." Silverman hands the flowers to Una. "Good grief Mr. Silverman, take these damn flowers with you."

At that very second, the front door opens and Una hears Mr. Barton's leather shoes slapping on the hardwood floors. His voice echoes down the corridor, "Is lunch ready? I'm starving."

Una slams the kitchen's storm door to hide the thwarted expression on Silverman's face from Mr. Barton's eyes.

"Good gracious girl. Why on earth are you closing that door on a hot day like this?" Barton barks.

"A mouse." It's the first thing that comes to Una's lips. She grabs the broom and pretends to be chasing it.

"A mouse in the house in this heat? Do kangaroos swim?" Barton grumbles, "Open the door for Christ's sake."

Una opens the door ever so slowly. "Yes, Mr. Barton. Whatever you say."

"That's better. Now open the front door and we'll get a cross breeze going through the house." Barton sees Una staring out the kitchen screen door. "What are you waiting for? Hell to freeze over?"

On her way to the front door, Una stops Mrs. Barton who is headed toward the dining room. Una looks at her directly, and in a whisper, she carefully enunciates each syllable, "Mis-ter Sil-ver-man was here."

Mrs. Barton gives Una a wide-eyed look of surprise. "Cold cucumber soup. Sounds delicious. Thank you, Una. Why don't you take the rest of the day off? You've earned it."

Una dashes to her third-floor room to collect her bathing suit and towel, then back downstairs to the kitchen. She grabs an apple, a chunk of cheese, and a thick slice of bread. She spreads butter and honey on the bread and wraps it in paper.

"Oh Susanna, Oh, don't you cry for me, 'cause I come from Alabama with my banjo on my knee." Una fills a mason jar with water and puts everything into her canvas shoulder bag. Peering around the corner of the parlor she sees Mr. Barton flick the pages of a newspaper while Mrs. Barton slouches on the divan, her eyes fully closed.

"Have a lovely day," she chants, "I know I will."

Una swings open the kitchen door, goes over to the shed, and picks up her bicycle.

There you are my lovely. We are going on an adventure, my friend. So glad I had you sent up by rail from the munitions plant this Spring. Oh, Susannah…

Una feels more alive than she has felt in quite some time. Her legs eagerly pump the pedals, and the wind blows her hair from her face.

So many beautiful wildflowers in the fields, blue Chicory, purple Astor, yellow Black-eyed Susan. Oh, look at that. Vultures circling on the air currents over by that stand of pine trees. Something must be dead over there. Porcupine, squirrel, who knows?

Suddenly Una pushes back on the brakes. Inches away from her front tire is a huge brown snake. For a fraction of a second, it freezes then quickly slithers across the road and disappears into the shrubbery.

I wonder when you'll shed your skin. I can hardly wait to shed my clothes and go for a swim. Although I'd rather not meet you there.

Back on her bike, Una stands up and turns the pedals with even more vigor, until at last, she rounds a bend and coasts downhill toward the lake.

Several families have the same idea this fine morning. The air is filled with children laughing and shouting as they splash one another. Someone has rigged up two sheets on the trees, one at either end of the beach to act as change areas, women on one side, men on the other. Una drops her bicycle on the grassy area. Just as she reaches the women's area, she bumps into Judith emerging from behind the sheet.

"Fancy meeting you here," Judith snips, stepping aside to let Una go behind the sheet. "If I'd known you were coming, I would have offered you a ride."

"I came on my bicycle," says Una eager to avoid a conversation with Judith.

"Goodness, you must be covered in dust." Judith scans Una from head to toe.

"What's that at your feet?" Una says alarmingly.

Judith immediately jumps around and shrieks, "Where? Where? Get it off me. What is it?"

"It was just a frog," says Una in a teasing manner. "but don't worry, it's gone now."

"Thank goodness," responds Judith clutching her towel to her bosom, "I'm going for my swim now. I hope there aren't any water snakes. I detest slimy things."

"Is that so," says Una. "I just saw one crossing the road not far from here."

"Disgusting."

"Like people, some are," says Una.

Autumn 1919

The days are getting shorter. The nights are getting longer. It's so dull outside. I wish I could just say in bed all day. But no. I need to light the fireplace in the parlor for Mr. Barton, the curmudgeon himself. Anything to keep him from grumbling. Open the blinds to let the morning light come in. Put the kettle on but leave the whistle off. Make one soft boiled egg for Mrs. Barton, two for Mr. Barton. Two French toast each, fresh blueberry jam, a small pitcher of maple syrup. Butter. Don't forget the butter cut into perfect little squares. Coffee, black for his majesty, and tea with sugar for her highness.

Una sits up in her bed.

I had better get started before I fall back asleep.

"Where are my slippers?" Mr. Barton's baritone voice erupts from his bedroom. Una puts on the speed and dresses as quickly as she can.

I'd better get to the kitchen before they come down to the dining room. My word, there they go, bickering again.

"Your slippers are exactly where you left them," says Mrs. Barton.

"Where might that be?" he grumbles.

"How should I know. I don't wear them. You do," she snorts.

"My feet are freezing goddamn it. They're not under the bed. Not in the closet," he grunts as he bends down to take a second look. "Oh, my sciatica."

"Did you look in the loo?" Mrs. Barton yawns. "I keep tripping over them at night. One of these days I'm going to fall and break my hip."

"Then I'd have to shoot you," snaps Mr. Barton. "They shoot horses, don't they?"

"You are the most disagreeable cad I've ever known. You only married me for my money."

"Una," Mr. Barton shouts, "where in God's name are my slippers?"

Una raps on the bedroom door. Angrily Mr. Barton swings the door open to reveal Una holding the slippers in her hands.

"Coffee in five minutes, sir."

Flustered and red in the face, he grabs the slippers and slams the door shut.

Breakfast clean up first. Laundry needs to be washed in that Thor washing machine. Hope I can make it work. It's better than scrubbing by hand, that's for sure. Tidy the bedrooms. Why Mr. Barton insists on leaving his soiled underwear on the floor and not in the hamper is beyond me. Do light dusting as needed. And today Mrs. Barton has asked me to wash the kitchen floor and wax it. At least they are going away for a few days to see the colors in the Algonquin region. Then I can have a break from all this drudgery.*

By midday, Una's tasks are done, and a rare peacefulness fills the house. All that can be heard is the gentle ticking of the grandfather clock in the downstairs hallway, and chickadees chirping as they gorge themselves on the last of the berries on the bushes in the garden.

Three days to myself. I can't remember the last time I had a break like this. But what is there to do? I guess I could go see Edith and the baby. Maybe not. I could go for a walk. But I've walked everywhere there is to walk. Maybe I could call on Archie. No, he said he was going to Toronto. What am I going to do with myself?

Una climbs the stairs, slips into the master bedroom and pauses briefly before going into Mrs. Barton's dressing room. She cannot believe her eyes. *So many clothes. So many colors, pink, yellow, green, purple, blue. What a gorgeous evening gown. I had no idea anyone could own so many dresses and skirts and blazers and coats.* Una strokes the fur-collared coats, and the rich textures. Tweed, linen, cotton, silk. *Twenty-two pairs of shoes and look at that - a dozen or more hat boxes on the top shelf.*

Standing on her tip-toes Una pulls down one of the hat boxes.

I really must try one of her hats.

She lifts the lid, pulls out a large straw bonnet with a wide robin egg blue ribbon wrapped around it. Una places it on her head.

How elegant. I wonder what other hats she has.

In the next hatbox, she finds a forest-green felt cloche with fabric apple blossoms all along one side. Una tries it on, but it is too large for her head and it droops over her eyes.

A black hatbox with gold trim stands apart from the others.

I wonder what's in here.

Cautiously Una lifts the lid. She reaches in and pulls out a long sheer chemise with the slightest bits of lace strategically placed to cover the breasts and pubic area.

So, this is what you must wear for your gentlemen callers. How risqué. Now I know why I'm asked to go on errands instead of making tea. "Take your time," you tell me. "Go for tea at the diner. Don't be back too soon."

Una caresses the undergarment against her body, then gently drapes it on the dressing table chair.

Oh my, Mrs. Barton, you are a naughty woman. What do we have here? White hosiery, elbow-length red gloves, a large ostrich plume, and a glittering rhinestone tiara. What mischief have you been up to?

At the bottom of the hatbox Una spots a rectangular box with a label that reads "Macaura's Pulsocon Hand Vibrator". Una removes the device from the box and turns the crank.

So, this is what a vibrator looks like. Some of the women at the munitions factory talked about such things but, I've never seen one before. I wonder?

A thrilling cocktail of curiosity explodes in Una's brain, and a shivering sweat takes over her whole body. Heat swells in her groin. An erotic intermingling of excitement and trepidation pulses in her veins, a sensual height she experienced only when Angus touched her. And now, more than anything, she longs for his kisses and caresses.

In her hunger for that feverish passion, Una strips off her clothes and lets the silky chemise fall over her naked body. Slowly she rolls the hosiery to above her knees. She slips first one hand, then the other into the red gloves, and lastly, she places the tiara on her head. Looking in the bedroom mirror, Una admires her smooth slender body. Then lying on the bed, Una takes the vibrator and pleasures herself in a way that demands she do it again. And again.

Winter 1919-1920

December 2, 1919

Merry Christmas Angus,

I hope this arrives before the 25th. So sorry my love. I don't know where the time has flown. I had been meaning to put this parcel in the post last week. There are lots of goodies for you to enjoy, but not all at once.

Will you be going to England soon? Do send me a postcard when you arrive. I will add it to my collection of cards you have sent from Belgium, Holland, and France. I've kept them for you to see when you come home.

The Imperial Theatre opened in November. It is a lovely facility. Our band played for the opening ceremony. Everyone was dressed to the hilt. There are quite a few performers lined up for the Spring including 'The Dumbbells'. I remember you telling me about them. And Friday is movie night. Won't it be fun for us to go together?

Our church services have moved to the theatre. They have a splendid organ which Mr. Brentwood is thrilled to play.

A group of women in town has organized a community Christmas party. There will be humbugs, candy canes, and a gift for every child. The teacher, Miss Preston, has organized some skits to be performed by the children and I have agreed to play piano for the carol sing. Guess who is going to be Santa Claus? Charlie! The only thing missing is you, my love.

So Merry Christmas my sweet and a very Happy New Year. I hold onto the memory of your kisses and so desire to be touched by you again.

with love, Una

February 14, 1920

Una pulls her wool scarf tighter around her neck as she walks home from the Valentine's dance, the light of the full moon casting long shadows on the snow.

Bear Moon. Nokomis, remember, this is the time when we can communicate in silence. I am sending Angus a love message with my mind. Do you hear me, my love? I'm glad the dance is over. The only couples there were the railroaders and their wives plus a bunch of old folks. I kept wishing you were with me Angus. Wishing we were dancing arm in arm as we did in Parry Sound.

When Una arrives at the Barton's she spots a letter that has been slipped under her bedroom door. *I've been so looking forward to hearing from you Angus. Please tell me you are coming home. Please tell me.*

January 15, 1920

My dearest Una,

Your package arrived on December 24th. The handkerchiefs are very special. I will keep them unused until I come home. The knitted vest fits me perfectly and how did you know that I like indigo. I have been nibbling on the fudge, a little bit each day but I fear it will be gone soon. So delicious. Thank you, my dear girl.

We are billeted with families in the outskirts of Paris. Johnny Sinclair, Billy McIntosh, and I share a room in an old stone house. We have a fireplace in the room so at least we aren't freezing like we were last year. Monsieur La Roche is a mining engineer. Between my broken French and his little bit of English we talk about the copper and ore mining operations back home and in France. His wife is an excellent cook, and they have three teenage daughters. We spent Christmas with them. I even went to Catholic mass. Don't tell mother.

Must close now my love so that I can mail this in the village before we get back to working the rails.

Yours always, Love Angus

A slip of paper falls onto the floor. Una picks it up and reads the pencil scratched note.

On my way to the post office, I heard from one of the chaps that we will be moving to the Salisbury Plain in England sometime in late February. From there it is only a matter of time before we can cross the ocean. How great it will be to see you, my girl. And better still to hold you in my arms. And to kiss you all over. xxxxoooo.

Una clutches the letter to her breast. And as she has done so often since discovering her pleasure, she rolls onto her hands and finds the release that gives her that moment of ecstasy she longs to share with Angus.

April 12, 1920

The applause dies down.

"That was a good first set. One more to go." Archie places his saxophone on the stand as he scans the crowd inside the Imperial Theatre. "Looks like the whole town is here."

"I'm not surprised. Mr. Emerson is the CN Supervisor after all," Una says as she sorts her music on top of the piano.

"Was," corrects Archie. "This is his retirement party, remember? Nice little bonus for the band from the CN tonight. We are getting paid double."

"Really? That's great Archie." Una sees Judith stagger toward the stage.

"Look who's dressed to the nines, and slightly sloshed," Una whispers aside to Archie.

"Mr. Brentwood, how lovely to see you this evening," garbles Judith leaning affectedly over Archie's shoulder. "The band is playing divinely this evening. Oh, hello Una." Judith waves her hand dismissively at Una.

"Now seeing as it is my father's retirement party, I was hoping I might convince you to accompany me on a special little song?" Judith bats her eyes. "I know you know it because I've heard you play it." Judith sings the words like a child on the playground. "I'm Always Chasing Rainbows".

"We know that one. I can play it for you, Judith," offers Una.

"No, not you." Judith abruptly turns her back to Una. "I want dear Mr. Brentwood to do the honor. You will, won't you?"

"Yes, of course." Archie looks at Una and shrugs. "Now Judith? Shall we do it now?"

"You're such a sweet man. I don't know why some woman hasn't snatched you up. But maybe you are in love with Una?" Judith flashes a nasty smile.

Ignoring her comment Archie leads Judith to where she can stand beside the piano. "Are you ready?"

"Yes, yes, I'm ready." Judith clears her throat. "Play the first note."

Archie obliges. He plays a short introduction and waits for Judith to begin.

"Now? Oh, silly me. Do it again," stammers Judith.

This time Archie starts to sing the song so that Judith knows where to begin. She slides up to the note and warbles with a forceful vibrato.

> I'm always chasing rainbows
> Watching clouds drifting by,
> My schemes are just like all my dreams
> Ending in the sky,
> Some fellows look and find the sunshine
> I always look and find the rain,
> Some fellows make a…

Judith suddenly forgets the words. Una sings them to her. "I know, I know," Judith sputters.

> Some fellows make a winning sometime,
> I never even make a gain, believe me
> I'm always chasing rainbows
> Waiting to find a little bluebird in vain.

Judith stops abruptly when she realizes that no one in the auditorium is listening to her. She shouts to her father who is obviously engaged in a conversation with another man.

"Daddy, Daddy, I'm singing this song for you," she shouts. Fuming, she yells at Archie, "Play it again."

> I'm always chasing rainbows
> Watching clouds drifting by,
> My schemes are just like all my dreams
> Ending in the sky...

Judith becomes more and more maudlin and is no longer able to sing. She runs off stage toward the women's powder room.

"I'd better go and see if she's alright," Una tells Archie.

She catches up to Judith who stands in front of a mirror dabbing her eyes with a handkerchief.

"Are you okay?" Una asks.

"Never better," Judith sniffs.

"I'm sorry your father wasn't listening," says Una trying to console Judith.

"He never does. He doesn't care what I do, and now we're moving to God knows where. Somewhere in Manitoba."

"I see." Una crosses her fingers behind her back because the truth is, she won't be sorry to see Judith go. "Maybe it won't be so bad."

Judith throws Una's words back at her in a taunting voice, "Maybe it won't be so bad." She wipes her nose with the handkerchief. "At least you must be happy."

Una seems puzzled. "How so?"

"Angus is coming back in May. And I won't be here. But you will," Judith goads.

"Coming back? In May?"

"Don't act like you don't know. I saw Mrs. McFadden yesterday and she was all excited to tell me. She had a letter from Angus. She had it right in her hand. So there."

Nothing.

"Well, aren't you going to say something?" Judith scowls.

"No, Judith, I'm not."

That night Una arrives home late. Tired. Confused. She turns off the lamp in her room and sits in darkness at the end of her bed.

I don't understand. Why didn't Angus tell me first? Why didn't Mrs. McFadden tell me that she got the news? Maybe a letter is on its way. That must be it. A letter is on its way. It has to be.

PART FOUR

For people who love even water is sweet.

Chinese Proverb

31

August 1930   **The Asylum**

Dr. Harrington, a graciously tall woman with red hair that defies being restrained in a bun, invites Una to step into her office. It is the first time. The other times they have spoken have been on the women's ward or in the cafeteria. As she closes the door, she indicates to Una that she is welcome to sit on the sofa next to her desk.

"This time is just for the two of us. We can leave the door open if you prefer."

What is going to happen to me? I don't have any reason to be here. None. Sit. She wants me to sit. Sit.

Una picks at a loose thread on the cuff of the blouse they have given her to wear. She sits on the sofa and nervously glances about the room. It is colorful and vibrant. Unlike the rooms in her ward, the office walls are covered in a pale blue and gold embossed wallpaper. A marble fireplace is stationed at the far end. Above the mantle hangs a large oil painting of trees with the St. Lawrence River in the background. A small plaque reads "Pickens Point, Site of the New Asylum".

Framed photographs of exotically dressed people and mysterious places hang behind Dr. Harrington's desk. Una recognizes the Egyptian Pyramids and the Sphinx. Her eyes are drawn to a photograph above the bookshelves. The Eiffel Tower.

Dr. Harrington immediately notices Una's curiosity and senses it as a positive indication that perhaps this will be the day that Una will choose to speak with her.

"This one?" Dr. Harrington walks across the room and takes the picture down. She hands it to Una. "Do you know where this is?"

Una nods, an indication that she recognizes the structure.

"Can you tell me?" Dr. Harrington gently urges Una to answer. "It's alright Una. We are safe here. Do you know where this is?"

Again, Una nods.

"Can you tell me?"

Una stares at the picture. A word whispers from her lips, "Paris."

Dr. Harrington professionally holds back any expression of delight. It is the first time she has heard Una speak since her admittance to the asylum in late June.

"Yes, Una. It is Paris. I was there attending a seminar. How do you know Paris?"

"Photograph."

"Photograph? You have a photograph of Paris? Did you go there?" Dr. Harrington knows that it is very unlikely that Una has ever ventured outside of her home province, let alone across the Atlantic Ocean, but this might encourage a conversation.

"Angus."

"Your husband."

"During the war," Una hesitates, "Angus came back from the war." Her voice disappears into uncontrollable sobs.

For Emma Harrington, this is a most profound joyous moment. More than anything she wants to keep Una from losing her memories, something that happens far too often when the asylum doctors treat their patients with electroshock therapy. She has vehemently argued against the treatment for Una.

Emma hands Una a cotton handkerchief. "You have every right to cry. Every right in the world."

After a moment Una asks, "Do I have to go to the showers. I don't like them. I don't like being strapped to the chair. Why are they doing that to me?"

"Sometimes we, the doctors, make decisions that," Dr. Harrington falters slightly, "that help some of our patients, but in your case Una, I believe we can forego the water therapy. We can do other things." Dr. Harrington hands Una a soft-covered notebook and a pencil. "Perhaps we can start with you writing down how you are feeling, or memories, or anything that comes to your mind actually. Would you like to try that?"

"Will you read it?" Una asks cautiously.

"Only if you want me to," Dr. Harrington assures Una. "I understand you are a musician. Did you notice the piano in the auditorium? Would you like to play it sometime?"

Una nods without looking up from the floor. "That's okay? I'm allowed to do that?"

"Yes, Una. I'll go with you if you like. Tomorrow. I'll come by your room in the afternoon. I'm sure the other patients will enjoy hearing your music too."

Dr. Harrington stands. Una stands.

"You are getting better every day, Una. I look forward to seeing you tomorrow.""

Una walks toward the door. Stops. "Thank you, Dr. Harrington. Tomorrow?"

"Tomorrow."

32

May 1920

Una paces back and forth in front of her bedroom window. She stops to glance out at the train station.

Today is the day. I've waited so long for you to come home my darling. I know the train isn't due for some time yet, but I can hardly wait to see you. I've put on my very best outfit, just for you, my love.

Una pulls out the last letter she received from Angus. He wrote it to her at the end of March. It had arrived a few days after Judith had spilled the beans at her father's retirement party. Her nights had been restless, and her days distracted until it arrived a week later than the letter he wrote to his mother.

Deborah G. Dunleavy

March 03, 1920

My darling Una,

How excited I am to tell you the good news. I will be leaving England in two weeks. Our first port of call is St. John, New Brunswick. From there we will be transported by rail to Toronto. I will send a telegram to let you know when the train is due to arrive in Capreol.

It has been a very tedious time. We know that most of the troops have already returned home and some of the boys are pretty agitated. Sinclair and McIntosh got into head-butting some Brits at a local pub last week. That won them three nights under lock-up.

The officers do try to keep us occupied with fitness programs and sports. I am learning to play cricket, what little good that will do back home. A group of us took a day trip to see Stonehenge, not far from our camp. The stones are enormous, as you can see on the postcard. They tower over the people posing beside them. It's hard to imagine how it was built thousands of years ago. Hell, we have a hard enough time constructing trestles with all our mechanical advancements.

How wonderful it will be to be back home again my darling girl. All I think about is being with you. Have you heard this song? It's popular over here. And I send it to you with all my love.

All aboard for home sweet home
Again to the girl I left behind,
I'll go sailing 'cross the foam again,
What a welcome there I'll find,
And the day that I return to her

I will make that girl my own,
Hello, dear hometown, I'm homeward bound
All aboard for home sweet home.

Yours always, Angus

Una slips the letter into the envelope and puts it in the shoebox with the other letters and photographs Angus had sent during the war. She adjusts the shoulders of her favorite dress, the blue one with small white butterflies.

In the downstairs foyer, she peers into the mirror and brushes her bangs back under the cloche that Mrs. Barton had given her. 'You'll want to look sophisticated my dear for when your sweetheart arrives,' she had said with a knowing twinkle in her eye.

Una checks the time on the grandfather clock as she puts on her white cotton gloves. The train is due in half an hour. The station is only a ten-minute walk away, but Una can't hold herself back any longer. She sets out to meet her one true love. Her Angus is coming home.

The station platform swarms with people, all dressed in their Sunday best, ready to greet the hometown heroes. Even mothers and fathers with the funeral armbands are there. Una wonders if they have lost more than one son and perhaps another is coming home or are they there to see who has survived the campaign.

Una waves to Edith and Charlie who proudly holds little Carol in his muscular arms. She wears a bright yellow dress with a white lace collar.

"You look as lovely as a daffodil." Una gives the baby a kiss. "How are you, Edith? Charlie?"

"Fine," Edith answers while gazing down the line. "You?"

"I am so looking forward to seeing Angus." Una tugs at her gloves. "Where are Mr. and Mrs. McFadden?"

"They'll be here shortly, I hope. Mother has been busy preparing a tea for his arrival," Edith says without looking at Una.

"A tea? I didn't know. I could have lent a hand." Una tries to maintain her composure while feeling awkwardly shunned. *Why didn't they invite me? Is it because I work for Mrs. Barton? Is it because I play music with Archie? Why?*

"We managed." Carol fusses in her father's arms and Edith reaches for her. "You are invited to join us, Una. You know that."

No, I do not know that.

"Angus will want you to be there," Edith says while looking down the tracks.

The station master checks his pocket watch. "It's on time," he announces at the top of his voice. "It should be pulling in soon."

Cheers erupt from the crowd. A man shouts, "I see the smoke coming from the stack." A young mother hoists her toddler onto her shoulders. The rumble on the rails grows louder and louder until the exhilaration of the moment makes Una feel somewhat weak in the knees.

Finally, the train pulls into the station. Soldiers lean out of the passenger car windows waving their hats and calling out to family and friends. A blast of steam emanates from below the engine. Una searches in vain to find Angus in the foggy mist. And when she cannot see him a moment of panic strikes at her inner core.

What if he missed the train? Oh, God, please let him be here.

The train comes to a halt and the soldiers leap onto the platform. Hugs, laughter, tears. Una strains to find Angus somewhere in the chaos of the crowd. She sees a soldier in uniform leaning over to kiss someone.

There he is. There's my darling Angus. He's with his mother and father. He's picking up Carol from Edith's arms. Should I go over? Should I wait? What am I supposed to do? Maybe he thinks I haven't come to meet him.

She watches tentatively as Angus gives Carol back to Edith. Then it happens. His eyes meet her eyes, and his smile says a thousand words of love. He weaves his way through the crowd toward Una. They embrace.

"Welcome home my darling," Una says wiping a tear of joy from her cheek. "I thought this day would never come."

Angus steps back slightly still holding Una by the hands, "Una, look at you. You're so, so," Angus searches for a way of expressing his deep feelings for Una, "beautiful."

"And you are as handsome as ever." Una steps up on her tiptoes and kisses Angus fully on the lips.

"Come you two. There will plenty of time for that sort of thing later." Charlie gives Angus a shove. "Good to have you home. Let's get you fattened up. "

The McFadden home is crowded with family and friends who have come over to see Angus. While they hover around the dining room table loading their plates with food, they fire one question after another at Angus, asking details about his time overseas.

Una stands off to one corner. Watching. Longing to be alone with Angus. Feeling like a stranger in a crowd, she wanders outside.

"What was it like over there?" A matron in a burgundy suit asks.

"There's no way of describing it really." Angus takes a bite of the egg salad sandwich. "Delicious, mother. I could eat a whole loaf."

"Are you glad to be home?" asks another of his mother's friends.

"Couldn't be happier." Angus smiles.

"What are you going to do now?" she prods for information.

"Not really sure. I'd like to get hired on with the railroad. I hear they need more trestles built up north of here." Angus looks around. He turns to Edith, "Have you seen Una?"

"Not sure. She was here a second ago." Edith holds out the plate of cookies to her brother.

"Not just now. Thanks, Edith." After looking about the house Angus finally walks out onto the front porch where he finds Una sitting on the stoop. Smoking.

"There you are." Angus plunks down beside Una. "Do you have another one of those?"

Una reaches into her pocket and hands Angus her silver cigarette case. "Rolled these this morning."

"When did you take up smoking?" Angus asks lighting his cigarette from the end of Una's.

"At the dances," Una pulls a bit of tobacco from her lips. Glances straight ahead.

"Look angel, I know this is really awkward, but family is family." Angus takes another drag then turns to face Una. "I so want to be alone with you, to laugh like we used to laugh and to do all the thing I promised I'd do."

Una smiles, "Me too, my love. Me too."

"Let's go for a walk. I'll just let the folks know I'll be back in a bit." Angus stands. "Don't go anywhere. I'll be right back."

Una waits for what seems to be forever and a day. She finishes her cigarette, drops it on the ground, and uses the toe of her shoe to grind it out in the dirt. She picks the butt up and places it in a small empty peppermint tin that she slides into her handbag. Conversations from inside the house seep out the windows and doors.

I wonder what is taking him so long.

After some time, Angus pushes the screen door open. "That took longer than I expected."

"If I can wait for the war to be over, I guess I can wait a few more minutes to be alone with you." Una removes her hat and gloves and tucks them into her handbag. Her hair falls into her eyes. Angus brushes her hair over her ear then takes her by the hand and leads her to the rear of the house.

"When I was a boy, I went swimming in this river," Angus tells Una as they follow a pathway that descends toward the riverbank. "One summer I got hold of some scrap lumber and I strapped it together to make a raft. The thing was as soon as I stepped onto it the current caught the darn thing and I had to be rescued a mile or so out of town."

Una stops Angus suddenly. She hears the snap of twigs coming from a stand of trees only a few feet away. A doe and its fawn peer out from behind the branches. Arm in arm Una and Angus silently watch the pair. After a few moments, the doe and fawn slowly move on.

Without another word Angus passionately pulls Una into his arms. They tumble to the ground, embracing and kissing, and soon nothing exists in the world but this precious moment.

33

July 1920

A downy woodpecker feasts on ants in a tree outside of the bedroom window. Una leans on the sill to watch the bird peck at the bark. The morning sun sends shimmering shadows of flickering leaves on the wall of the white garden shed. Sudden nausea fills her whole being and before she can make it to the washroom, she regurgitates all of her oatmeal porridge onto the floor. Stunned. It is the third time this week. And it is the second time that Una has not had her monthly menstruation.

Not now. How can I tell Angus? I don't want this right now. I don't want to have a baby. Not until we are married.

Repeatedly, as Una goes about the morning chores, she is forced to stop and take deep breaths to avoid vomiting. Just as she is about to sit on the lower steps of the stairwell, she hears Mrs. Barton calling from the kitchen. Una stands up and immediately the linoleum tile flowers swirl around her head. She clutches the end of the banister.

Again Mrs. Barton calls out, "Una! Mr. Silverman has delivered a basket of blueberries. They need preserving. Una!" Mrs. Barton peers out of the kitchen and down the corridor toward Una. "Goodness girl. You look like you've seen a ghost. Are you not well? Oh dear, do you have a fever? Let it not be that dreadful influenza. Come sit down before you fall down."

Mrs. Barton leads Una to a chair in the parlor but before Una can sit, she feels the bile rising in her throat. She covers her face with the dust rag and rushes from the parlor to the kitchen sink. For a second time this morning, she vomits, and her whole being breaks out in a cold sweat.

"Should I call for the doctor? Are you going to be alright?" Mrs. Barton shows grave concern. When Una does not answer she asks again, "Should I call for the doctor?"

Una lifts her head from bending over the sink. "That won't help."

"What do you mean?" Mrs. Barton seems quite puzzled.

Una strokes her stomach. "Am I showing yet?"

"Una. You poor thing. Why did you not take any precautions? At least coitus-interruptus." Mrs. Barton sighs, "I suppose that is a little too late now. Have you told Angus? It is Angus who is the father, isn't it? Not Mr. Brentwood."

"Angus is out of town. Near Cochrane. He's due back tomorrow. How am I going to tell him?" Una asks.

"Have you considered terminating your situation?" Mrs. Barton gets right to the point. "You're still not married after all."

Shocked by the bluntness of Mrs. Barton's proposal Una responds quickly, "I could never do that. Never." Una explains, "My mother had an abortion. I wasn't very old when it happened, but I remember she was gravely ill afterward. I don't want to do that." Una pauses. "But what if Angus doesn't want this baby? What if he decides that he doesn't want me?"

"If you ask me Angus is completely in love with you. I know men. My husband loves me despite our constant squabbling. He'd do anything for me. We haven't had sexual relations in years, but he'd never leave me.

And, well, I do look after myself. He might know that too, but honestly, he sees that I am much more amenable to his way of thinking than if I were left unsatisfied. You do know what I mean."

When Una does not respond Mrs. Barton continues, "So, here's the plan. You don't tell him right away. That's never a good idea. Don't let on a thing. Be happy. Make love with him as soon as you can and then tell him how excited you are that you are carrying his child."

"That'll work?" Una asks.

"What choice do you have?"

The next day, after the dinner meal, Una cleans up the dining room and kitchen as quickly as possible. Angus has promised to call on her. Upstairs, she slips off her house dress and freshens her face and underarms in the bathroom sink.

It's a good thing I only get sick in the morning.

She dabs bright red rouge on her lips, brushes her hair, and examines a blemish under her chin. *This is so ugly. But it is the least of my worries. Don't be nervous. Act as if everything is fine and dandy. Fine and dandy. What shall I wear? Something light.*

Una pulls her new green gingham dress over her head and adjusts the dropped waistband's bow at the back. She hears the clip of horses' hooves outside.

That must be Angus. I must tell him. I have to tell him.

Walking toward the house, Angus removes his tweed cap and smooths his fresh haircut. He raps on the frame of the screen door and a moment later Mr. Barton comes to the door wearing a sleeveless undershirt beneath his black suspenders, a newspaper in his hand, and a cigar dangling in the corner of his mouth.

"Is Una home?" Angus asks politely.

Mr. Barton hollers, "Una, you have a caller," then turning to Angus he grumbles, "You may as well come in. Women. It takes them forever."

By this time Mrs. Barton has come into the foyer. "Angus McFadden aren't you looking dashing this evening. Any special plans?" she asks coquettishly.

Angus looks down and fingers his cap apprehensively. "Not really Ma'am. I mean yes, I suppose so. I thought Una might like to go for a ride to Lake Wanapitae before the sun sets. " Angus gestures to the horse and cart at the front of the house.

Una skips down the stairs. Mrs. Barton stops her before she reaches the landing and whispers, "Remember what I told you."

"Of course, Mrs. Barton. I'll take care of the silverware tomorrow." Una says the first little white lie that comes to her lips.

"You look especially lovely this evening Una. A new dress?" Angus asks as they jostle down the road.

"I ordered it from the Sears Roebuck catalogue." Una fusses with the collar. "How was Cochrane?"

"Too many black flies to count," answers Angus pulling slightly on the reins to get the horse to turn. "How have you been? Any more dances coming up?"

"Yes, actually, next Saturday we are playing an outdoor concert at the baseball diamond after the women's soft ball game. You will come, won't you?" Una puts her arm through Angus's arm.

"As long as I'm not sent back north. Yes. I'll be there."

"Angus," Una starts.

"Yes, my girl?"

"I have something I need to talk to you about," Una hesitates.

Angus pulls up on the reins. "Good. Because, well," Angus hesitates slightly, "So do I."

"So do you what?" asks Una.

"I have something I need to talk to you about," he says. The horse comes to a full stop. For a moment they stare at each other neither one knowing where to start.

Eventually, Angus is the first to speak. "I know I've been away a lot since I got home. And I am thankful that the Canadian National hired me on. But you know how I feel Una. At least I hope you do. What I mean to say is that I've been thinking." Angus scratches his chin as he gathers his words.

Una blurts, "I'm pregnant."

"Already?" Angus appears to be happily surprised.

"You're not angry?" Una blushes.

"Angry? No, Una," Angus tips his head to the side. "Well, that just makes what I want to say a whole lot easier.

"What do you mean?" asks Una.

"We'll get married. I was going to ask you tonight when we got to the lake," Angus falters. "It's just that I don't have a ring yet, and we haven't got our own place what with me still staying with my parents."

"A ring doesn't matter to me, Angus. You are all that matters." Una throws her arms around Angus's shoulders. "So when? how? where?"

"So many questions. Let's think this over, shall we? We want to go about this the right way." Angus flicks the reins. "We can arrange something private. I think given the circumstances that might be best, my dear. Do you agree?"

"I do Angus. I very much agree."

Spectators cram the baseball bleachers. Fans from Sudbury sit at one end while local supporters take up the other end. The crowd is so immense that they spill over onto the ballpark sidelines. Some have even brought their kitchen chairs to sit on. It is the bottom of the final inning of the Women's Softball Championship game between the Capreol Cardinals and the Sudbury Sparks. The score is twelve to eleven for the Sparks. Two out. Two players on base. One on first. The other on third.

Una stands behind the Cardinal's bench with the members of Archie's band. She feels the hushed tension in the air. "Gosh, I sure hope they win. There won't be much of a celebration if they don't."

"Strike one!" the umpire shouts. The Capreol fans boo and hiss. Sudbury fans whoop and cheer.

"Maybe we should consider not playing if they lose," Archie tells the band, "We don't want a mess like last year when they lost to the North Bay Pikes."

"Ball!" Again, the fans express their approval and disapproval. Someone shouts at the umpire, "You ought to get your eyes checked."

"Is Angus here?" Archie asks.

"He's back in Cochrane," Una says while watching the pitcher wind up. Crack. "Look, Archie. Look. It's going over the fence. Home run. We won. Oh my God, what a game."

The Capreol fans storm the field. Una suddenly swoons, "Archie I think I'm going to be sick."

"Too much excitement for you?" Archie teases.

Una abruptly turns away and barely misses spitting up on Archie's shoes. "Oh, I am so sorry Archie. I don't think I can play piano today."

"No, I should think not." Archie leads Una away from the spill. "Did you eat something rancid? You look awfully pale. We'd better get you home."

Una avoids eye contact.

"Oh, I see. You're not? Are you?"

"Yes. Angus says he wants to marry me, but he hasn't told his parents. He still lives with them you know. Archie, what am I supposed to do?"

Archie stands tall as if in charge of the situation, the way he always poses during a crisis or when the church choir fails to pay attention. "Right after the concert you and I shall have a little chat. Are you sure you can't play?"

"Actually, I feel much better now.

"Right, then, what are we waiting for?" Archie leads the band toward the platform stage behind the bleachers. Let the music begin."

After the band packs up their instruments and loads the piano on the back of a wagon Archie takes Una aside. "I've got a plan for you my dear girl. You know for certain that Angus wants to marry you?"

"Yes, of course. But he's away so often it is difficult for us to make the arrangements." Una adds, "We don't really want anyone to know. Yet. He needs to break it to his parents. You understand, don't you Arch?"

"Exactly. That's why you and I are going to meet with Reverend Albright after service tomorrow. You are a faithful singer in the choir, and I am sure he will see that you and Angus can take your nuptial vows. In a very private way. It won't be the first time. I can tell you that. It happens more often than you know up here. I'm glad I will never have to deal with this sort of challenge myself." Archie gives her that knowing look that the two of them share.

August 1920

August 8, 1920

Dear Eva,

Your letter arrived this morning. I am so thankful to finally have your new mailing address. The sunsets you describe in Goderich sound magnificent.

I have very wonderful news to share with you. Angus and I were married last Saturday. It was a small, private wedding held in Reverend Albright's parlor. My dear friend Archie was a witness as was the minister's daughter Sarah.

I am pregnant. It came as a surprise for both of us, as you can well imagine, but we are happy. Angus has a job as a pile driver operator with the Canadian National. He is often away for weeks at a time, and I do miss him. He still lives with his parents, and I am still living and working for Mrs. Barton. We will tell his family at the right time. Hopefully, before I out-grow my skirts.

Things are really changing in Capreol. The Moose Mountain Mine closed in Sellwood and new families are moving to Capreol in the droves. We now have sidewalks and electricity. Mrs. Barton has all the new electric appliances, even an electric wringer washing machine. I really look forward to the day when Angus and I can have our own home. Maybe an electric wringer too.

I hope we can come and visit you after the baby is born. I would love to see you, Eva. You are always in my mind and heart.

Love, Una

"We have to tell them, Angus. I really am starting to show." Una pulls her dress tight around her middle to reveal the tiny bulge.

"You're absolutely right." Angus leans against the oak tree beside Barton's garden shed. He pulls Una toward him. "Tonight, at dinner, you'll come over and we'll tell them our plans."

"Plans?" Una asks curiously. "What are our plans, Angus?"

"I'm sure you can move in with my family. You won't want to keep working now that we are married and especially once the baby is born." Angus sees the uncertainty in Una's expression. He caresses her hair with both hands. "I know it's not ideal right now. But I have put in an application for one of the new boxcar homes. They're supposed to arrive by October. We can have our own place then."

"That will be wonderful," Una pauses for a moment, "then we can play music together like we promised one another. I would love to do that Angus."

"Why don't you bring your mandolin and banjo to the house. I'll invite Edith and Charlie to come over. He plays a mean set of spoons. And after dinner, I'll pull out my guitar and we can have a real sing-along. What do you say?" Angus beams from ear to ear, his blue eyes sparkling.

"Alright, if you are sure it's a good idea." Una looks up at Angus expectantly.

"Sure-as-shooting." Angus takes Una by the hand. "Let's go down to the river."

"We don't need to," Una teases, "The Bartons have gone to Sudbury for the day. We can go up to my room."

"I'd follow you anywhere my girl."

The silence in the McFadden dining room is deafening. Una holds Angus's hand under the table. Waiting.

"I guess that settles it, now doesn't it," Agnes McFadden passes the wedding certificate to her husband. "Well Obadiah, it looks like another grandchild is coming."

Una looks baffled. Angus had not mentioned the fact that she was pregnant.

"You have that glow about you," says Agnes. "Why else would Angus have married you so soon, and he with no home of his own for a family."

"Mother," Angus says sternly. "I love Una. I have since the day I set eyes on her."

Without another word, Agnes starts to clear the dinner plates from the table.

"Here, let me help you," Una offers.

"Just pile them up." Agnes shrugs, "I'll do them in the morning. I've got some patchwork to do." Agnes picks up her sewing bag and takes it with her to the summer porch.

"Don't mind her," Obadiah finally speaks up. "She's not been the same since Andrew died. His birth was a bit of a surprise at our age, but it was God's will that he not live long." Obadiah pulls his pipe out of his pocket, flicks a match, and inhales the sweet amphora. "She'll come around. You'll see." His chair screeches on the floor as he stands. He gestures to Angus and Charlie, "Let's go out back. Got some chores for you boys to do next week sometime."

Edith finally speaks up, "Let's do these dishes Una. Then we can have some music. This is an occasion to celebrate. I'll wash. You dry."

Una senses that Edith is warming up to the idea that she is her sister-in-law.

"If it is a girl, you can have Carol's clothes. She's growing so fast. She's already too big for most of her early things. I'll set them aside for you. But if it's a boy? Oh, who cares. Babies are babies. Have you told your parents?"

"Not yet. I suppose I should," Una says, "I haven't spoken with them in quite a while."

"How so?" Edith asks.

"I guess when I moved out to work at the munitions plant, I moved out in more ways than one. It was the war, I think. It changed everything. But," Una gives it a second thought, "you know Edith, my mother and I, we never saw eye to eye. It's hard to explain. We don't get to choose the family we are born into, do we?"

"Well, you're part of our family now. I mean it." Edith empties the dishwater. "I know I was harsh with you before. But this town can be nasty if you're not careful."

"Don't I know it," admits Una.

"But that's in the past," says Edith. "You've got more to think about now. Having a baby changes everything. Everything. Believe me."

Una does believe Edith. That only makes her more uncertain, but she does not let on.

I'll have to give up playing in Archie's band. What if the baby is sickly like Carol was? I love Angus but this is happening too fast. Agnes is mad at me, but it's not my fault. I didn't get pregnant on purpose. I didn't know you could get pregnant the first time.

The following morning over breakfast Mrs. Barton strikes up a conversation with Una. "Be thankful you don't have to wear a corset, my dear. My poor dear mother never let on she was ever pregnant with any of us. It was as if the stork really did drop us down the chimney. At any rate, I am very happy for you my dear, although you will be missed. It's hard to find reliable help anymore. So, what are your plans?"

"I'll be staying with the McFadden's, at least for a little while," Una says. "Angus has applied for one of the boxcar homes. I hope they arrive soon. I want to get things ready. For the baby."

"You are surely blessed." Mrs. Barton looks pensive. "Mr. Barton and I tried but I guess it wasn't meant to be. Maybe that's just as well. I do like my freedom to come and go."

"I'll still come over in the mornings for a while if that suits you?" Una is hoping that she can save some of her earnings to set up house.

"That would be fine. But you mustn't strain yourself," Mrs. Barton adds pragmatically. "I suppose you will need a few things to get started."

"We'll manage," Una states proudly.

"I've been wanting to perk the place up a bit." Mrs. Barton looks about the parlor. "You can have the settee. It is a little worn, but a blanket can make it look fine. It should be just the right size. I understand the boxcar homes are small. It won't take up too much room. And the washstand in the guest room? Take it. There's an old kitchen table in the shed. It just needs a fresh coat of paint. You can pick out whatever sheets and towels you need. It will give me an excuse to order new ones anyway."

"Mrs. Barton, you are too kind," Una bows her head slightly, "I don't know how to thank you."

"No thanks needed. Not a one."

Mrs. Barton dramatically changes her tone of voice to the one to which

Una is accustomed, "Laundry needs doing. Then Mr. Barton needs two of his shirts ironed for his trip to Toronto. Gone again. Lucky me."

September 12, 1920

Dear Mother and Father,

I know it has been some time since I last wrote to you. I received a letter last week from Colin telling me that father's goiter is giving him trouble again. I hope it clears up soon. It is a shame Eva Stanton is no longer living nearby. She would be able to make some herbal remedies for him.

I hear Martha is pregnant again. And I have some rather good news too. Angus and I are married, and our baby is due in February. We are living with his parents until October when we will move into our own place. Lots of folks up this way live in converted boxcars. My sister-in-law Edith has fixed hers up nicely.

Angus has been working for the Canadian National for some time now. He is often out of town, but I keep busy. I'm still working for Mrs. Barton, at least until we move into our place.

Not much other news. The poplar leaves have all turned yellow, but I do miss the maples. I'm still playing music at home but have stopped playing for dances. I'm learning to crochet. Not that I'm very good at it but it does help to pass the time.

Last week Angus and I went fishing. We caught two pickerel. What a feast.

Happy Thanksgiving. It's a few weeks away but I wanted to wish you well.

Love to all,

Una

34

October 1920

"I'll be back in seven days," Angus kisses Una on the cheek and gently places his hand on her growing abdomen. "Soon we will be a family."

Una sees the joy in his eyes, and it temporarily dispels any fear she might have about what will happen when she goes into labor. Angus steps outside. Una closes the door behind him and watches as he heads down the road toward the train station.

He's so handsome. I do love him. I just wish he didn't always have to be going away to work. At least we have a home of our own. Living with his parents was dreadful.

Una slides her hand along the kitchen table that Mrs. Barton had given her. After she painted it white it almost looked brand new. So many people have given them things to get started - - cutlery, dishes, linens.

Una feels a sense of pride about the way she has everything arranged in their boxcar home. She's put pictures on the walls and embroidered a few pillow cushions for the settee.

At the same time, there is an uneasy emptiness that seems to dampen her spirits. More and more Una talks out loud to herself.

I'll just take these breakfast dishes to the sink and pump some cold water to put on the woodstove. I wish to God we had electricity and hot running water. Then I could have a wringer washer, the same as Mrs. Barton has.

I always have to trudge over to Archie's to play his piano. We need one here. When Angus gets back, I will ask him to buy me a piano. There's room. I will make room.

Tell me, what are you going to do with yourself today? Go for a walk? Play your mandolin? You haven't touched it in ages. You'll need to tune it up. It's been so long. Oh, I guess I should make the bed. Maybe I'll just go back to bed. Why does Angus have to be gone for so long? You know why. Do you want a piano or not? I want a piano.

"I want a piano, Archie. I can't keep coming over here to play," Una says as soon as she enters the apartment.

"Of course, you can," Archie says.

"No, Archie I can't. I'm a married woman now and I know I shouldn't even be coming over here now, especially since Angus is out of town, but I thought that maybe you could help me find a piano. I've got to do something Archie or I'll go stark raving mad. Angus is away. Again. This time for seven days."

"Well, have you considered the cost of a piano?" Archie settles into his armchair. Tamps the amphora into his pipe. Lights up.

"No. Not really," Una confesses, "but I've saved a little bit."

"Yes?" Archie exhales the sweet tobacco smoke.

"I've saved ninety-five dollars," Una says proudly.

"Well, let's see," Archie opens the seat of the piano bench, "I just happen to have a Beckwith Piano Catalogue."

"What does it say? How much for an upright?" Una asks, the excitement building in her voice.

"Some pianos are more expensive than others, Una, close to three hundred dollars. Wait a minute. Here's one. It's a Maywood upright in a mahogany veneer. It costs one hundred and fifty-eight dollars. Now you can order it, Una, put a down payment on it, and then pay the balance at a rate of five dollars a month." Archie reads on, "Boxed, shipped from factory, freight charges are added. Freight charges must be paid at time of first payment."

"Archie, you will help me, won't you?" Una sits on the edge of his chair. "Surely my ninety-five dollars will cover the down payment and the freight. Please, Archie. You know I will absolutely die if I don't have a piano."

"You do have a persuasive manner about you, Una." Archie gives her a sideways glance. "Alright. I will put the order in for you, on the condition you can actually cover the initial expense, and you don't tell Angus I did it."

"My lips are sealed." Una hugs Archie. "You are a dear friend. What would I do without you?"

"Lots, I can imagine."

November 1920

"A piano," Angus cannot help but see it as he comes into the house. The upright sits directly across from the front door. "I go away for a few days, and I come back to find a piano in my living room. Una, how on earth did you pay for this?"

"I ordered it last month. It arrived yesterday. I wanted to tell you. Honest, Angus, I really tried to but it's just that you're always away and I love my music. You've always known that about me." Una takes a breath, "Besides, it's mostly paid for already." Una avoids looking Angus.

"Mostly? What do you mean mostly?" Angus hangs his coat on the hooks by the door.

"I saved every penny from working for the Barton's. We only have to pay five dollars a month for eighteen more months." Una tries to make light of the situation.

"You can't be serious. Una. Five dollars a week. That's nearly half my weekly wage." Angus lets the silence hang in the air. "What were you thinking?"

"I was lonely."

"Lonely."

Angus walks over to Una and lifts her chin so that her eyes meet his. "You know what this means, don't you?"

Una looks confused and guilty all in one.

"I'm going to have to get more work. Cutting ice this winter. Anything. And it means I'll be out more." Angus shakes his head. "But I know you love your music, Una. Sometimes I think you'd even give up food if meant you could play your music."

"I've made baked ham and scalloped potatoes. Are you hungry?" Una says coquettishly.

"Yes, my girl, that I am."

After dinner, Una and Angus fall into each other's arms. They caress and kiss one another, and soon the piano purchase is forgiven and forgotten. Una looks deep into Angus' eyes and sees the endlessness of their love.

December 1920

All the storefronts in town boast colorful Christmas displays. Una peers into the frosted window of Plexman's General Store. A sign reads: *'Get Your Son Something He Wants'*.

I wonder if you are a boy or a girl. Next Christmas I will buy you something special.

Red paper bells decorate the corners, and green garlands drape from one side to the other. A shiny blue bicycle leans against the back wall, and a miniature train set complete with engine and boxcars takes up the floor space in the window. Placed side by side are three life-sized dolls with matching dresses and bonnets.

Una is hoping to find some inexpensive decorations and a little something for Angus. She has four dollars that he gave her on his way out the door this morning, plus the two dollars she found when she put her hands in the pockets of her winter coat.

I must have left the change in my pockets after buying groceries last week. Now I can even buy some Christmas cards.

Una kicks the snow from her boots as she steps into the store. Several townsfolk seem to have the same idea – last minute shopping. Mothers with children tugging at their coattails beg them to buy one toy or another. Confused husbands look at various items including gloves, scarves, perfume.

"How are you today Mrs. McFadden."

Una quickly spins around to see Archie standing with a new pipe in one hand and a box of chocolates in the other.

"Archie, you never call me Mrs. McFadden."

"I know but I thought I'd try it out," Archie winks. "Which should I buy for my friend in Toronto? Chocolate or this pipe? I'm heading down there right after our service on the twenty-fourth. You will be joining us in the choir, won't you?"

"I could be if you don't mind that I look like a plump turkey," Una sighs.

"I'll put you behind Mrs. Chartrand. No one can see past her girth," whispers Archie.

Una stifles her laugh, "Now that's just not nice Mr. Brentwood. Of course, I'll be there." Una looks around. "Did you see where the Christmas cards are?"

"Two aisles over, just past the kitchen utensils." Archie tips his fedora. "Must be going. Lots to do to get ready for the holidays."

"Chocolates," Una says. "Everyone loves chocolates. Buy them for your friend and his wife will think you bought it for them both."

"Clever girl."

Una places her parcels on the kitchen table. She admires the one and only decoration that she could afford, a large red paper bell, and the few Christmas cards that she bought.

I ought to send one to my parents. I'll add a note for Colin and Martha and their families. And this one with the horse and sleigh, I'll send it to Eva. And this one to Emily. I hope I still have her address. And of course, I'll give cards to Archie, the Bartons, Edith and Charlie, and Angus' parents. Did I miss anyone?

Una opens a tiny blue cardboard box and pulls out her gift for Angus, a shiny Douglas lift arm lighter. She tosses thirty-six cents on the table, just enough to cover the cost of postage.

Suddenly Una feels a kick in her womb.

You want to be a dancer, do you? I bet you'll be a fine one too.

Una places both hands on herself to feel for another kick.

Let's go for a walk. Let's go and gather some decorations from outside. Maybe some fallen birch branches and red berries and vines. We'll make it nice for when Daddy comes home. We are going to have the best Christmas ever.

January 17, 1921

Dear Emily,

How lovely to get your letter. I was afraid that my card might not have reached you. It seems you have settled in well, with your job as a telephone operator. We don't have a phone yet but one day I am sure we will. And when we do, I will phone you first thing.

Angus and I had a marvelous Christmas. We had venison. He shot the deer with his bow and arrow. He's quite the marksman. At the Community Christmas Celebration, my brother-in-law dressed as Santa Claus again and only a handful of older children guessed who he really was. Next year we will have a little one to take to the festivities.

Angus is very busy with his railroad work, and he's also taken on a few other odd jobs. Now that the river is frozen solid, he helps out cutting ice. And he sometimes does deliveries for Plexman's General Store. I hardly ever see him.

I sang with the church choir on Christmas Eve. I think I mentioned in my card that I had been in a small band. That's been put on hold for a while as I am about to become a "mommy". Who would have guessed?

On New Year's Day, there was an outdoor exhibition hockey game and of course, Angus was right in there scoring two out of five goals for the local team. I nearly froze my toes off, but it was great fun.

Do you ever think about those days in Nobel? They seem so long ago. I have lost track of the other women. Do you ever hear from Evelyn or Maisie? Do keep in touch. Let me know what you are up to. Anyone special?

Must go now. I'm making cornbread muffins to go with rabbit stew. Angus' father traps them for us.

Your friend always, Una

PS: Angus helped me buy a piano. I am one lucky woman to have such a loving husband.

35

February 1921

It can't be happening. Oh my God, not now. Angus isn't here. He's snowed in some place outside of Kirkland Lake. Oh Jesus, Jesus, the pain, the pain.

Night has fallen. Still in her nightrobe and slippers Una stumbles out the front door and wades through the deep drifts of snow toward her neighbor's place.

I've hardly spoken to them before. They just moved here from northern Quebec. I only know a few words in French. Bonjour. Merci. Please be home. Please.

Frantically Una bangs on their door. A young woman about Una's age cautiously opens the door, a coal oil lantern in her hands. She too is in her night clothes, but as soon as she sees that Una is in distress she cries out.

"Mon Dieu. Maurice. C'est notre voisin. Elle a une bebe. Maintenant. Vite. Entrez. Come in. Come in."

Una moans desperately, "I need my sister-in-law. She lives in the last house on the street." Una points, "la maison. The far one. Her name is Edith."

"Oh, oui, yes, we know Edith. Come, you lie down on my bed. You are Una, non? I am Jocelyn. You be okay." She orders her husband, "Maurice, va chercher Edith et le docteur."

Since the day she found out she was pregnant, Una has been dreading this moment. Her mother's difficult labors have been haunting her at night and more than once her crying has awakened her. Angus holds her and tells her she is going to be alright.

Oh, God. The pain. The pain. What if I can't do this? I don't know if I can do this.

Una cries out loud, "I need Rachel Little Feathers. Nokomis, I need you. I need you now."

Twelve hours later Doctor Smitherin closes his bag and heads for the door of Una's home. He reassures Edith and Jocelyn, "She's going to be fine. It was a difficult birth but with you two helping out I am certain she will regain her strength. The baby is small. Make sure she is kept warm at all times. It is a good thing that the mother can breastfeed. I'll bid you two ladies good day. Oh, my, I am hungry. It's noon already."

Dr. Smitherin shuts the door behind him sending a wisp of snow into the room.

"I can stay here for a few hours," Edith offers Jocelyn the opportunity to go home and take a rest.

"You stay? I go?" Jocelyn asks.

"Yes," Edith agrees. "I'm not sure when Angus will be able to get home." Edith sees by the look on Jocelyn's face that she does not understand. She points to the clock on the shelf. "I will stay until four." She holds up four fingers. "Can you be here from four to ten?"

"Oui, Oui, I can do this. Mais, what about tonight?"

"I will come back," Edith says.

"Bon. Such a beautiful baby. She is so lucky to have a baby. Me and Maurice. Non. But we still try. Okay, I be back at four."

Edith looks down on Una's newborn, wrapped in a flannel blanket and tucked neatly into a dresser drawer near to the woodstove. "Welcome little one. We will take care of you and mommy."

Una is flying, soaring above the lake. Below she sees the scow on the Lake of Bays. Rachel Little Feathers sits on the roof, smoking her pipe. Una lands beside her. "Ninniijaanis, you come to visit me?"

Una cannot speak.

"You know I am dead."

Una wants desperately to tell her, "I have a baby Nokomis. I have a baby girl."

Rachel Little Feathers points to the sky, "See that hawk. See how she soars. But you, Little Goose, you cannot be here. You not dead yet."

Una awakes sobbing, tears pouring onto the pillow, "My baby," she cries, "Where is my baby?"

Edith rushes to Una's bedside. "She's resting Una. She's okay. Everything's okay."

Una suddenly realizes that she is no longer dreaming, and that Edith is sitting on the edge of the bed. "Oh, Edith, where is my Gavina?"

"Gavina? You've found a name for her already? Do you think Angus will like it?"

"I don't know?" Una admits, "Rachel Little Feathers came to me. In a dream. Just now. We saw a hawk."

Edith knows that Una had been delirious throughout the birthing and many times she called out for Rachel. "I have never heard of anyone calling a child Gavina."

"My father knew some Gaelic that he learned from his father," Una recalls, "When I was young, he would tell me the names of birds. Gavin is a boy's name. It means white hawk. See how blond her hair is. My baby girl is Gavina."

Una hears familiar foot-stomping outside the door, a habit Angus always does before entering their home. It has been several days since the baby arrived. She drops her spoon in the stewpot and rushes to open the door. She throws herself into Angus' arms.

"It's a girl Angus. We have a baby girl."

"My dear, dear girl, how have you managed? If only I could have been here. Are you okay?" Angus barely waits for an answer. He sees his daughter sleeping soundly by the woodstove and without hesitating to remove his coat or snow-covered boots, goes directly to the child. He picks her up and holds her to his chest.

"She's as delicate as a butterfly."

"A butterfly that fills her diapers." Una leans her head on Angus' shoulder. "Her name is Gavina. It's Gaelic for hawk. Do you like it?"

"I guess I had better, hadn't I?" Angus knows all too well that if Una has her mind made up about things, there is no changing it. Still, he teases her, "Now you didn't think to call her Mary, Jane, or maybe Sally?"

Una pokes him in the ribs. "Hand her over. Let her rest before she cries for my breast."

"I can hardly wait to be at your breast." Angus flirts as he kisses Una on the cheek.

"You might just have to wait your turn," Una flirts back and gives him a wrinkle of her eyebrow as if to say I miss you too.

August 1921

The train comes to a stop at the Owen Sound Station. With six-month-old Gavina on her lap, Una looks outside the window and scans the platform to see if Eva is waiting for their arrival. Angus jostles to get their luggage down from the rack above their heads.

"There she is," Una shouts pointing to Eva Stanton. "I knew she'd be here. I've wanted you to meet her for so long my love."

Angus leads the way down the aisle to the passenger car door. He exits first then places their luggage on the platform before reaching up to take Gavina from Una's arms. Una steps off the train and goes directly over to where Eva sits on a bench. Awkwardly Eva uses her cane to come to a standing position. Right away Una can see that the years have taken a toll on her long-time friend. Her face shows the lines of aging, and her posture appears far more curved than the last time they were together.

"Una, you look absolutely radiant, and this handsome man must be Angus. I've heard so much about you, young man. Hello, little one. Gavina. Now isn't that a lovely name. And your cheeks are as rosy as a peony in bloom. Are you hungry? I know it is a long journey and we still have quite a long drive before we reach Goderich. My goodness Una," Eva says quietly, "Are you with child again?"

"Yes, I am. The baby is due in December. If it is no trouble, we could use something to eat, a bowl of soup perhaps, something light. Is your cousin here?"

"I didn't want to worry you, Una," Eva takes a breath. "Caroline passed away a few weeks ago. I didn't tell you. I thought you might change your mind about visiting."

"I am so sorry, Eva." Una, unlike Eva, is lost for words.

"It's fine. Really. She'd been sick for some time. It was one of the reasons I moved here. To help her, you know. That's what families do. I was always fond of Caroline. She never married either and we both shared a passion for gardening." Eva leans on her cane. "Shall we? I know a lovely spot to take you to. My treat. Caroline did very well for herself, frugal to the point of stingy sometimes. Bless her. She left me a little extra. I even have a driver and a car now whenever I need one. He's parked at the rear."

During the car ride, there is much sharing of events in each other's lives. Eva speaks passionately about her garden and how she is the president of the local horticultural society. Una brags about Angus' skills as a hockey player then teases him about being away too often working in the backwoods.

Eva seems keenly interested to know the details of his work on the construction of railroad trestles. Much to Una's surprise he gives her a very detailed account interspersed with humorous tidbits about the black flies and the silly capers that some of the men get up to including a play-by-play retelling of how one night a group of men locked the superintendent in the outhouse.

"You never told me that," Una laughs, "Did you get caught.

"I still have my job, don't I?" Angus says.

Una explains that she doesn't miss working for the Bartons even though Mrs. Barton has been generous with handing down her old furnishings.

"I do miss playing in the band," Una adds "but, Gavina comes first, and now that another baby is coming, I don't think I'll be able to join the band again for a while."

"Yes, I suppose so," Eva seems slightly distracted as she looks ahead down the road.

"I do have a piano," Una says, "And Angus and I play music together now and again, don't we?" Una waits for a response but sees that Angus is looking out the window as well.

"Here we are. Goderich." Eva speaks directly to the driver who has been respectfully silent for the duration of the trip. "Take them on a quick tour around the town square before going down Wellington Street."

Una is impressed by the strong stone buildings and the circular treed central square.

"Eva, it is so wonderful to be here. What a stunning town. A breath of fresh air from where we live."

After few minutes, the car pulls up to an enormous red-brick Victorian house boasting a tall mansard roof tower at one end. Una points up to the iron cresting that has the appearance of a crown on top of the patterned shingled roof. Two while pillars stand on guard at the front door.

"Oh my, Eva, what an exquisite house. It looks like something out of a fairytale."

"It is a very unique home. Caroline's father, my father's brother, did very well for himself as an architect. I must confess that now, with Caroline gone, I sometimes feel a little overwhelmed by its emptiness." Eva gathers her composure. "I am so pleased that you have come for a visit. Let's go and get settled in. Mrs. Abernathy will have prepared dinner."

"You have a cook?" Una asks with surprise.

"I do," Eva admits, "Caroline hired her a few years ago and I know Mrs. Abernathy still needs the employment. She has four children all under the age of ten, and her husband was severely injured in a farming accident."

"You do have a big heart Eva," Una says.

"And she is an excellent cook." Eva walks slowly up to the front door. "Later you will want to go for a stroll down by the lake. The sunsets are magnificent. I used to go regularly."

It is difficult to say goodbye, as it is clear to Una that Eva Stanton is not the independent woman she had once known as a girl. Eva had possessed a strong and willful determination that she had so admired. She fights back the tears as she bends over to give Eva a farewell hug, a hug that she senses may be the last one. And when she does let go of Eva's maternal embrace, Una sadly recognizes the aging loneliness in her dear friend's eyes.

"It has been so wonderful to have you here with me these past few days," Eva says. "My driver will take you to the station. I'll stay here. It is a long trip. You understand. At any rate do come back again soon, perhaps after your second child is old enough to travel." Eva turns to Angus, "And you, young man take good care of your family. They mean the world to me, and I am holding you responsible should anything happen."

"Yes ma'am," Angus salutes. He knows the order is said out of love and besides, Eva has been teasing him the whole time they have been with her.

"Now in you go." Eva points to the idling car. "Write soon."

The car makes its way to the end of the drive. Una and Angus look back and wave until the car turns onto the road, and Eva and her house disappear behind the row of houses.

"I'll never see her again, " Una says despairingly.

Angus places his hand on her knee to comfort her, "Now we don't know that, now do we?"

Una looks longingly out the window. "I just know. I feel it in my bones."

October 1921

Una's breasts ache. Her nipples stand out enlarged and tender. Her ankles are swollen, and she is constantly having to urinate. At seven months pregnant Una is already counting the days until the baby is born and with each day, she prays that the delivery is easier than it had been with Gavina.

Angus comes into the bedroom to find Una sitting naked on the side of the bed, her head hanging down. He lifts her chin. "You are my beauty. You will always be my beauty."

"How can you say that? Look at me. I am swollen and fat and ugly." Una grabs the sheets and throws them around herself."

"Not to my eyes." Angus sits beside her, "I think you are the most beautiful woman in the world. When I was in Paris, I saw paintings of royalty and goddesses and none are as beautiful as you, my girl. None. Now come and lie down beside me."

Angus folds Una into his embrace. He strokes her hair tenderly until she falls into a gentle sleep. Then he too nods off.

Suddenly Angus shouts, "Jesus Christ get down, get down." He tries to push Una off the bed. "Oh my God. No. Move it."

"Angus wake up. It's me, Una. Angus. You're hurting me." Una tries to get Angus to come to, but he is paralyzed by the frightening memory of the war. Una sings as she has done in the past. "Let me call you sweetheart, I'm in love with you. Let me hear you whisper, that you love me too…"

Angus shudders and slowly comes to, confused, covered in sweat.

"You had a bad dream, my love," Una reassures him. "You are with me now. The war is over. Everything is okay." Whenever this happens it takes some time for Angus to settle down. Una puts on her dressing gown. "I'll heat up some milk. Would you like that? There is a full moon. We can watch it if you like."

"I don't know what I'd do without you my girl," Angus says joining Una in the tiny kitchen. He stands behind her and rests his head on her shoulder.

"Nor I," Una says. "We are better for being with one another, aren't we?"

"We are."

December 1921

"It's not supposed to be like this," Una rocks back and forth, the lifeless body of her seven-day-old infant in her arms. "What did I do wrong?"

Edith and Charlie have come over. To offer support. To make tea. To talk about other things. Angus jostles Gavina in his arms. She squirms and giggles as she tries to grab his hat from his head.

"I don't want them to take him away. Not yet." Una is adamant. "Connor hasn't even been baptized. He needs to be baptized. Please, Angus. Don't let them take my baby away."

"He has to go to the vault at the cemetery," Edith says consolingly, "We'll have a funeral in the spring."

"So tiny, so, so tiny. My poor baby." Una watches in horror as the undertaker walks away with the body of her newborn.

No words erase the sorrow. No caress removes the guilt. Nothing catches Una from her cascading fall into depression. Even Angus is unable to offer her some comfort. Una's heart is a closed-door sealed with unspeakable grief.

For days she refuses to get dressed. Angus does his best to prepare the meals, yet Una sits at the table unable to bring herself to eat. When Gavina cries, she ignores her wails. Angus has come home several nights to find Gavina still in her playpen, soiled and sobbing.

More than a week has passed since Connor died. Angus tells Una he has to go up north again. That night as Una lay with her back to him, he knows what he must do. In the morning he will ask Edith to take Gavina until he comes back, and Una is well enough to look after her again.

It isn't until noon that Una finally wakes up. Immediately she realizes that both Angus and Gavina are gone. Her heartbeat quickens with fear.

Why would he do this to me? Where is my little girl? Where has he taken her?

Archie opens the door to his apartment to discover Una shivering from the cold. No winter coat, her hair a tangled mess, her eyes dark and sullen.

"He's taken Gavina," Una sobs, "my baby died and now he has taken Gavina."

"Let's just have you come inside, and we'll sort this all out Sweet Pea. I am sure Angus would never abduct your child. There must be some other explanation." Archie leads Una to the sofa and puts a blanket over her. "I am so sorry about the loss of your baby. I can see this has not been easy for you Una. You look dreadful. But let's put our thinking caps on. Where would Angus take Gavina?"

"Up north." Una fearfully concludes.

"I doubt that. You and I both know the railroaders are not allowed to bring their families. Besides, who would look after Gavina while he worked?" Archie's direct approach seems to be lifting Una's emotional malaise. "So, who would look after Gavina?"

"Edith?" Una asks.

"Most likely my dear. Now we need a plan." Archie sits across from Una.

"You need to stay here and have a relaxing bath. It always helps me when I feel blue. I'll go and fetch some fresh clothes from your place, and we'll call on Edith." Archie taps his fingers impatiently on the arm of his chair. "Well, don't just sit there. Run a bath. There are fresh towels on the shelf. And don't worry I won't look in on you."

Una soaks in the warm soothing water, her eyes closed. Her last bath had been during her visit with Eva Stanton. The boxcar home is too tiny for a bathtub and washing at the kitchen sink is the best she can do.

Memories flood Una's mind. Memories of swimming naked off the scow and the fresh feeling of the water as it rushes past her youthful, naked body. She sees herself paddling on the lake with Rachel and catching fish to fry. She vividly recalls that one time when the baby's casket passed through the window and her mother wept for its lost soul. Now Una understands. Now she knows the pain her mother had to endure so long ago. But she also knows it is too late to make amends.

I cannot go back in time. I cannot change what has happened. I must find a way to move forward. I will find a way. I will.

February 18, 1922

Dear Una

How are you? It has been a long time since I last heard from you. Your little Gavina looks adorable. Thank you for sending the photo. Did you knit the sweater and bonnet? You last wrote that you were about to have another baby. Boy or girl?

Now that the war is over several of my women friends have found themselves without work. At least I still have a job. Some, who have married keep harping on about, when am I going to get married. My parents pester me constantly and keep inviting sons of their friends for dinner. Even if I were inclined that way none of them are to my liking, not even as human beings.

One chap, Frederick, he's an accountant, bores me to tears when he starts talking about his hobby, homing pigeons. I do see him occasionally to make appearances, but I would never dream of marrying him just to please my parents.

By the way, I saw the most splendid Mary Pickford film last week. You know how much I adore her. She plays a boy in Little Lord Fauntleroy. Be still my heart.

There's going to be a reunion of the gals from the plant in Nobel in May. It's being held in Parry Sound. Did you get the notice? I'm not sure about going. You?

Please drop me a line when you are able. I can only imagine how busy you must be with two little ones.

As always, Emily

March 25, 1922

Dear Emily

You are such a dear friend to keep in touch with me and I have been so slow to write back. Much has happened since my last letter. In December I gave birth to a beautiful baby boy, Connor. My darling child died seven days later. It still breaks my heart to think about it.

Gavina is completely unaware of what happened and is a cheery little girl. I am so thankful for that. She keeps me on my toes now that she is a toddler. The other day she took hold of the tablecloth and started pulling it down. I caught her just in time before dinner ended up on the floor.

Yesterday I heard geese heading north. Seems a bit early for up here but maybe they know something I don't know. I can hardly wait to collect pussy willows, hopefully before Easter. It's late this year, April 16. Do you have plans? We will go over to Angus' parents' place. I've promised to bring butterscotch cake.

Haven't seen a movie in ages. You must keep me up to date. I hear Rudolph Valentino is in a new one. I'd like to see that.

I haven't received an invitation to the reunion. It could be they lost track of me. Who knows? At any rate, I won't be going. Angus is away quite a bit and I have Gavina to look after. If you do decide to go give the gals my best.

Take care, Una.

36

August 1930   **The Asylum**

I've been trying to write. Nothing comes. I just stare and feel empty, empty like this blank page. A white nothing. That's what I am. Nothing.

Una places the pencil inside the notebook and closes the pale green cover.

'Don't worry,' she says. 'Give it time, the words will come.' I know she means well, Dr. Harrington, and she tells me it is good for me to write, that it will release me. Release me from what? How can I be released from what I no longer have? My heart aches for his touch.

Una's pain scalds like a lump of hot coal searing deep within her soul and she fears she is turning to ash and drifting away. She bends over the round oak table and places her head upon her crossed arms.

"Having a rest?"

Startled Una looks up to see Dr. Harrington standing beside her, the light streaming through the sunroom windows creating an aura about her.

Una thinks she is seeing an angel.

"I have some very special news for you, Una." Dr. Harrington stands across the table from Una. "Your children can come and see you on the weekend. Would you like that?

"Are they okay? I love them you know." Una wrings her hands with embarrassment and the shame of not being able to care for them again. "I would never abandon them. It's just that…"

"You've had a great shock Una and you are still grieving. But I see an improvement each day, especially since you started playing the piano." Dr. Harrington pauses. "So, shall I arrange an afternoon tea for Saturday, say, at three?"

"Yes, yes, I do miss them so. Will Edith be there too? I want to thank her for coming all the way to Brockville. It is a long trip from Capreol you know. And she has a little girl of her own…" Una stops short.

"What is it, Una?" Dr. Harrington asks.

"My hair. I look horrible. I don't want them to see me like this. They can't. I can't let them see me. Maybe it isn't such a good idea."

"Una, you are far too hard on yourself." Dr. Harrington continues, "We do have a salon you know. I can make an appointment for you to have your hair done on Friday. And this afternoon you can go to the Women's Auxiliary Shop. There are some lovely new donations. I'm sure you will find something suitable. But then again if you aren't feeling ready to see your children, I understand, but Una I am sure they'd love to see you."

Of course, I want to see them. I've been so selfish. I need to be strong for them now. I need to do this. Angus would want me to be here for them.

Una nods, "Yes, you are right Dr. Harrington. I will. I will see them."

"Call me Julia," Dr. Harrington suggests, "and please keep writing in your journal Una. It may help you see things more clearly. Sorrow is long-lasting. And you have suffered an enormous loss." Dr. Harrington checks the tiny watch pinned to her lapel. "Forgive me Una but I have another patient to see. I'll drop by the salon on my way and make an appointment for you."

Una calls after her as she walks away. "Dr. Harrington, I mean Julia –"

Dr. Harrington waits in the doorway. "Yes?"

"Thank you." Una holds the journal in her hands. "I will try. And thank you for arranging to have the children brought here for a visit. Thank you."

"Not at all. No thanks needed. I shall see you on Saturday for the tea."

37

December 1922

Everyone in the McFadden household is laughing, spinning tall tales, and eating second helpings of Agnes' Christmas pie. Gavina chases her older cousin Carol around and under the dining room table.

"Cheer up Una. It's Christmas. Have another shot of crème-de-menthe," Charlie chortles as he takes a swig.

"Thank you, no, Charlie. I'm fine," Una smiles feebly as she holds two-month-old Sean in her arms.

They're all acting as if it didn't happen, that I should be just fine. My baby died last year. Connor died.

The previous December the unbearable sorrow of losing her baby had left Una feeling completely separated from her own body. The Christmas gathering at the McFadden's played out like a bizarre movie where Una watched from the sidelines. And the guilt of not being able to recover gnawed at her appetite. She pushed the turkey and mashed potatoes with gravy from one side of her plate to the other long after everyone had gone finished eating. Disgusted with life and everything to do with it, the mantra *'why didn't I die too'* rattled in her brain like a never-ending roll of the dice.

She could tell that the family was walking on eggshells by the way they overcompensated with their tenderness. She knew they were judging her for having abandoned Gavina. She was aware that they never approved of the time she was a housekeeper for Mrs. Barton and that they deemed her frivolous for dressing in flamboyant costumes like the ones Mrs. Barton wore.

When Edith gave Una a parcel of baby clothes that had been intended for Connor she had said, *'One day, I am sure you'll have another baby.'*. Una sharply flew into a rage and stormed out of Edith's house.

As it turned out, two months after Connor died Una was pregnant for the third time. Once again, she feared that she would die from the pain of childbirth or worse kill the baby during the delivery even before it could take its first breath. But after ten hours of agony, Sean was born with a full head of black hair and blue eyes that sparkled like his father's.

"Una, would you like some pumpkin pie?" Edith offers. "Una? pumpkin pie?"

Una snaps to. "Sean is hungry. I'm just going to take him to the parlor. Thanks anyway."

While holding Sean to her breast, Una hears snippets of the conversations going around the dining room table.

"Angus, we're going to the hunting camp. Why don't you come with us," Charlie enthuses.

"We'll have to see, " Angus replies hesitantly.

Maybe he'll say no. I hope he says no. I need him home right now.

Una overhears Agnes. "They've asked him to leave."

"What a shame," says Edith, "He's a fine musician. Mr. Brentwood has served our congregation well. Why would they ask him to leave?"

"Because he's a blooming dandy," quips Charlie gulping down the homemade cider.

"Now Charlie, nobody knows that for certain," Edith retorts, "Just because Mr. Brentwood is a gentle creature does not mean he is a homosexual."

"Well, we can't be taking any chances," Charlie adds, "he could be messing with little boys."

Una rushes into the room. "How dare you say these things about Archie. How dare you. He is the kindest, most sincere person I have ever met, and he wouldn't hurt a fly. Besides he's in love."

"In love? Who with?" Charlie demands, "You?"

Una suddenly realizes she has broken her promise to Archie, to never reveal that he is a man who loves men.

"No, not me. Don't be ridiculous. He has a special friend in Toronto. He told me so. But this friend is married. You people. Why would you treat him like this? He is my only friend in this God-forsaken town." Profanities and insults fly out of Una like speeding bullets. "You idiots, you two-faced lying bastards, I know you hate me."

Angus steps up and leads Una to the front door. "We'll be going now."

"They hate me, Angus. They hate the fact that you married me."

"Let's just get the children and go home. You're exhausted, that's all. I know," he says calmly. "Everything is going to be fine. You're going to be fine. Nothing that a good night's sleep won't fix."

"I've always known," Angus says as he climbs into bed beside Una. "I knew from the moment you introduced me to Archie, at the dance that time, remember?"

"But how? I made a promise and now I've broken it." Una clutches her pillow. "He'll never forgive me. And your family. I yelled at them, Angus. I couldn't help myself. All the things they were saying."

Angus pulls Una closer. "Look, they were out of line. It's over. You can forget about it. I know how close you are with Archie. And I knew he would never, I mean never, cross the threshold with you. He's just not made that way. People around here have been saying things for a while now."

"But if he leaves, and with you away so much, I just, I just..." Una buries her head in Angus' shoulder.

"I know my girl." Angus strokes her back. "At least I have work. Think of it. You've seen them, the men who can't find a job, men like me who fought that damn war and are scrambling to get work, anything." Angus lifts Una's chin and looks her in the eyes. "That's why I have to go where they send me."

Una senses that Angus is holding something back. "What is it? Angus? Tell me?"

"I was going to surprise you. Tomorrow. On Boxing Day." Angus teases, "But now, I guess I have to tell you."

"Tell me what," Una squirms with anticipation, "Tell me, tell me, tell me."

"I bought you a guitar. You've always wanted one, ever since you taught yourself how to play mine. It's a Regal Parlor guitar, just the right size for you."

"Oh, Angus, you did? Where is it?"

"Under the bed."

Una leans over to see it but is immediately pulled back by Angus. "I expect you to be playing all sorts of chords," Angus slips in, "by the time I get back."

Una slumps onto her pillow. "Where this time?"

"I've decided to go hunting with Charlie and the boys. It'll only be for a few days. Now come over here." Angus fondles her breasts, kisses her neck.

"Be gentle," Una says wrapping her legs about his waist.

As their words melt into more kisses, Una feels the intimate rapture of their oneness. She swells with an endless emotion of loving and longing, and a deep desire to never let go.

38

March 1923

March 28, 1923

Dear Eva,

    The children are finally asleep, and I have a quiet moment to jot a line to you. How are you? This winter seems to be going on forever. Another blizzard came as a surprise yesterday. In like a lion, out like a lamb, although it is the other way around this year. It is so cold up here. I had no idea. I'm still wearing leggings under my skirts and two pairs of wool socks most days.

    If I recall, you wrote saying you have a kitten. That must be nice to have a little friend to keep you company. One of my closest friends moved to Toronto. I hardly see anyone these days. My neighbor Jocelyn is very sweet but she barely speaks a word of English and you can imagine how horrible my French must be.

Gavina is into everything now that she is walking and I'm still breast-feeding Sean. Plus, I am pregnant again. So much for the wives' tale that you can't get pregnant while nursing. Angus says that all he has to do is hang his trousers on the bedpost and there's a bun in the oven. To be honest, I hope this is the last one.

I play music at home when I can, but I do miss playing for dances. Angus bought me a parlor guitar. We sometimes play old-time tunes together.

I would love to come and see you when the weather warms up if you'll have all four of us. I am due in August so it might be best to visit in May if that is alright with you. I'd invite you here, but we are living cheek to jowl just now. There is a hotel in town, but it has a bar on the lower level and it gets pretty rowdy at times.

So, my dear Eva, I do hope my note finds you in good spirits and dreaming of all the flowers that will soon be blossoming in your garden.

Affectionately yours, Una

April 1923

"How long?" Una stops doing the dishes and wipes her hands on her apron. "You're going where?"

Angus downs the last of his coffee. "It's an opportunity I can't turn down. I know it's longer than usual."

"How long? Two weeks?"

"Four, maybe six." Angus starts to put on his coat.

"And what am I supposed to do?" Una folds her arms across her chest. "Damn it, Angus, I waited through that whole goddamn war for you, and now every time I turn around, you're off to someplace. God knows where this time. Where is this place Agate anyway? And why can't you come back on weekends?"

"Una, my girl, you know I will miss you," he says as he puts his hands on her shoulders, "but what choice do we have?"

Una waits.

"I'll come with you. If you are going to be away for that long a time, then the children and I will come too. For a visit."

"Una, you can't. They won't let you. I could get fired and then where would we be?" Angus tries to explain.

"That's a chance we'll just have to take. Sneak us in. Who says the big wigs in Toronto or Montreal, or wherever they are, have to find out?" Una stands her ground, "I can be discreet and so can you. I'm sure you can persuade the foreman to turn a blind eye." Una coos as she presses her body against Angus, "Please Angus do this for me. Please. Do it for Gavina and Sean."

"I'll see what I can do. No promises. But I need to warn you, it's rough up there. I'm telling you, Una. Nothing but a lean-to squatter, no running water, and we'll be cramped into half of a boxcar, all four of us. The only other women are the cook and her daughter."

"As long as I'm with you, even for a week or so, that's all I am asking for Angus. I do love you so."

"Was there ever any doubt?" Angus tips his hat the way he did in those early years. I knew what I was in for the day I married you, my girl. And by the way..."

"Yes?"

"I love you too."

Una waits eagerly on the train platform in Capreol. Angus, who has been gone for just shy of two weeks, has planned for Una and the children to travel in a caboose attached to a CN freight train heading north. In his note, he warned Una that it would likely be dark when she arrives.

Una has gone to great lengths to dress the children and herself in their Sunday best. Gavina twiddles the large white buttons on her in a new navy blue, wool coat.

"Leave them alone Gavina. You don't want them to fall off before we see Daddy." Una adjusts her daughter's pink cloche with yellow daisies embroidered on one side. She leans over and pulls down the sleeves of Sean's new beige sweater-coat. "You are a handsome one, just like your father, you are."

The weather is unseasonably cool. Una has decided to wear her black sheep's wool coat with the red fox cuffs and collar. Angus bought it for her with a bonus he got from CN for working overtime, plus some pay he earned doing odd jobs in and around town. To top off her attire Una proudly wears a brocade cloche and a long white silk scarf. She is determined to make an impression even if it is for a bunch of railroaders wearing greasy coveralls and grimy shirts. All that matters to Una is that she makes Angus proud to have such a fine-looking family to show off to everyone, though it is a secret that they are going to be there at all.

As the train pulls out of Capreol the sun is already setting in the west, casting crimson light through the black silhouetted trees. Una rocks Sean who is fussing. Gavina leans against Una and soon is lulled asleep by the motion of the train.

How did I get to be like this? A mother? I never wanted to be like my own mother. One baby after another.

The trees and rocks flash by the tiny caboose window like a motion picture that is falling off its reel. *Click, click, click.* Una's head drops onto her chest. She straightens up with a start. In the darkness, she checks to see that Sean is fast sleep. Gavina lay curled up on the bench beside her.

My babies. So innocent. So sweet when they sleep.

It does not take long for Una to succumbs to the motion of the train until hours later the train stops and the stillness wakes her up. She peers out the window into the pitch black. Nothing. Not a single star shines through the clouded sky. Then, in the distance, she sees what looks like a swinging lantern getting closer and closer.

Angus opens the door to the caboose. "You made it," he says. "Welcome to the middle of nowhere."

Before the sun rises, Una wakes to find Gavina staring up at her, crying. Una whispers, "She's wet the bed. Angus. Wake up. Gavina has had a little accident. Where do I wash things?"

Angus rolls over, "The cook."

"What are you saying?" Una starts to undress Gavina. "Angus. I've got to get these things washed."

"Wrap them up and I'll give them to the cook. She does our laundry too." Angus pulls on his work pants. "Cook will have a fire going. I sure could use a hot cup of coffee."

Una picks up Sean who has been whimpering for her breast. "What will we do today Angus?"

"I'll be working up the line most of the day," Angus says mindlessly as he brushes his hair. "I suppose you can look around the camp but don't let the children wander off. Maybe you can visit with the cook. She'll be making our breakfast in about an hour. You'll think of something."

Una gathers up the soiled sheet and Gavina's things, then dresses herself and the children.

"Goodness Una," Angus clicks his tongue, "You all look like you're dressed for church."

"Only the best for you, my love." Una proudly adjusts the buttons on Sean's sweater. "Ready when you are."

In the dining-shack the men do a double-take at Una and the children. Una holds her head high and sits at one end of a long table as if she is dining at a banquet. She will not let her pride be squelched by a bunch of railroaders whispering under their whiskers.

She looks at them, "Good morning gentlemen. Lovely morning."

"If you don't mind the black flies," mumbles one.

"Damn near sucked the blood right out of my bones," says another.

"You'd best stay indoors or get eaten alive," chuckles an older chap with a beard that reaches his chest.

"They're right Una, it can be pretty miserable out there." Angus delivers a plate of bacon, eggs, and toast to Una. "Cook says you can stay here if you like. It's either that or in our quarters."

"I see," Una looks at the meal. "This is huge."

A burly woman wearing a stained apron comes by with porridge for Gavina. "Working men need big meals," she says in a strong accent unfamiliar to Una's ears. "Little girl gets little meal. You need warm milk for your boy?"

"That would be lovely if you have some. I've been trying to wean him," Una replies.

"I give you goat milk. We got two goats out back. You know what you needs to do? You needs to put vinegar on your teat. It work for Magdalena my daughter." The cook gestures to her plump teenage daughter serving coffee to the men. "She a big strong girl, no? Like Russian father. But he dead. Die in train derailment last year. But me. We okay. I got good job here. You want more coffee?"

"Yes, thank you."

It finally dawns on Una that she has landed in a place like no other. A place with nothing to do and nowhere to go, and she wonders why on earth she came here in the first place.

"This wasn't such a good idea, was it? My coming here."

"Let's talk about it when I get back." Angus wipes his chin. "You can have lunch here. Cook will see that you get fed. I'll be back for dinner." Angus pushes in his chair. He tussles Gavina's hair and pinches Sean's cheek, "Take care of Mommy until I get back." He leans over and quickly gives Una a peck on the lips.

"Look at the little love birds," the older man teases.

"Cut the crap, Smitty." Angus puts on his tweed cap. "We need to take the gas car up line before the freight train comes through from Manitoba."

Angus lowers his voice for Una, "Don't mind him, he's just an old codger who doesn't know any better."

Una and Angus lay side by side in the cramped single bed. They decide that it would be best for her to take the children and return to Capreol on the next southbound train. Una admits that Angus was right. She should have listened when he had tried to discourage her from coming.

Angus sees disappointment in her eyes, and he assures her that his love for her is deeper than the sea. Gently placing his hand on her swelling, he croons, "Soon we will have another mouth to feed."

"Maybe then you can work closer to home," Una says hopefully.

"I hope so too my girl. I hope so too."

39

May 1923

On Saturday mornings like this Una is glad to be alive. The warm Spring air blows through the screens on the windows and doors. Angus wears an apron and busily scrubs the dishes after their breakfast. Sean babbles to himself and plays with his rattles in the playpen. Gavina sits beside the piano strumming the home-made guitar that Una fashioned out of an old cigar box and a few rubber bands.

"Let's have some music this morning," Una says, her fingers dancing across the keys of the piano. "Strum along Gavina."

> The Camptown ladies sing this song,
> Doo-da, Doo-da
> The Camptown racetrack's five miles long,
> Oh-de-doo-da-day.
> Going to run all night

Going to run all day
I bet my money on a bob-tailed nag
Somebody bet on the grey.

At every "doo-da" Angus looks around the corner of the kitchenette and hoots like a train whistle which sets Gavina off in a fit of contagious giggles. As soon as his hands are dry, he gets out the guitar and together they play one song after another, "Skip to My Lou", "Hand Me Down My Walking Cane", and "Casey Jones The Brave Engineer".

"We ought to go on a picnic. It's warm enough. What do you say? Lake Wanapitei? " Angus suggests, "I'll go over to Dad's and hitch up the horse and wagon."

"I think that's a splendid idea," Una beams, "I'll rustle up some sandwiches and we can purchase some Root Beer and tarts from the grocers. I'd like to stop by the post office. I haven't picked up the mail for a few days."

Within the hour Angus pulls up, sitting tall with the reins in his hands. Una stands outside with Sean and Gavina at her side. She has everything ready - the wicker picnic basket, two old blankets, and a tote bag filled odds-and-ends. Her hair is tied up in a bright orange bandana and her smile radiates joy beneath the round sunglasses perched on the end of her nose. Una is ecstatic. Family time, a rare treat.

"Pull over at the post office please," Una asks as they approach the red brick building.

"Yes ma'am," Angus says pretending to be a chauffeur.

"I'll just be a minute." Una hands Sean over. "He's as squirmy as a fish today."

Mr. Finch, the postmaster, is a beanpole of a man with a pencil-thin moustache and balding brow. As Una approaches the counter he seems slightly distracted.

"Any mail this week Mr. Finch?" Una inquires cheerfully.

"Just a minute young lady. Oh dear, where did I put those overseas stamps? Mail? For you Mrs. McFadden? Let me see." Finch looks through

Unsayable Absence

a pile of general delivery letters. "No, no, oh, yes, here's one. It's a return to sender."

Finch hands Una the familiar envelope. Right away Una sees that it is the very letter she had written to Eva Stanton in April. Someone has written Return to Sender. Deceased.

Overcome by the sudden unexpected message Una rushes out of the post office and quickly steps up to the cart. She sits beside Angus. Speechless, she stifles her shock.

The last thing I want to do is let the children to see me so upset. I won't let this day be ruined. I won't.

She hands Angus the envelope.

"Oh, my girl. I am so, so sorry. I know how very fond you are of Miss Stanton." Angus places his hand on her knee and gives her back the letter. "Maybe we should go home?"

"No, let's go. This is our day. I'll be okay." Una hugs Sean, "Are you my beautiful boy?" She reaches to Gavina, "And you are my beautiful girl."

"Mommy why are you crying?" asks Gavina.

"I'm just so happy that we are all together and we are going on a picnic." Una wipes a tear from her cheek. "Aren't you happy?"

"Yes, Mommy. When we get there can I build a sandcastle?" asks Gavina.

"Of course, and we will pick wildflowers and make it the most wonderful castle ever."

Wildflowers for Eva, columbine and lady's slippers, snapdragons and lily of the valley, and all the flowers the earth has to offer.

That night Una dreams she is walking through a large open field that shimmers with golden sunlight. The wind blows the tall grass and the field rolls like waves on an endless ocean. Una floats backward onto a bed of soft hay. Eva looks down on her. She is dressed in a flowing white robe, and she is so young. She carries a basket of flowers over one arm.

Then Rachel Little Feathers appears with a raven on her shoulder. Both women radiate an intense love that Una feels surging through her body. Their lips move but Una has trouble hearing them. *What are they saying? I want to know.* Una hears them whisper, 'Everything is alright. We will be here for him when he comes.' *Who will be alright? Who are you talking about?* Una tries to reach toward them, but they dissolve into a fog. In desperation she tries to call out their names, but her voice gets stuck in her throat. *Eva, Rachel, don't go. Come back. Come back.*

"Una, wake up. Wake up, Una. Are you okay?" Angus reaches across the bed.

Slowly Una emerges from the visitation in the ethers.

"I was dreaming. I saw Eva and Rachel. They came to me Angus. They came to me in my dream."

"You're going to be fine. It was just a dream. Come here. I'll rub your back." Una curls up, her back to Angus.

"They were trying to tell me something," Una whispers.

"I know my girl. I know."

Una once more falls asleep. She tries to bring her dear friends back to her dreamtime but like a mist dissolving on a cool summer morning, they had already risen and were gone.

June 1923

June 22, 1923

Dear Archie,

I am so sorry I have not written sooner. Your letters mean the world to me. I am so happy for you that you have found a church that appreciates your musical talents. And it is the same church that your friend attends. Some things are

Unsayable Absence

meant to be.

So much has happened since you last wrote to me. My dear friend Eva Stanton passed away this Spring. She was the person I told you about. I stayed with her for many years before the war.

Angus still goes away to work the rails. I took Gavina and Sean with me to one of the camps. Big mistake. It was in the middle of nowhere and the black flies were dreadful. Poor little Sean was covered in bloody bites. I came back to Capreol after only one day.

Are you in any bands or orchestras? Our little ensemble still plays here and there but I haven't been able to join them. Motherhood takes up most of my time. And I am due in August. I already look like a great big pumpkin.

I miss your laughter, your music, and your fine cooking. Angus and I play music at home. Did I tell you he bought me a guitar? My fingertips are still sore from playing chords.

Well dear friend, do take care and drop a line when you can. I so look forward to your letters.

Yours truly, Una.

Una slips the envelope into her purse. Angus, who is home for a few days, left an hour ago with the children. He decided to take them to a farm a few miles out of town where they could go for a hayride. Una wisely decided that it might not be all that comfortable, being pregnant on a hot day, and riding on a jostling hay wagon. At any rate, she wants to pop by the post office and pick up a few things from the store.

On her way downtown, she waves to Jocelyn who is busy sweeping the grit from her front stoop. In the distance she sees a bright, yellow Roadster Convertible coming toward her. Sitting in the passenger seat is Mrs. Barton accompanied by a handsome young man at the steering wheel.

Una waves and smiles. She knows that Mrs. Barton doesn't care what anyone says. She had once told Una, 'What Mr. Barton doesn't know won't hurt him, or me for that matter. Anyway, he would never leave me or my inheritance.'

In the village, the store window boasts a poster that announces a free concert at the park pavilion.

That's this evening. How perfect. We can go as a family.

After collecting her few groceries Una heads over to the post office. She walks through the door and catches Mr. Finch off guard swatting flies with a rolled-up newspaper.

"Good day Mr. Finch. How are you this fine day?" Una asks cheerfully.

"Pesky flies," Finch utters as he resumes his postal charge behind the counter."

"Beautiful morning we're having," Una says.

"You'd think so," scoffs Finch. "If people would only remember to put stamps on their letters my job would be a whole lot easier. I've got six of them right here. It's not my fault if I can't post them." Finch shuffles the letters. "Here's one from Father Finnegan. You'd think he'd know better. And this one is from Old Lady Spencer, blind as a bat she is, I can barely make out the address."

Finch stops his rant, "So what can I do for you, Mrs. McFadden."

"Postage to Toronto please," Una says placing three pennies on the counter. Finch hands her a stamp which Una wets and places on the envelope. "Hope your day gets better."

"Humph."

On her way home Una passes by an alley between two stores where an elderly woman sits on a blanket, a mongrel curled up at her feet.

Her raspy voice calls out, "Missus, missus you want to buy this basket. Beautiful basket."

Right away Una thinks of Rachel Little Feathers and her heartbeat quickens. The old woman's face shows years of hardship, every line on her face telling a sad story.

"You gonna have biibii-yag. You gonna have a baby girl. She rides low. I know." The old woman holds up her basket. "You want basket? Only one dollar but for you fifty cents."

"Aho, yes," Una reaches into her purse and pulls out a one-dollar bill.

"You speak my language?" the old woman seems pleased.

"Only a few words." Una hands her the dollar. "What is your name?"

"Waabigwan. It means flower. But me, I am old dried-up flower. Soon I go to winter garden," she laughs a dry coarse cackle. "Them nuns take my name away. They call me Rebecca. They try to take my name from me, but they no take my spirit." She reaches up. "Take two basket. You nice woman."

"Thank you Waabigwan. It was nice to meet you. The baskets are beautiful."

Una walks away. Looks back. The old woman tosses a crust of bread to her dog.

I wish I could do something for her, anything.

"You've certainly changed." Judith suddenly appears out of nowhere. "When is this one due?" she chirps caustically. "I hear you have two other babies. What are they? A boy and a girl?"

"What brings you back to Capreol?" Una says ignoring her remarks.

"My fiancé wanted to see where I grew up. I told him it wasn't worth the drive, but he insisted." Judith clicks her tongue as she glances up and down the street. "I must say I don't miss it here."

Una wants to say, *"And we don't miss you"* but utters, "Well then you probably want to be going. Soon." With that Una simply walks away.

In the early evening following dinner, Una and Angus take the children to the outdoor concert. The band plays an array of popular marches and familiar music from the cinema.

I do miss playing music with the band. But I am here with Angus and that matters more than anything. I wonder if he ran into Judith. I don't trust her even if she does say she's getting married. Who knows what she's likely to do?

"I saw Judith today," Una prods for a reaction.

"Oh yes," Angus says mindlessly. "Quite the turnout this evening."

"She's getting married."

"Who?"

"Judith."

"I pity the poor man. She can be a real troublemaker. Look at Gavina and Sean, marching like little soldiers to this tune."

Right away Una's insecurities scatter to the wind. There is no doubt in her mind that Angus loves her. And he loves their children.

After the concert, they stroll home together watching the setting sun ignite the clouds in a prism of rainbow colors. No need for any words. With tenderness in their hearts, they stroll arm in arm, Gavina prancing ahead, and baby Sean fast asleep in his pram.

40

July 1923

"There's a registered letter and a parcel for you Mrs. McFadden. It's from someone in Goderich." Mr. Finch pushes them toward Una. "I'll be needing your signature for the letter. Sign here." Finch points to the line with his crooked, arthritic finger.

Una asks for a pen which Finch reluctantly gives to her. Holding onto it, he barks like a dog that has been stepped on, "Don't be walking away with it. I've already had to replace two pens this month."

"No. I won't. Thank you." Una immediately sees that the letter is from a solicitor and likely has something to do with Eva's estate.

"That parcel's pretty heavy. Maybe you want someone to bring it to your place. I mean," he stutters, "in your condition."

"I'm fine. I can place it under Sean's carriage." *Good grief I'm not an invalid. Just because I'm pregnant.* "Gavina, you hold the door for mommy."

"What's in there?" Gavina asks.

"I don't know. We can find out when we get home." Una places the parcel on the rack under the carriage. "First I want to go to the cemetery."

"Why?"

"Your baby brother is buried there."

"Why?"

"He wasn't strong like you and Sean."

"Why?"

"Connor was born that way." Una pushes the carriage across the street toward the cemetery gates. "Let's gather some fallen branches to make a wreath. Go over by that willow. See what you can find."

Gavina skips away, stooping here and there, filling her arms with several willow branches.

Further along, Una stops beside a small flat grave marker. She lifts Sean from the carriage and places him on the grass. Una reads aloud the words on the marble stone, '*Connor McFadden. Age 7 days. A twinkling star in heaven rests.*'

"Is Connor a star? Gavina asks innocently. "What is heaven like? Can we go there and visit him?"

Una twists and braids the tender branches and tries to explain death to Gavina, "Heaven is a beautiful place. It is everything wonderful. But it isn't a place we can get to while we are living."

"Can we see Connor tonight? Is he one of the stars?" Gavina asks as she hands her mother another branch.

"I like to think so, but there are millions and millions of stars. He's probably playing with them every night."

Una takes the delicate wreath, kisses it, and places it on the grave. Gavina, copying her mother, picks the wreath up, kisses it, then gently lays it back down.

Gavina pleads, "Can we see Connor tonight? Can we look for him in the stars?"

"Yes, we can try. But he likes to play 'hide and go seek' up there," Una says light-heartedly, though her heart weighs heavy. So many people have died. Her brother Robert, Rachel Little Feathers, Connor, and most recently Eva Stanton.

"Time to go home. You must be ready for lunch. Good thing I made a pot of soup this morning. Chicken noodle."

After lunch Una tucks both Gavina and Sean into their cots for an afternoon nap. In the quiet moment, Una retrieves the items from Eva's parcel and lays them out on the kitchen table. She finds an old book entitled *The Ladies' Companion to The Flower-Garden by Mrs. Loudon*. How well Una remembers leafing through it and admiring all the vibrant floral prints that Eva delighted in describing in great detail.

Una picks up a small, embroidered pillow sham with yellow daisies, the very one that had always been on the bed where she slept. Wrapped in a tea towel, Una immediately recognizes the sterling silver cake server that came out for special occasions. Una had always admired it.

One more item. Una gasps as she unfolds the tissue paper. A silk scarf lay neatly folded as if it had never been worn. It matches the one that, years ago, Eva had made for Una from her Japanese kimono. Una was devastated when she lost hers at a dance in the Village Recreation Hall outside the munitions factory in Nobel.

She tenderly picks it up and holds the smooth fabric to her cheek. It smells like rose petals. Una sees a yellow envelope with her name written in pencil. She opens the flap and pulls out a petite note card.

December 14, 1922

My dearest Una,

    I am setting these few things aside for you for one day which I hope will not be too soon. I need not tell you what joy you have brought to my life and how very happy I am to know that you are now well-loved by Angus and your children.

Be happy, and whatever you do, don't be maudlin when you get this. My life has been grand.

Yours fondly, Eva Stanton

Una takes a sharp kitchen knife and slits open one end of the registered letter from Eva's solicitor. She skims the message that has been typed on the legal stationery.

> Please find enclosed a certified cheque for five hundred dollars payable to Una McFadden. Proceeds are derived from the sale of Miss Stanton's furnishings.

Over dinner, Una shows Angus the gifts from Eva Stanton. Then without saying a word she slips the certified cheque across the table.

Angus's eyes open wide. "My word Una this is more than,"

"I know." Una finishes his sentence, "It's more than two month's wages. I've been thinking that maybe now you can take some time to find a job in town. I really don't like you being away so much, and with the new baby coming any day now I need you to be here. Not just for me Angus, but for the children."

"I don't know Una. I've looked. There's no work for me here. Nothing. At least nothing with the kind of benefits I get working for CN. If anything ever happened to me at least you'd have some compensation."

"What do you mean?" Una feels uncertain.

"There's a death benefit if I'm killed on the job." Angus steps away from the table, scratching his unshaven beard. "You remember Mike Macintosh had his leg severed last October. Happened up near Kirkland Lake. Got blood poisoning. You remember. I told you. His widow got money from the death benefit."

"But..." Una starts.

"No, I won't leave the CN. Not just now." Angus states firmly. "Let's put that money away for a time when we might need it. But I know you've been talking about wanting to buy a few new things for yourself. After the baby is born treat yourself to a new outfit. You deserve that my girl."

Una starts to clear the table when Angus puts his hand on her arm to stop her. He takes the plates and puts them back down.

"This may not be the life you thought you would have but you need to know that I think you are the most wonderful girl in the world. I am so thankful to be able to come home to you and the children. I don't know what I'd do without you, Una. I love you. I'm doing the best I can for all of us."

"It's just that I get so lonely sometimes and I miss playing music with other people." Una's eyes well up. "I'm afraid you won't be here when the baby arrives. What if this baby dies like Connor? I'm scared, Angus. I'm so scared."

"I'll think of something. I will." Angus pulls Una toward him. "I have some time owing to me. I'll be here. You don't need to worry. We can do this together. Can't we?"

Una nods, then laughs through her tears, "I've slobbered all over your shirt."

October 1925

Over two years have passed with the seasons since Eva Stanton's money arrived. Una's fingers trace the rippling motion of the raindrops as they fall down the outside of the windowpane. Beyond the watery smudges, it seems as if the dank autumn morning has covered the town in an old gray army blanket.

She presses her forehead against the cold glass and watches Angus head toward the train station. Again. This time he'll be away for five days.

The previous night he had told her that he had been offered a permanent posting in Hornepayne, a railroad junction further to the north.

"I can't go," she had said, "I just can't do it. I'll go mad Angus. I will lose my mind. Anywhere else. Isn't there somewhere else?"

Angus had pointed out to Una that he wouldn't have to be away as often if they moved there. He could be home for the children, for her. And this morning, just before he left, he mentioned it again, but Una refused to say anything. She'd been clear enough already.

Two-year-old Fern tugs repeatedly at Una's skirt.

"Oh Fern, I feel like a bear this morning."

"Okay. You mommy bear," Fern babbles, "me, baby bear."

Una picks up her daughter. "You are one funny girl. Did you know that? Now go play with Gavina and Sean. Mommy Bear has chores to do." Una places Fern back on the floor. "Off you go baby bear. Off you go."

Una stands beside the piano.

I've hardly played you at all lately. When did my music die? How did I let it go? I need my music. If we move up north, I will never play again. I just know it.

June 1926

With each passing day, Una's mood-swings have been getting more and more exaggerated. At times Angus loses patience with Una's persistent demands, but he never leaves for work with a rift standing between them. He still has words to calm her rages, and a touch that soothes her nagging fears.

Una is thankful to have such a loving husband and decent provider but, increasingly, she feels disillusioned, caught in a never-ending downward spiral. Then, just when Una is certain she will never leave the north, Angus comes home to the dinner with a special announcement.

"How would you like to move south? I've been given a posting down on the St. Lawrence River."

June 12, 1926

Dear Archie,

    We are leaving Capreol. Finally. The CN has given Angus a posting in Brockville, south of Ottawa. Have you heard of it? I went to the library and saw it on a map of Ontario. It's not far from Kingston. Thank God. I was so afraid we would have to move further north.
    I got the program for your concert with the Kingsway Jazz Orchestra. I do miss those days when we played for dances. Maybe I can meet some musicians in Brockville once we get settled. The town is a lot bigger than Capreol. Angus went down there last month and found a lovely apartment on the top two floors of a house. It has three bedrooms, one for the girls, a tiny one for Sean and a large one for us. I'll have space in the parlor to set up my piano and Angus tells me the kitchen has all the modern conveniences. Oh yes! Indoor plumbing!
    Maybe you can come by train one day for a visit. There are three fine hotels where you can stay. And I understand the river is quite beautiful. It is in the Thousand Islands. Can you imagine that? One thousand islands? I hear movie stars live on some of them. I am so, so happy to be getting away from here.
    I've enclosed a picture of Fern. Edith took it when we went looking for pussy willows. Edith is probably the only person I will miss up here.
    As soon as we get settled, I will send our new address. Have a wonderful summer dear friend and do keep in touch. Any new music I should order? I have been out of the loop

Deborah G. Dunleavy

the last little while.

All best wishes,

Una

PART FIVE

In rivers, the water that you touch is the last of what has passed and the first with that which comes, so with present time.

Leonardo da Vinci

41

August 1930   **The Asylum**

Una slams her journal shut. Angry. Eleven-fifteen. For over 20 minutes she has been sitting at the cafeteria table twiddling her pencil and staring at the blank page of the journal.

How could she? Edith knows they are all I have left in the world, my children.

We had a lovely tea together, at least I thought we did. It was so wonderful to see my sweet babies, growing up so fast. Poor little Fern kept asking, when is Daddy coming home. I fell apart. How do I tell my children that Angus is gone forever? He's never coming home. Never.

Just as they were leaving, Edith tells me she's taking them with her. She's taking my children back to Capreol. What if I never get to see them again? Oh God, if you believe in me, help me now. I am their mother. Please God, I have to get my children back.

All those times. I should have listened. The tarot cards told me. My dreams told me. Rachel tried to prepare me. Why didn't I listen? I could have stopped it.

Melancholia. That's what Julia, Dr. Harrington, tells me I am suffering from. She says that I do not need to have electroshock therapy. Thank God. I have seen what it does to the patients here. They sit around like empty shells with their insides torn away.

I hate this place. It's crawling with crazy people. I'd better write something. Anything. I try to write most days. Like today. But I can't. It won't bring Angus back. It won't stop Edith from taking my children. I thought I could trust her.

I suppose I could write about last night. They showed a movie called 'Coquette' starring Mary Pickford. I had no idea her voice would sound like that. I think I liked her better before the talkies. Should I write about that?

"Una, you'll have to leave now."

Una jumps. "You frightened me. You shouldn't sneak up on people like that."

"Sorry my dear, but we need to set the tables for lunch. Unless you'd like to help?" Miss Graham, a round, middle-aged woman tugs at her apron. "We can always use an extra pair of hands," she says encouragingly.

"I suppose I could," Una hesitates, "if that's alright. I mean, do I have to get permission?"

Miss Graham puts her hands on her hips and with a twinkle in her eye she says, "As Matron of the kitchen, dining room, sewing room, laundry, and housekeeping, I hereby give you authority to place the cutlery on the tables."

Miss Graham reminds Una of Doris Finnegan, the change room supervisor at the munitions factory. She had been strict but compassionate at the same time.

"Well, are you going to leave or be useful?" Miss Graham's voice strongly suggests that "useful" would be a good idea. Una follows Miss Graham to the cutlery drawers.

"Put a fork on the left, prongs facing upward," she says clearly. "A knife goes on the right with the curved blade toward the plate."

"And the soup spoon to the right of the knife and the dessert fork above the plate," Una continues, "Do we need salad forks too?"

"Not today," Miss Graham cocks her head to one side, "I see you are going to be of great help here Una."

I need to be. I've got to get out of here before I go mad.

42

August 1926

Every window in the upstairs apartment is fully open yet the still stifling air of summer does little to offer any relief from the sweltering heat. Una wipes the sweat from her brow as she unpacks the last of her dishes and puts them on the shelves in the kitchen. Her new home.

The move could not have happened any sooner. Una had been feeling trapped like a fly in a spider's web for months when Angus finally announced they'd be leaving Capreol. The Canadian National had taken over several smaller railroad companies in Eastern Ontario and was looking to hire more crew to work the lines. Angus jumped at the opportunity. He knew that Una was more than ready to make a fresh start.

Since moving into the apartment two weeks ago Una has tastefully decorated the living room and dining room on the second floor. Her piano and array of instruments take up one whole side of the living room. She has mounted pictures in the three bedrooms on the third floor and hung curtains on all the windows.

In an attempt to get some relief from the heat Una pours herself a cool glass of iced tea and sits at the new oak table.

I must drop a line to Emily. This place has more than twice the space of our boxcar home, and we have electricity. I must tell her about the porcelain light fixtures, and the luxury of having a flush toilet in the water closet.

Una takes the last swallow of the iced tea and heads up the stairs to her third-floor bedroom. She strips off her sweat-stained house dress and puts on a sleeveless floral summer dress. Standing at the large bay window she glances out over the rooftops toward the river.

It's a perfect day to pack a picnic. I'll take the children for a swim at St. Lawrence Park. It's only a short walk away. I'm told it is a lovely spot with tall trees, and a pavilion. Sometimes bands play there in the evening. Maybe I can meet some musicians.

"We had a wonderful day at the park." Una tells Angus over dinner. "It is such a lovely spot. So popular. I think we got the last picnic table. It was packed with people, my love. And tomorrow night there is a concert in the pavilion. We must go. Angus, I don't remember feeling this happy for so long."

"Things work out as they should," Angus agrees. "Let's go for a walk down by the docks. We can watch the sailboats and steamers. In any case, it's a lot cooler down by the river."

"Yes, let's. It will be good for the children to have some fresh air before tucking them in."

August 24, 1926

Dear Edith,

We have finally unpacked everything and are settling in quite well. Angus likes the new posting and I love that he is home for dinner most nights. The children enjoy going on picnics at the park down by the river. And my what a river. It is quite something. You can see the United States on the other side.

How are you? I imagine Carol will be looking forward to school in September. Gavina is beginning this year. How the time flies. I guess Charlie will be off hunting soon.

Last week we attended an outdoor concert. The local Brockville Band is quite splendid. I hope I can meet some musicians soon and find an opportunity to play for dances again. Angus thinks this is a good idea too.

On Sundays, we attend Trinity Anglican Church which is very close to where we live. The children go to Sunday school. Even little Fern is welcome. I find great comfort in going as a family, something I never really appreciated growing up. My mother was so strict. I think I told you that. But times change. Angus and I feel it is important to have this family time together.

It would be swell to have you come for a visit someday. We have room to put you up. There are plenty of stores on King Street where we can go shopping. There is a row of mansions that you wouldn't believe, nothing like you'd ever see up north. The Victoria Building, our town hall, has a clock that chimes every hour on the hour, even at night, but I am getting used to it.

Please pass our love to Mother and Father. Let them know we are doing fine.

Bye for now,

Una

October 1926

Saturday morning. The scents of ripe apples, plump pumpkins, and fall flowers waft through the warm autumn air. Even before the clock strikes seven the local vendors have come in by horse and wagon to set up their produce in the market square. Townsfolk stroll from one stall to another, buying the last of the harvest vegetables and homemade preserves.

Una and Angus walk arm in arm while their children scamper freely about. Standing at the top of the street Una looks down toward the river. Sunlight glistens on the waves.

"Is this not a day meant for heaven," she sighs blissfully.

"With you by my side every day is like a day in heaven," Angus teases.

"Every day?" Una asks.

"Every day," Angus replies.

"Angus, look," Una points to a man standing at the flower stand across the road. "Isn't that the conductor of the Brockville Band?"

"I believe so," Angus confirms.

"I'll be right back."

Una crosses the market square and approaches the distinguished-looking gentleman, handsomely dressed in green cuffed trousers and a matching mackinaw jacket. He appears to be examining a vibrant display of chrysanthemums.

"The rusty orange ones look lovely, don't they?" Una says as a way of engaging him in conversation.

"I suppose you're right. Were you going to buy them? If not, I'd like to take them to my wife," he says in a distinct English accent.

"No, no. I was just admiring them." Una clears her throat. "The truth is I saw the Brockville Band this summer and I believe you are the conductor? I quite enjoyed the program. Do you play elsewhere in the cold weather?"

"Yes. quite often at the Armories and other places." He hands the money to the vendor and picks up the potted flowers. "Why do you ask?"

"I played in a band during the war, an all-women's band, when I worked at a munitions factory in Nobel, and later with a group up near Sudbury." Una doesn't stop to take a breath. "We, my husband and I, we just moved here a few months back. He works for the CN. And I have yet to meet anyone who has a dance band that I might fit in with. Well at least try out for, or even some musicians to share music with."

The man jingles the change in his coat pocket as he listens. Finally, he asks, "What instrument do you play?"

"Several. Piano, banjo, mandolin, guitar, autoharp," Una pauses briefly, "and I sing."

"I guess you can see that the concert band is probably not what you are looking for unless you play tuba," he jests with a wry smile. "However, a group of us have a band that plays the occasional dance. Popular songs mostly. In fact, we are playing for a dance at the Grand Central Hotel next Friday. Why not come out and see if you like what you hear?"

"I'd like that very much," Una tries not to wiggle like a girl on her first date. "I'll be there. By the way, my name is Una McFadden. You are?"

"Ward, Dr. Steven Ward. I'm a dentist when I'm not conducting or playing my clarinet."

Una extends her hand, "Lovely to meet you, Dr. Ward. I look forward to hearing your music on Friday."

October 22, 1926

Dear Archie

    It has been ages since I sent you a note. How are you? What musicals are you playing for these days? Was 'Our Nell' a success for your operatic society? I wish someone would do a Gershwin musical in Brockville.
    There is a fine opera house on King Street. I understand the stage is one of the largest of its kind in Ontario. They

often get touring troupes traveling between Montreal and Toronto.

I have great news. I have finally met some musicians who have a small dance band with saxophone, clarinet, piano, drums, and guitar. Last Friday night I went to hear them. I knew several of the numbers. They used to have a piano player, but she moved out west. I suggested that perhaps I could give it a go and so they have invited me to come to a rehearsal in November.

Have you ever been to Brockville? It is quite a smashing town with all sorts of stores and parks. Like you, I am so glad we moved down south.

Must go. Gavina will be home from school soon and she'll have lots to tell me about her day.

Yours musically, Una

December 1926

The smell of hot cider and fresh spruce fills the whole apartment. The previous evening Angus brought home a lush spruce tree that reached up to the ten-foot ceiling leaving barely enough space for a star to be placed on top. In their boxcar home, they didn't have room for a tree. Still, Una always found things to hang the decorations on. Curtain rods, doorways, and even the bedposts. Come Christmas morning Angus and the children would wake up and find brand new decorations and candy tucked into their shoes.

On this dark, early evening a gently falling snow drifts past the windows of their apartment. Una and the children sit around the dining room table busily stringing popcorn garlands and pulling out ornaments saved from past years, a reindeer with a red bow on its neck, a snowman with a top hat, a penguin, a ballerina, and a toy drum. Meanwhile, Angus unveils a brand-new set of tree lights, the first they have ever owned. Green, yellow, red, blue.

"This is going to be the most spectacular tree ever," Angus boasts as he plugs them into the socket. In no time the tree stands fully decorated with all the lights glistening brightly.

"Come over here. I have a story to tell you." He says to the children, "Would you like that?"

Gavina runs to her father. "Yes Papa. Please."

Sean and Fern chorus in, "Please Papa. Tell us a story."

Una playfully shrugs. "They said the magic word. You have to tell them now."

"Good then. But right afterward it's into your nightclothes and off to bed." Angus gestures for them to sit at his feet. Una joins them with Fern nestled between her legs.

"Do you know why evergreens don't lose their leaves?" Angus asks. "When autumn comes, the cold north wind blows all the other leaves away, all the maple, birch, and oak. Remember how we played in them? And the birds? Where have they gone?

"South," says Gavina.

"Yes, they have. But one year there was a tiny bird who had a broken wing, and it couldn't fly away with the other birds. It was getting very, very cold. The bird needed shelter from the harsh wind. So, it hopped and flapped its way to a tall birch tree, and chirped, 'My wing is broken, and my friends have flown away. May I stay with you for the winter?'."

Angus asks, "Do you know what the birch tree said?"

The children shake their heads and Angus continues in a very nasty voice, "No! I have enough birds to look after already. Go away."

Again, Angus softens his voice, "So the poor wee bird hopped and flapped its way to a huge oak tree and cried, 'My wing is broken, and my friends have flown away. May I stay with you for the winter?' And the oak tree said, 'No! You might eat up all my acorns. Go away.'."

"So… the poor wee bird hopped and flapped its way to a willow tree and the bird cried…" Angus gestures for the children to help him. " 'My wing is broken, and my friends have flown away. May I stay with you for the winter?' And the willow tree said…"

The children shout, "No."

Angus waits, then continues in a cruel voice, "You are a strange little bird. I do not like strangers. Go away."

"The tiny bird was shivering and trembling. It was so, co cold. But then it heard someone calling, 'Come here little bird. You can stay in my warm branches all winter if you like.' It was the spruce tree, just like our tree, inviting the little bird to hop onto its branches. Then another tree spoke to the little bird, 'I am the pine tree. I will protect you from the winter storms with my thick branches.' And a third tree called out, 'You may stay with us all winter long. I have plenty of Juniper berries that you can eat.'"

"That night there was a strong wind that blew and blew until every leaf from every birch, oak, and willow tree fell to the ground. But the wind did not blow the leaves from the spruce, the pine, or the juniper. Do you know why?"

Angus waits for a moment.

"Well, let me tell you. Jack Frost saw that those trees had been kind to a poor little bird, and because of that, he gave them the gift of being green all year round."

"Is that true, Papa?" Sean asks.

"Does it feel true?" offers Angus.

"Yes."

"Then let it be so." Angus stands up. "Skedaddle now. Off to bed. Sleep tight. Don't let the bed bugs bite."

The children hug their father and Una shoos them up the stairs to their bedrooms. She whispers into Angus' ear, "I do love you, Mr. McFadden."

"That's good because I love you too."

Winter 1927

Febuary 3, 1927

Dear Emily

Thank you for the lovely Christmas card and note. You must be so happy to have a special friend like Lois in your life. She seems to be quite the adventuresome soul, convincing you to go downhill skiing. I can't picture you doing that, but you did. Bravo!

Winters aren't nearly as cold here as up north, but we still get plenty of snow and the river freezes over all the way to Morristown in Upper New York. People sometimes take their horse and cutter across. There is a small bay below the town hall that is kept clear of snow. Folks skate on it. I took the children there the other day and we could see right through the ice. A huge pike swam by, right under where we were standing. Fern was especially excited about that.

Angus has a good job with CN and is away far less than before, just the occasional overnight. He is back playing hockey with a team in town and is scoring like he did when we saw him play in Parry Sound.

For Christmas Angus bought me a used but handsome parlor organ. In fact, he brought it home before Christmas. It was wonderful to play carols on it for the children to sing along. Gavina has a lovely voice and Sean likes nothing more than to beat the small drum I bought for him last year.

And the other bit of good news is that I now play piano for dances with a small ensemble called the Riverside Jazztones. It reminds me of the good times we had at Nobel.

Remember our shenanigans.

I've gone on far too long about me. What about you? Hope you are still enjoying working for the phone company. Drop a line when you have time.

Keep on the sunny side!

Una.

Spring 1927

The bright Spring morning is awake with birdsong. Una and Angus have decided to take the steamboat to Kingston for the day. Afterwards, they will ride back by train. It has been quite a while since they have had time together without the children.

Una has arranged for Mrs. Cook, the landlady who lives downstairs, to take them for the day. She had shown great affection for them since the first day they moved in, giving them candies from her candy jar. Her only son, a single man, had died in the war and her husband passed away the previous year. She had said on numerous occasions that she would be happy to look after the children, and finally Una is taking her up on the offer.

"Thank you so much, Mrs. Cook. Now don't go spoiling them with all those candies."

Una straightens Sean's hair by wetting her finger and flattening his cowlick. She turns to all three children, "I expect you to behave properly. What Mrs. Cook says, goes. No arguing. I will hear about it if you do. Now go on. Be good."

One by one she kisses each child on the forehead.

Angus hands Mrs. Cook a crumpled-up dollar bill. "For ice cream."

"That won't be necessary," Elva Cook objects.

"Please take it." Angus puts the bill in her hand.

"Very well," she says reluctantly. "It's just a joy to have them here with me. Now you two run along before the boat leaves."

The blast from the steamship's whistle echoes up Market Street. Una and Angus rush past the horse and buggies at the wharf and scramble up the plank in the nick of time.

Winded, Una's heart beats in her chest. "We made it," she gasps. "Let's stand at the rail."

She takes Angus by the hand and together they look back at the Brockville skyline, the church steeples getting gradually smaller until, finally, the steamer slips between the islands and the town can no longer be see.

Several smaller boats dot the river, taking full advantage of the clear blue skies and warm weather. Gulls swoop alongside the steamer and mallards float closer to shore. Una closes her eyes and takes a deep breath of the fresh river air. With Angus' arm around her waist, Una feels as blissful as she did when he gave her those first kisses.

We're sailing away, leaving every care in the world behind.

By the time the train pulls into the station, it is close to midnight. Mrs. Cook had suggested the children could spend the night with her. She would make up the sofa and the double bed for them. "Don't worry," she said, "we'll go to the park after supper, and I'll let them run around. Then we'll play games and listen to the radio before calling it a day."

Angus quietly turns the doorknob to the foyer where a small table lamp has been left on for them to see the note. 'We've had a gay old time. I'm making pancakes in the morning. Come and join us. Elva.'

They smile at one another, then head up the stairs to their apartment.

In the kitchen, Angus pulls Una toward him and slowly unbuttons her blouse. He places his hands on her breasts. Then Una undoes his trousers and slips her hand between his legs. Kisses replace words as they spin their way to the bedroom and fall deeply into each other's being.

43

September 1927

September 2, 1927

Dear Archie

    Where has the summer flown? The nights are chillier but still lots of sunshine. I received your postcard from Niagara Falls. I'd love to go there one day. I must ask Angus if there is a train that runs to Niagara.
    We have had the best summer ever. CN gives Angus rail passes so we have gone on a few jaunts around Eastern Ontario. In July we took a train to Cornwall which is a rather industrial town and not at all what I expected. The train is known as "The Moccasin". It does a milk run, stopping at farms and villages. The scenery along the St.

Lawrence is spectacular.

In August we went on another trip up the Brockville Westport route. We hopped out at a little place called Delta. They have a wonderful agricultural fair. There were all sorts of contests. Everything from pumpkins to apple pies. The children especially loved looking at the animals. Fern keeps asking for a pet lamb.

What are your plans now? Are there any more musicals that you are accompanying? How is your friend?

I'm really enjoying playing music with the Riverside Jazztones. Last week we had an engagement on the 'Kingston' Steamship. People danced while the boat took us around the islands. Angus has been so sweet, staying home with the children when I go out to these events.

On Labour Day, next weekend, the Railroaders will hold their family picnic at St. Lawrence Park and our band will be at the Pavilion. Wish you could be there to join in. Another saxophone would do wonders. And I'd love to see you, my dear friend.

Musically yours,

Una

Labour Day 1927

Una and the children mingle with the crowd that has come to St. Lawrence Park to enjoy the Labour Day Picnic. On this late but warm summer day folks line up on the dock. Some of the women don their bathing suits and others wear sleeveless dresses, while the men sport white shirts with ties, and have their caps tipped back on their heads. Children gleefully splash about closer to the shore and a few adults swim toward the deeper parts.

"Gavina," Una hollers at her daughter who paddles about. "Keep an eye on your brother and sister. I need to set up for the concert."

"I'll look after them." Elva Cook, wearing a floppy straw hat, and a huge floral dress that billows like a sail in the breeze, comes alongside Una. "I don't mind."

"Elva, I do appreciate that. Their towels are in here." Una hands over a bulging tote bag.

The clink of metal on metal as horseshoes hit the pole can be heard in the distance. The men cheer loudly.

"Angus is pitching horseshoes with his team. The railroad construction workers are taking on the engineers' team. I think he has a bet going on the tournament. If he is as good at horseshoes as he is at hockey, they're bound to win," Una boasts.

"After their swim would you be willing to take the children to the playing field? They want to enter the races and contests, you know, the potato sack race, three-legged race, wheelbarrow race, and the messy egg toss contest. There's sure to be laundry to do after that."

"My pleasure. We'll meet you after the concert, shall we?" Elva says holding her dress down from a gust of wind. "Oh my, did my slip show?"

"Not that I could see. You are an angel, Elva. Thank you ever so much."

Una heads up the stairs of the band pavilion and sets her music on the music stand, pinning the pages open with clothespins in case a gust of wind should blow them down.

"There that should take care of it. What are we starting with Steve?"

"'If You Knew Suzie'." Steve Ward adjusts the reed on his clarinet. "Looks like it's going to be a grand day for making music."

"You have no idea how I love being with the band," Una says gleefully.

"We're just glad you came along at the right time Una. You're doing a fine job," Steve says. "Looks like we've got plenty of folks ready to enjoy themselves. Let's give them some toe-tapping tunes."

By late afternoon families begin packing up their blankets and folding their tablecloths. Children scurry about with endless energy until their parents finally start to leave. One by one the swimmers emerge from the river, their laughter and cheers rising up above the treetops.

"We won," Angus hollers to Una who is still in the band pavilion collecting her sheet music. "We beat all five teams. 1927 Horseshoe Champions." He proudly holds up a bronzed horseshoe mounted on a wooden base. "I could hear the band. You sounded great Una. Did you have a good time?"

"Best ever. I am so glad we moved here." Una skips over to Angus. "Have you seen the children?"

"They're in the playground. Sean is flipping on the monkey bars. You should see him. Gavina is pushing Fern on the swings. Mrs. Cook is watching them. She looks exhausted. Perhaps we can all go out for supper at the hotel."

Una slips her arm through his. "That sounds delightful. This is the best day ever, my dear. The best day ever."

November 1927

"I have to leave first thing in the morning." Angus hands the newspaper to Una. "They need every crewman available."

Una reads, "Flood Sweeps Across Vermont. Thousands of people left homeless. Whole buildings swept away by the raging rivers."

"There's miles of CN line torn up down there. And God only knows how many bridges have been destroyed. They'll need men to operate the pile drivers. I may not be able to get a letter to you right away. You know that my girl. But don't worry I will send one as soon as I can."

Una puts the paper down and quietly walks toward the window. She looks out at the dark, looming clouds.

"I don't like it."

No response from Angus.

"It's too dangerous. You could drown."

"Did I not survive the war?" Angus stands behind Una, his arms around her slender body. This is a piece of cake. And I won't be dodging bullets."

"I know but..."

"But what?"

Una turns to face Angus. "I don't have a good feeling about this. It just doesn't feel right."

"Are you having those dreams again? Did someone from the grave come to you again?" Angus asks.

"No."

"Then you have nothing to worry about," Angus says reassuringly. "I'm only sorry I won't be here for the dance this Friday. You'll be great. You always are. Now look, I'd better get packed. We head out at the crack of dawn." When Una doesn't say anything, he adds, "I'll be fine."

"He's been gone five days." Una looks in the empty mailbox beside the front door. "No word yet."

"Don't you worry. It's going to take time," Elva Cook offers comfort to Una. "By all accounts, the phone lines are down and everything in Vermont has come to a halt. You just go ahead to the dance tonight. Have yourself a good time. The children have already asked me for some Velveeta Cheese and crackers to have while we listen to *Amos and Andy* on the wireless.

"Don't go spoiling them," Una says as she adjusts the clip in her hair. "Do you like it? Angus gave it to me for my birthday last year."

"I believe he spoils you," Elva replies, a twinkle in her eye. "Have a good time. Join us for breakfast."

"Thank you. You must come to one of the dances sometime," Una suggests.

"With my sciatica. No, my dancing days are long gone. Besides someone has to look after these hooligans."

At the dance Una's mind is far away. Twice she forgets what the next number is. The third time Steve Ward gives her a look of disappointment. On the break, he joins her for a cigarette.

"Something bothering you tonight?" he asks.

"Sorry, Steve. Angus has gone to Vermont."

"Oh, the floods."

"I'm worried." Una takes a drag on her cigarette. "What if something horrible happens? What if he gets swept away? What if he drowns? I haven't heard from him since he left. If anything happens to him, I couldn't go on Steve. I just couldn't bear to lose him."

"Don't worry, Una. He's fine. Angus knows what he's doing," Steve says to console Una. "Come, I'll buy you a soda. What do you say?"

"I know. I'm over-reacting. But sometimes I get this feeling that..."

"That what?"

"Oh, nothing. You're right. He's going to be fine," Una says trying to convince herself. "What are we starting the next set with?"

" 'Shine On Harvest Moon'."

Una has become obsessive, checking the mailbox almost every hour. Two weeks pass and still no word. The newspaper continues to report the damage with photographs of the devastation. Several show the rising waters in Montpelier, the capital of Vermont. The buildings stand half-submerged by the raging waters, the streets littered with debris.

Sitting on the divan Una skims an article, "Two thousand men are now at work with complete equipment of steam shovels, pile drivers..."

Angus is one of the pile driver operators. This ruined train trestle could be one that Angus has to reconstruct. My God what if, what if...

A sudden rap on the apartment door causes Una's heart to skip a beat. Mrs. Cook, dressed in her favorite bird-patterned apron, opens the door a crack.

"Postcard for you my dear. He told you he'd write as soon as he could."

Una snatches the card and rushes back to the divan to read it.

Nov. 12, 1927.

My dearest Una.

We arrived at Island Pond safely. Going down to Wells River tomorrow. Travel is difficult but we are managing. It may be a while before I can send another card. You are always in my heart and mind. Hugs for the children. Say a prayer for these people. It is a terrible disaster. Your loving husband, Angus

That evening Una shows the children the postcard that Angus sent and tells them that Daddy is building railroad trestles. Una draws them close to her on the sofa.

"When I was a little girl, I had a friend who lived in the woods. Her name was Rachel. She used to teach me things."

"Like what Mommy," asks Fern.

"She taught me how to skin a rabbit, and how to cook fish on a fire pit."

"I'd like to do that, " says Sean.

"Not me," says Gavina.

She also told me wonderful stories. Would you like to hear one?"

"Yes," they chorus.

"One day turtle was wandering along slowly, slowly. A deer leapt across the field. 'I wish I could leap like that,' said turtle. Then she saw a fish swimming in the water. 'I wish I could swim like that.' Turtle looked up and saw birds soaring in the sky. 'More than anything I wish I could fly like a bird.'"

"At that very moment, two eagles landed on the branch of a tree right beside turtle. *'Eagles, will you teach me how to fly?'* asked turtle."

" 'You're too heavy,' said one of the eagles."

" 'You don't have any feathers,' said the other."

" 'But it looks like so much fun,' cried turtle. 'Please, please, please. Please.'"

' "Alright,' said the eagles. 'Put that stick in your mouth and we will take hold of each end and take you up into the sky. But you must promise one thing. Do not open your mouth when you are flying.'"

"Turtle was so excited. She could hardly wait. She clenched her jaw around the stick. The eagles grasped the stick in their talons and flew up, up into the sky. They went over the treetops, above the hills, and almost through the clouds. Then they swooped over a place where children were playing. The children pointed up at turtle and yelled, 'Turtle, you can't fly.'"

"Turtle said, 'I can too.'"

"Poor turtle opened her mouth. She fell, down, down, down. Crash. Turtle landed on a rock and her shell broke into hundreds of pieces."

"Oh, no Mommy," Gavina gasps.

"Poor turtle," Fern says.

"That must have hurt," says Sean. "What happened?"

"Well," Una explains, "all the little birds, the chickadees, sparrows, and finches picked up the pieces of the shell and put them back together."

"They did?" asks Fern cheering up.

"Yes, they did. Turtle crawled into her shell and was very happy to go back to her pond." Una waits a moment. "Rachel told me that's how turtles got those cracks on their backs."

Sean tugs at Una's sleeve. "When is Daddy coming home?"

"I don't know for sure, but won't it be a lovely thing to have him tell you his stories too." Una kisses his forehead. "Good night my son. Maybe an animal will speak to you in your dreams. Good night Gavina. Good night Fern. Sleep tight."

"Don't let the bed bugs bite," the children chorus.

Una crawls into the cold emptiness of the double bed and pulls Angus' pillow into her embrace. Moonlight streams through the curtains and shines on the tears that dampen her cheeks. *Come home. Please come home safe. I miss you so.*

Finally with a deep, sad sigh sleep comes to Una and she sails away with her dreams.

She's standing in the middle of a downtown street, a place she has never been to before. There are no other people. Only abandoned buildings. She looks at her shoes and realizes they are fully submerged in rising water. Walking becomes impossible as the waters swell around her. She feels herself floating away with the current. A man comes by on a bicycle that rides on top of the water. 'No trains today,' he shouts. 'No trains tomorrow.'

Una wakes with a start, drenched in perspiration. In the distance, she hears a train rumbling on the rails. She tosses the sheets aside and with her arms wrapped about herself she rocks back and forth on the edge of the bed.

Angus is fine. He knows what he is doing. Angus is fine. He'll be home soon. Angus is fine. Angus is fine. Angus is fine…

December 22, 1927

The first flakes of snow swirl in the diffused light of the streetlamp outside the apartment. The children are fast asleep, and the house bears an uneasy quietness that causes Una's ears to sizzle. She paces the kitchen floor waiting for the kettle to boil. So many nights spent waiting and worrying.

It is the longest that Angus has been away since the war and Una has taken to smoking more cigarettes than usual. She looks at his last note, a colorized postcard of the ornate state capitol building in Montpelier, obviously taken before the flood. She flips it over and reads it again. It had taken ten days to get to her.

Dec. 2, 1927

My darling Una,

Thank God I packed my long johns. Things are getting pretty cold in these parts. We've just about finished at Wells River. The Red Cross has arrived. A lot of folks have lost their homes and there is a food shortage. I swear it looks as if there has been a war. Don't worry. I'm fine. CN is making sure we get fed. But no more beans for a while. If all goes well, I'll be home for Christmas my darling. Love to the children. Love to you too. Angus

Una is about to turn the kitchen light off for the night when she hears familiar footsteps echoing in the stairwell. She throws the door open.

"My God, you're home," she cries.

Angus drops his satchel on the floor and hugs Una with such force he nearly knocks her over. "Oh, but it is good to see you, my girl."

"And won't it be good for you to take a bath. You smell like rotten radishes." Una scratches his rough beard. "And come to bed right after. You must be exhausted."

"Not too exhausted," he says teasingly.

"I've been worried sick," Una stops herself. "Do you have to go back?"

"No, my love. I'm home now. Just in time for Christmas." Angus kicks off his boots and throws his work coat over the back of the chair. "How are the children?"

"They ask about you every day. They will be thrilled to see you in the morning."

"As will I be to see them."

44

August 1930   **The Asylum**

I've got to get out of here. My children. They need me. I need them. Angus would want me to be strong. I must be. I have to be. I am not, I am not, I am not crazy.

"There you are." Miss Graham taps Una on the shoulder. "I've been looking all over for you. Are you coming to the concert this afternoon? Dr. Ward and his band are playing."

I can't go. Look at me. Steve will think I've gone off the deep end. Oh, why did I think those words, the deep end? I. Am. Not. Crazy.

"Is that a yes?" Miss Graham asks. "Come with me to the laundry. I've got something I think you'll want to see."

Be normal Una. If you want to get out of this place, for God's sake, be normal. You're fine. Everything is fine. Fine. Fine. Fine.

"Well?" Miss Graham waits patiently.

"Yes, thank you, Miss Graham."

"Here, try this on. I think this dress will suit you." Miss Graham fusses with the lace collar. "It has such a delicate floral pattern, and the dropped waist is all the rage it seems."

Una strokes the soft, cream-colored, crepe fabric. "It feels brand new."

"That's because it is." Miss Graham continues, "Mrs. Hollingsworth, who owns the dress shop on King Street, brought it in. It has a little tear under the arm. Can you imagine that? I mended it and thought who better to have a cheerful new outfit than you Una."

"Why me?"

"Why not. You've been through hell and high waters. And…" she hesitates, "word has it, that you were in Dr. Ward's band. Perhaps you will want to join in with them this afternoon."

"Miss Graham, I can't. I haven't played with them in so long. I, they may not want me to play."

"You never know. I've heard you on the piano in the auditorium when no one else is around. Isn't it like riding a bicycle, although I never could master those things, what I mean is, once you learn how to play an instrument, you never forget? Do you? At any rate, you deserve a new dress. And that's all that matters."

Una waits outside the auditorium smoothing the dress along her hips.

I hope to God he doesn't think I'm nuts. I'm not. I can do this. I can go inside.

Steve Ward sees Una standing in the doorway. He leaves the stage and comes toward her. "How are you?" he asks.

Una cannot look him in the eyes. "You know."

"It cannot have been easy for you."

"Guess not, or they wouldn't be keeping me here," Una tries to make light of her situation.

"Would you like to sit in, play a song or two? The boys would love that."

Una hesitates, "I think I'll just listen."

"Well, if you change your mind, let me know."

"I think I'll just listen."

Una offers a feeble smile and walks toward the rear of the auditorium. She chooses a chair close to the door. While it isn't long before the auditorium fills with the other patients, Una can't sit still. She crosses her legs one way, then the other. She fusses with the collar of her dress and repeatedly puts her hair behind her ears.

I'm going to jump out of my skin if the band doesn't start soon.

Una's squirming takes over her whole body so much so that she is overwhelmed with a great desire to escape from herself. But then, just as she is about to stand up, the band is introduced. When they break into their first number, Una slowly relaxes into the music. She recognizes each song. The melodies spark memories that carry her heart to happier times. She recalls fondly the times they played in the pavilion at the park, and for the dances on the steamboat. Una hears the opening chords to "What'll I Do" and immediately a bolt of terror races through her body.

This is our song. We sang it together all the time. 'What'll I do when you are far away, and I am blue, what'll I do?'

Una's chair topples onto the floor. Startled, the band stops. Everyone cranes their necks to look at Una as she stumbles out of the auditorium.

"He's never coming back," she screams, "he's never coming back."

The ward lay in complete darkness save for the moonlight that spills through the trees and cascades on the walls of Una's room. Comfort does not come to Una. For hours she repeatedly gets out of bed and paces about her room, then crawls back into bed. Out, then in again.

The sheets are strangling me.

Una kicks them to the floor. She squeezes the pillow in her fists, heaves it onto the floor, then thrashes until she is worn out. When at last she succumbs to exhaustion, she slips deeply into her dreamtime.

I'm swimming underwater. Everything is so clear, and fresh. The sun glistens like gold flakes all around me. Look. Tiny-blue green fish. That larger one looks like an owl with mother of pearl scales. I can hold my breath forever and ever and ever. Every part of me tingles, and oh, there's a rippling of waves between my legs. It is as if I am making love with you Angus. I feel you. You are here with me, aren't you? Oh my God, I see your face, your blue eyes shining like stars. Angus. No. Don't go. Don't go. The river is washing every part of you away, your hair, your skin, your bones, all washed away to the sea. My love, my love, my love.

45

October 1929

October 16, 1929

Dear Emily

How are you, my dear friend? Hope you had a lovely Thanksgiving.

It has been three years since Angus and I moved to Brockville. Can you believe it? Seems like only yesterday you and I were cycling down the road to Parry Sound, treating ourselves to desserts in the cafes.

The children are growing like wildfire and are all in school now. The apartment feels a bit empty but at least I have time to do things I've been meaning to do. I cleaned out all the closets and patched Angus' work pants. And I've taken up pressing flowers again. I used to do that when I lived with Eva Stanton. I made this notecard with wildflowers that I collected in the summer. The purple asters turned out well, I think.

Most weekends I play for dances with the Riverside Jazztones. There is some talk of doing a recording, but we'd have to go to Toronto for that. I'll let you know if it happens. Maybe you could meet me there.

Angus can't wait for the winter to come so he can get back to playing hockey. He joined a baseball team this summer, mostly made up of railroaders. In September they played Donkey Baseball against the opposing firefighters' team as a fundraiser for the hospital. It was hysterical. I laughed so hard I cried. Whenever a batter hit the ball, he had to climb on a donkey and ride it to first base. Angus nearly fell off but still made it because of a playful fumble by the other team. The children loved it. That and the hot dogs sold at the concession stand.

I trust you and Lois have been enjoying the autumn leaves. Drop a line when you can.

As always, Una.

One-thirty. Just enough time to go to the Post Office.

Una admires her brand-new hip-length coat and matching beret that she recently purchased from the Eaton's catalogue. She tucks her hair under her hat and examines her stylish attire in the downstairs hall mirror. She'd shown it to Angus when it arrived last week. He expressed his surprise at the cost but still flattered her with his words, 'You'll be the smartest dressed woman in town.'

Una is about to leave the building when the door swings open. Angus stands on the other side of the threshold, his cap in his hand.

"Why are you home at this hour?" Una says, perplexed by the grim expression on his face. "Are you not feeling well?"

"Come up to the apartment." Angus brushes past Una and climbs the stairs.

"Go ahead. Put your feet up. Make a cup of tea. I'm going to mail this letter to Emily. I'll be right back."

"No, Una." Angus's voice trembles with anger. "Come upstairs." He slams his metal lunch pail on the kitchen table with such force that the salt and pepper shakers fall over. "I've been laid off."

Startled, Una is unable to respond. She has never seen this volatile side of Angus before.

"Twelve of us. We've been let go." Angus clenches his fists.

"Let go?" Una asks in dismay, "For how long?"

"For God knows how long." Angus pulls out a chair and slumps into it.

"Last week we heard rumors of a crew being fired up near Belleville. Yesterday several men were let go just this side of Cornwall. Damn it. It's not good, my girl."

"We'll be okay Angus. We'll find a way, won't we?"

"How?"

"I can get a job," Una offers.

"If men can't get work what makes you think they are going to hire a woman."

His words sting. Una resents what he is saying even though she knows it's true. When the men came back from the war women were forced out of their jobs. And ever since the Stock Market crash in September the newspapers have been reporting that factories are slowing down production. Men are already heading out west in hopes of finding work.

"Will we have to move?" Una says, dreading that it might mean going back north.

"I don't know. Where? It won't change anything." Angus rubs his brow. "Some of us boys are going to meet up tomorrow. Frank Shipman, the fireman on the trains, he's been let go too. Anyway, he says there's talk going around about a drill boat that might be coming here before the freeze up. They'll be dredging a channel for the ocean going vessels.

Maybe there's work to be had on it. Who knows?"

"We can hope." Una puts the kettle on the stove then sits across the table from Angus. "Everything is going to work out fine. You'll see."

"How's that?"

"You know that jewelry box you gave me for Christmas last year? I've been saving some of the money I was paid for playing at the dances. Saving it for a rainy day. Guess it's going to come in handy now. And I haven't worn this jacket yet. I'll get the money back. It doesn't fit right anyway."

"But I thought you loved it?" Angus tries to change her mind.

"I do, but I don't really need it," Una forces a smile. "I've got two other coats in the closet. Everything's going to work out just fine. You'll see."

November 1929

Una wraps her wool scarf around her neck as she goes down to the wharf to meet Angus. He's promised to take her out for dinner at the Central Hotel after his shift on the J. B. King Drill Boat - as a way of celebrating his new job.

"Who is this?" Una gestures toward a German shepherd standing beside Angus.

"The boat mascot, King." Angus tugs on the leash and the dog sits at his feet. "I said I'd take care of him. It's better this way, that one person looks after him."

"Is that so?" Una questions, "Is King coming for dinner at the hotel too?"

"Not exactly. But I have a responsibility to look after him. He latched onto me the moment I stepped onto the barge. He doesn't leave my side." Angus reaches in his pocket and hands the dog a piece of bread crusts."

"And is it any wonder?" Una teases. "What are we going to do during dinner?"

"I'll tie him up outside the hotel. He won't go anywhere." Angus speaks to the dog as they walk toward the downtown. "Where I go you go, right boy?"

"And after dinner, are you taking him back to the barge?" Una asks, one eyebrow lifted in skepticism.

"I thought he could sleep under our kitchen table," Angus says with confidence.

"Good," confirms Una, "as long as he doesn't share our bed."

"Thank you, my darling. That was the best hot turkey sandwich," Una says while sipping her strawberry soda. "I still can't get over it. That drill boat is enormous."

"They say the J. B. King is the biggest drill boat of its kind in the country," Angus proudly tells Una.

"I'm sure it is. Thank goodness you got hired to work on it. Will it be ready to start blasting this Spring?"

"That's the plan. You know they brought it here all the way from St. Catharines on Lake Ontario. Took them weeks. The crew comes from all over. There's this one fellow from Quebec, always singing some song or another, and a few boys have come up from the Maritimes. There's even a couple of blokes from Yugoslavia. They can't speak a word of English, but they sure play a mean game of whist. Lost two dollars yesterday."

"I'm glad you only have to do the day shift," Una admits.

"It's all working out." Angus gives Una his cheeky half-smile. "And no, King will not be getting between you and I tonight, not any night."

December 1929

December 12, 1929

Dear Archie,

 Can it be Christmas already? I've finished my shopping for the children. One special gift each and a few little things for their stockings. I bought Sean a tinker construction kit. Gavina is getting a new pair of ice skates, and Fern will be thrilled with the Raggedy Ann doll that she has been wanting. Hiding it from them is a challenge but they know that our bedroom closet is off-limits. I also got them a beautiful birch wood toboggan which our landlady Mrs. Cook is keeping for us in her apartment. There is a splendid hill at St. Lawrence Park where everyone goes sliding. I might even go myself.
 I wasn't sure we'd have much of a Christmas this year. Angus got laid off from the CN but landed a job on the J. B. King drill boat. They'll be blasting a channel in the river as soon as the ice is gone. There seem to be more and more layoffs in town. Our church is hosting a Christmas potluck supper this coming Sunday. I'm looking after the decorations.
 Do you have a New Years' dance to play for? Our group is playing at the Armories again this year. There should be a good turnout despite the hard times. Folks need cheering up.
 Bye for now, my musical friend. Hope you don't get a chunk of coal in your Christmas stocking.

As always, Una

March 22, 1930

It isn't the first time that Una has seen them leaving by the back door of the house. Hobos. For weeks now Mrs. Cook has been putting food in the rear porch. Soup and bread mostly. Una has told the children not to speak to them. Just leave them alone and they'll move on.

"You know, some of those men have come from as far away as places like Moncton, New Brunswick. Riding the rails of all things. In the dead of winter," Mrs. Cook explains as Una walks out behind the house to put the garbage in the bin. "Hope you're not throwing out food scraps. They'll be picking through it if you do. I'd rather have them come in here than see them be so degraded as to rifle through the trash."

"You're a good soul, Mrs. Cook," Una says closing the lid on the garbage can. "We give the scraps to King." Una suddenly feels embarrassed about feeding a dog before feeding a hungry hobo.

"I understand there's a camp set up down by the tracks just west of here," Una says. "Women and men. They must be freezing. The snow is melting but it still goes below freezing at night. I am so thankful that we're okay. When Angus was let go from CN last October, I was pretty scared, let me tell you, but I guess we are the lucky ones. I'm going over to the soup kitchen at the church this afternoon. I've made a pot of beef barley to take with me."

"I can give you some potatoes if you like." Mrs. Cook goes into the kitchen then calls back, "There's someone at the front door. I'll be right back."

A moment later Una hears Mrs. Cook frantically calling out, "Una come quick. It's Angus. He's fallen through the ice."

Una races to the front of the house just as four firefighters carry Angus inside. They've wrapped him in blankets, and his face is ghostly white.

"He's one hell of a lucky man," says one of the rescuers. "Apparently he was loading a piece of equipment onto the barge when the planks that were set up on the ice broke clean through."

"It's over twenty feet deep," adds another firefighter. "The crew said your husband went right under. When he came up, he was unconscious. If it hadn't been for that dog jumping in the water and hauling him over to the crew, it would have been game over. The papers are going to want to hear about this. That dog is some hero."

"Angus, Angus, speak to me. Say something. Oh, my God. Oh, my God." With lightning speed, the panic rushes through Una's body. "What do I do? What do I do?"

"Now Una," Elva says calmly, "we need to get him out of these wet clothes. Come on now. You run ahead to the bedroom and pull out something for him to wear. These gentlemen will carry him upstairs for us." When Una doesn't move Mrs. Cook continues, "I was married once. It won't be the first time I've seen a naked man. Go on now. Get him settled in before the children come home. Una. Now. I'll bring up some soup. We need to get him warm before things take over."

All that Una can think about is how Old Joe's body washed up against the scow. "Is Angus going to die?"

"No, but we don't want him catching pneumonia, now do we?"

"I couldn't bear it. I couldn't bear it at all."

As the firefighters leave by the front door, King slinks past them and immediately heads to Angus' bedside. Whimpering, the dog places his head and one paw on the side of the bed.

"He seems fine now," Mrs. Cook whispers to Una. "He's stopped shivering. The rest will do him good."

"Thank you. Thank you so much, Mrs. Cook. I am so sorry for how I reacted. You have been such a Godsend."

"It was quite a shock, I know. Well, I'll leave you now. You look like you could use a rest yourself. When the children come home, I'll give them a snack."

"If it's not too much trouble. Thank you again."

Una quietly closes the door behind her landlady then crawls in beside

Angus and presses up against her husband to give him the warmth of her body. He stirs slightly.

"What happened?" Angus asks softly.

"Jesus Angus, you fell through the ice."

"I did?"

"Yes, you fool. You ought to be more careful. I don't know what I'd do if you ever drowned."

April 3, 1930

Angus tosses the Toronto Globe on the kitchen table. "Look at this. King is in the papers."

"What does it say?"

Angus reads out loud, "When a member of the crew fell through the ice and sank in more than 25 feet of freezing water, King showed his quality. With a promptness that no human could expel this splendid animal sprang from the deck of the boat and dived after the drowning victim."

"It's true. King is a hero," says Una. "He can have as many treats as he deserves after dinner tonight." Una spots a white envelope on the table. "What's this?"

"Here," Angus says pushing the envelope toward Una.

Slowly Una opens the flap and pulls out a certificate. "Life Insurance?"

"You know all about explosives, Una, from making bombs up in Nobel. Most of the men on the drill boat are getting insurance." Angus senses trepidation on Una's part. "I mean nothing's going to happen. Right? We know that. I just thought that with the children, it makes sense, right?"

"I guess, but let's not think about this, okay. Let's just put this with our other papers." Una folds the document, slips it in the envelope, and puts in the top drawer of the china cabinet. "I pray I never have to look on that again."

"We are extremely cautious," Angus assures Una, "Just yesterday that bloke, Nielsen, the hot-headed one from St. Catharines, was fired. The foreman caught him smoking on deck."

"Seriously? With all that dynamite on board." Una shakes her head. "Some people have as much brains as a fruit fly. Honestly."

"You don't need to worry." Angus places his hand on Una's knee. "At least I can't fall through the ice, now that it's all melted."

May 1930

May 28, 1930

Dear Archie

How are you, my musical friend? What devilment have you been up to this Spring? Any plans to come for a visit?

I mentioned in my last letter to you that Angus is working on a drill boat on the river. They started blasting a few weeks ago. It is quite the undertaking, making this channel. Angus tells me that they drill right into the bedrock some 25 or 30 feet deep. The noise gives him a headache, especially since he works below deck keeping the machinery oiled and all.

There are twelve drills and when they are all drilling at the same time, we hear it in town. I'm getting used to it though. The barge is generally tied up to the nearest landmass, usually an island. They stuff the holes with dynamite and run wires up to the barge. Before they light the fuses, they undo the ropes and chains so that the barge drifts away from the blasting site. Quite the production if you ask me. Some blasts even rattle the windows in our apartment.

We sure are eating a lot of fish. Every day Angus scoops up a few dead ones left floating after the blasts. I mean, how many ways can a person cook a pike anyway?

    Times are getting tough for a lot of folks. At least you have your job at the church and with your band. People still need music, don't they? I've purchased a few recordings: "Happy Days Are Here Again" and "Puttin' on the Ritz". Nothing like a good song to help us forget these hard times. I am so thankful that Angus has a job.

Keep on the sunny side of life.

As always, Una.

46

June 26, 1930

Una, wearing nothing but her cotton slip, rinses the dishes in the sink. Lately, the weather has been increasingly humid. The previous night a tremendous storm ripped through the town wiping out the electricity. Fortunately, it has come back on in time for Una to make breakfast for Angus.

"I'm off now. See you for supper, my love. Hopefully, we can take the children for a swim before bedtime. They always sleep better afterward." Angus comes up behind Una and slides his hand under her slip and onto her bare breast. "I know what makes me sleep better," he whispers, then kisses the back of her neck.

"You rascal," Una squeals.

"By the way, our baseball team has its final game on Saturday. Hope it doesn't rain," he says heading out the door.

"Looks like rain again today. We need something to clear this air."

By late afternoon, the heat is unbearable. Una fills the bathtub with cool water. Twice she steps in to rinse the sweat from her body, and the children take turns as well. Splashing and giggling.

It's almost supper time. Angus should be back within the hour. But it is too damned hot to put the oven on. And fried fish is the last thing I want to cook. Creamed chipped beef on toast will have to do. And canned peaches for dessert. That won't take long.

Una sits at the piano playing a song from her new sheet music when an enormous blast shakes the floors and rattles the windows with such force that the open window beside Una crashes to the sill.

My word, that was huge. They've been blasting all day. That one sounded awfully close.

Una flips through a pile of sheet music that she has had for years.

These are the ones I played when Eva gave me lessons. My goodness, this one's from the 1890s. I remember it. "Clair de Lune" by Debussy.

Una plays a several more pieces then looks at the clock. *I wonder what's keeping Angus. He's usually home by now.*

Fern screams, "Mommy, Sean is splashing water all over the floor. I'm hungry. When is Daddy coming home?"

Una hears a rap on the apartment door. "Maybe that's him now. He must have forgotten his keys again."

Fern, dripping from head to toe and not a stitch of clothing on, runs to the door and unlatches the lock. "It's Mrs. Cook. She wants to speak with you. Can I have a piece of cheese, please?"

"Go help yourself. But just one small piece. You don't want to ruin your supper."

"Una," Mrs. Cook appears flushed, "It's the drill boat. It's gone."

"What? What do you mean it's gone?"

Mrs. Cook takes a deep breath, "The whole damn thing. It exploded. Just off Cockburn Island."

"Oh, my God. No. Not Angus. Is Angus okay? I have to find him."

Immediately Una runs down the stairs and races out onto the rain-drenched street, no shoes, no slippers, nothing on her feet.

The children come and look toward the landing just as Una heads out onto the street and disappears from their sight.

"Where's Mommy going?" asks Fern.

"What's happened?" Gavina steps forward.

"When's supper?" Sean asks.

"You three get dried off and come downstairs with me," Elva tells the children. "I've got a big pot of macaroni and cheese. Your mother will be back shortly." In truth, Elva Cook fears the worst.

The sun sinks low on the horizon. Una still has not returned. Acting cheerful, Elva sends the children upstairs to get their pajamas. "You can sleep over with me tonight. And we can listen to the wireless. I'll make popcorn. You'd like that. Now quick, go get you pajamas."

While they are getting changed, Elva phones the police. It takes several hours, but finally, the police return with Una, drenched to the bone and trembling uncontrollably.

"We found her huddled against a gravestone in the Anglican cemetery that overlooks Cockburn Island," says the young constable. "There's nothing left of that drill boat but a bunch of debris. They can't do a thing until daylight. If there are any survivors, it'll be a miracle."

"He's not dead. Angus wouldn't die," Una snaps.

"Oh, my dear," Elva says, putting a towel around Una's shoulders. "As the officer says, there's nothing we can do until tomorrow. So come along, and we'll tuck you into bed. The children are asleep in my apartment. Let's not disturb them until we know more."

It is the third day since the explosion. Una stands outside the Rowing Club, her gaze fixed on the river. She clenches her fists at her side, her heart beating like a drum in her ears.

They need to find him. I can't live without him. Please God, please God. Please.

Her eyes search through the bobbing wreckage that has been carried miles downstream by the swift current. Each time Una learns that a body has been pulled from the waters she holds her breath and swears that it can't be Angus.

He's not dead. I would know. I would know.

Families weep over the twisted bodies that have been pulled from the rubble. Una fights off the demon voice in her head.

They've missed him. He's alive. He's drifted further downriver. I'm sure of it.

The day grows long. One by one people leave the wharf. A diver carrying his heavy diving suit and breathing equipment walks past Una. She stands perfectly still, her jaw fixed with determination. *I won't look at him. If I take my eyes off the river, I might miss Angus.*

When darkness falls, one of the rescue workers approaches Una. His words to Una's ears sound muffled as if he is speaking through a wad of cotton batten.

"The search has been called off," he says. "There are no more survivors ma'am. Maybe you ought to go back home."

Una does not respond.

The man tries to explain, "There aren't any more bodies. Back where it blew up, the water is too dangerous. Our divers could get swept away. Look, I am terribly sorry. It's all we can do." He waits, and when Una still does not respond he offers, "Let me take you home."

Una watches his lips move. No words make any sense. She feels her heart fall into a dark abyss, so deep that it cannot be brought back up. Gone with Angus. Gone and never to be found. She closes her eyes and collapses in the stranger's arms.

For several days Gavina tries to get her mother to eat. Most of the time Una sits motionless in the chair by the side window of the living room.

Her arms twisted and folded under her left leg, she stares blankly over the rooftops toward the river.

"Mommy, please," Gavina begs, "I made you a sandwich Mommy."

No response.

"Why won't you eat?" Gavina tugs on Una's arm. Waits.

Still no answer.

Gavina goes to the kitchen and brings back a glass of water. Suddenly Una violently swats at the tumbler and the water spills all over her daughter. Una charges toward the piano. She throws the sheet music across the living room floor. She grabs the autoharp and hurls it against the wall. Terrified, Gavina takes Sean and Fern, and they huddle behind the kitchen table.

In horror, they watch their mother wrench the strings from the body of her banjo with such force that the neck of the instrument snaps off. Blood oozes from the slits on her fingers. Una abruptly freezes and collapses on the floor.

Gavina cautiously comes toward her mother with a tea towel to wrap around her mother's hand, but Una refuses to look at her eldest child. Gavina watches helplessly as her mother sways back and forth, back and forth, like an old tire swinging from a rope that's been tied to a tree.

This is the day that the doctor comes. The day that Una is taken away. Gavina holds Sean and Fern close as they watch their mother being led out of the apartment. Mrs. Cook waits with them until the door is shut. In the living room, she finds an address book on a side table.

"Is Edith your aunt?" she asks.

Gavina nods yes.

HEALING

River is time in water; as it came, still so it flows, yet never is the same.

Barten Holyday, 17th Century poet

47

September 17, 1930.   **The Asylum**

My Darling Angus,

    Tomorrow I will be going home. I've been at the asylum for over two months and Dr. Harrington says I am well enough to leave. I guess I'm ready, or at least as ready as I ever will be.

    Edith has been an angel. After I was hospitalized, she came down here from Capreol to look after the children. When it seemed that I needed to stay in the hospital longer she took them up north with her. At first, I was angry, but at the time there was no other choice.

    You will be pleased to know that the children arrive by train tomorrow afternoon. All by themselves. Aren't you proud of them?

I so look forward to being with them. Last week I received three of their homemade cards. Sean drew a bear that looked more like a dog, and Fern scribbled trees and ducks, I think. Gavina pressed some wildflowers and made a lovely card. If only you could be here to see the children when they come home. I know they miss you as much as I do.

A ceremony was held on Cockburn Island last week. I was told I could go. I couldn't do it. I hope you understand. They unveiled a huge commemorative plaque. A photograph was in this morning's paper. King's name is right below your name. I am not surprised. He never left your side.

I've been thinking about all the special times we had together like the time you met me in Toronto, you in your uniform, looking so handsome. And how you swept me off my feet at the hockey game in Parry Sound. I fell in love with you right there and then. I can't remember the last time we made love and that troubles me. But I do remember the first time as if it were yesterday.

You don't need to worry about me, my love. I will manage. Mrs. Cook has agreed to let me stay in the apartment at a reduced rent, and I will help by doing chores and cleaning for her.

I cannot pretend that this has been easy. At least during the war, I had always hoped that you would come back one day. But you, my darling, are well on your way to a place where I trust you will wait for me. I miss you so terribly my love. I wish I could hold you in my arms again.

Sometimes, at night I feel as if you are watching over me. Even now as I close my eyes, I sense your eyes looking deeply into mine. You are in my soul now and forever, and I shall love you beyond all time.

Your loving wife, Una.

September 18, 1930

The heavy oak doors to the asylum shut behind Una. She takes a deep breath of the fresh autumn air still chilled by the early morning rain. Nervously she clutches a small satchel to her side as feelings of trepidation swell in her gut.

Mrs. Cook is supposed to be here. I was told she'd pick me up and take me back to the apartment. I don't know if I can do this, but God help me, I am never going back inside this place.

"Una."

"Dr. Harrington. You startled me." Una gathers her composure. "Before leaving, I wanted to thank you for all that you have done for me this past while, but you weren't in your office. I'm so sorry. The nurse said you must have had another patient to attend to, and my ride is coming so, I came ahead outside."

"Nothing to apologize for Una. I was taking a bit of a break myself and wanted to see if last night's frost had destroyed the flowerbeds." Dr. Harrington brushes a lock of her red hair from her forehead. "You're all set then?"

"I suppose I am."

"Grief is a long lasting-companion, one that unfortunately we all must endure at some point in our lives. From everything you have told me you have many reasons to start anew. Your children, your music." She stops short. Waits. When Una does not respond she continues, "I know, words may console for a while, but time is the only true healer of sorrow. Never mind. You look better than you have in weeks. What are your plans?"

"I'm not all that sure." Head down, Una shuffles her feet. "I want to make things as normal as possible for the children. They're all I've got now." Una spots a black taxicab pulling into the drive. "There's my ride. My landlady doesn't drive. There she is waving at me from the back seat." Una starts to walk away, then looks back. "I'm not sorry to be leaving here. I admire your dedication, Dr. Harrington. Thank you again. I won't forget all that you have done for me."

Mrs. Cook is in a cheery mood. She leads Una through the front door and places her umbrella in the stand.

"I picked up a few groceries to get you started. And there's a pot of ham and bean soup for when the children arrive. The train should be here in a few hours. Do you need a rest? I've made a light lunch for us before you go to the station."

Una looks up into the dark stairwell.

"You go on up, my dear. I put fresh linen on the beds."

Una bites her lip. She knows that she left everything in disarray, the instruments smashed and all. "You tidied the apartment?"

"A few of the women from the church lent me a hand. It was no trouble, no trouble at all, not after what you've been through. It's just ten o'clock. Come down at noon. That'll give you plenty of time to head over to the station. I believe the train arrives at ten to two. You must be looking forward to seeing the children."

"Yes. I miss them terribly."

The uneasy emptiness of the apartment washes over Una, silent, save for the steady click of the clock on the mantle in the living room. Right away she spots Angus' shoes on the mat by the door. She closes her eyes and leans heavily against the wall, her heart overflowing with sorrow and longing.

How can I do this? How can I possibly be strong for the children?

In the kitchen, Una notices that several unopened letters have been left on the table. Sympathy cards. She opens one that has the town hall address on the envelope - from the Mayor's Office: 'Please accept our deepest sympathies over the death of your husband.'

Una reads the card from the Women's Auxiliary of Trinity Anglican Church. 'You have our sincere condolences, and we will keep you close in our thoughts and prayers in the coming weeks.' Tears well in her eyes. A third card bears the inscription, 'May God's love be with you at this time'.

Steve Ward signed it and added a handwritten message. 'When you are up for playing some music get in touch. We miss you.'

Una immediately recognizes Emily's handwriting on the next envelope. The card displays an elegant floral wreath and two brightly colored birds, and 'Thinking of You' printed in gold letters.

> May you see God's light on the path ahead
> When the road you walk is dark.
> May you always hear,
> Even in your hour of sorrow,
> The gentle singing of the lark.
> When times are hard may hardness
> Never turn your heart to stone,
> May you always remember
> When the shadows fall—
> You do not walk alone.

Una reads her friend's personal note.

July 15, 1930

Dear Una,

I cannot imagine how devastating this has been for you. I read about the disaster in the papers. It is unimaginable. Please know that my thoughts and prayers are with you and the children. If there is anything at all that I can do I hope you will reach out to me.

Yours ever so sincerely, Emily.

Em sent that two months ago. I must write her back. But how can I tell her? How can I tell her that I've been in the Asylum?

On the top shelf of the bedroom closet, Una pulls down a square cookie tin with a portrait of King George VI on it. She reaches into her satchel and retrieves the letter she had written to Angus just before leaving the Asylum. Opening the lid, she places her secret love note to Angus in with the letters that he had sent her during the war years.

I know you will never read this letter my love, but I need to believe that somehow your spirit lives on. Do you hear my soul crying out for you? I miss you so, so much.

Through her tears, Una reads his letters, one after the other - - the letter from Versailles, the one about the stray dog companion, and another about the time the train transported the Dumbbells after their performance for the soldiers. A flood of bittersweet memories overwhelms her heart. With her arms wrapped around Angus' old wool sweater, Una falls onto the bed. In fetal position, she chases after all the old times, trying desperately to hold onto them so that they don't dissolve like so many fleeting dreams. The first kiss. Watching him score at the arena in Parry Sound. Angus chasing the sleigh and disappearing into the darkness.

A sudden rap upon the door.

"Are you coming down for a wee bite?" Elva Cook calls from the far side of the apartment door.

"Yes, right away. Thank you. I'll be right down."

I see them now. Waving from the window.

Una runs alongside the train as it pulls into the station. When it stops, the train attendant lifts Fern down from the passenger car and she immediately rushes to throw her arms around Una.

"My sweet darling. How I have missed you." Gavina and Sean hug their mother with such force that Una nearly loses her balance. "Aren't you all a sight for sore eyes."

"Auntie Edith took us looking for wild blueberries and we saw a big black bear," Fern says excitedly.

"I caught a large-mouthed bass," boasts Sean. "It weighed five pounds and Uncle Charlie and me, we cooked it at his camp, and I got a fish bone stuck in my gums, but he pulled it out."

"Well, that's good," Una says.

Gavina stands quietly beside her mother. She holds out a tiny wreath of willow branches and wildflowers. "I made one for baby Connor like we did when I was little. Remember? Can we put this one on Daddy's grave?"

Suddenly Una feels as if she is suffocating in her sorrow again. Then, with a deep breath she says, "Daddy is in the river. Forever. The river is his grave. Why don't we go to the park and send your beautiful wreath out on the waves? Would you like that?"

"Yes, Momma. Can we do that now?"

"I think that is a grand idea."

"Mommy?"

"Yes, Fern."

"Can we have an ice cream cone on the way home?"

"Of course, we can."

September 28, 1930

Dear Emily,

I am so sorry for not writing sooner. I only received your card a couple of weeks ago. When they couldn't find Angus, I completely fell apart. I had to be hospitalized for over two months. But I am home again and doing my best to make life as normal as possible for the children.

They are doing quite well, considering. This afternoon my landlady Mrs. Cook has taken them to the cinema to see Our Gang in "Small Talk". I am ever so thankful to have her support these days.

I miss Angus beyond words, but I know he wouldn't want me moping around. I've been in touch with the fellas that I played music with, and I will be rehearsing with them next week. It's been quite a while since I tickled the ivories.

Hope all is well with you dear chum. I look forward to your news.

As always, Una

December 14, 1930

Dear Archie,

It seems like ages since I last heard from you. I think I am the one who owes you a letter, but no matter, I do miss your banter.

How are you? Well, I trust, and up to your musical mischief-making.

You may have read about the J. B. King drill boat explosion that happened last June. My poor sweet Angus lost his life. They never found his body. It was a tremendous shock as I am sure you can understand.

On the brighter side of things, my children have become the center of my life. Little Sean is the spitting image of his father with his sparkling blue eyes. Gavina has taken to the piano much as I did, picking up tunes by ear. My youngest, Fern, is a regular rascal always picking fights with her older brother and sister then running to me to settle the squabbles. But my what a curly top.

Yesterday I took them tobogganing at St. Lawrence Park. There is an enormous hill. They went flying down the slope so fast that they almost ended up in the river. My heart nearly stopped when I saw that. But of course, they were full of giggles.

I will be playing for a dance this New Year's Eve. I am really looking forward to it. What are your plans? Are you going to be traveling again this summer? I've kept all your postcards from your trip to British Columbia. How I would love to have high tea with you at the Empress in Victoria. And the Banff Springs Hotel certainly looks like a European castle. You really do travel in style.

Won't you come out this way for a visit? We can take a jaunt to the Parliament Buildings in Ottawa and, if we time it right, you can bring your saxophone and join in with the band.

Merry Christmas. Don't eat too much plum pudding. I always do.

As ever, Una

July 01, 1931

"We couldn't have asked for a better day," Steve Ward says as he lays his music out.

The bandstand at St. Lawrence Park is gaily decorated with red and white banners and tiny Union Jack flags. Dominion Day. Despite the hard times folks have come out in their Sunday best to celebrate the Nation's birthday.

"How are you doing Una? It's been just over a year since, you know…" Steve stammers slightly.

"It's hard to imagine really. Sometimes it feels like it was only yesterday and other times it seems like forever ago." Una leans on the piano. "They had an anniversary memorial service at Trinity Church on Sunday. I took the children but wish I hadn't. It made them sad."

"How so?"

"Fern kept asking questions about Angus - 'Is Papa watching from heaven?' That just about broke my heart. She's so young. She barely remembers Angus at all. But look at them now, playing on the swings. They'll be fine. They'll be fine," Una repeats as if telling herself that she too will be fine one day.

"Una," Steve points to a man standing at the top of the hill, dressed in a white suit and matching fedora. "He's waving at us. Do you know him?"

"My goodness. Yes. It's Archie. Archie Brentwood. He came."

Una rushes up the hill and throws her arms around her longtime friend.

"Hug me like that my girl and the whole town will be in an uproar. Do you want them spreading rumors about a new amour?"

"Let them yabber on. I'm just so happy to see you, Arch. And you did it. You brought your sax. Just in time. We're about to start. Come on. What are you waiting for?"

That evening after Una tucks the children into bed, she and Archie sit at the kitchen table. They pour themselves sweet sherry and make a toast to a wonderful day. Una is overcome with a lightheartedness that has been long missing.

"Remember the time I got the black eye and we had to share a room? Everyone in Capreol had something to say about that, I bet."

"We both gave them tons of fodder to gossip about." Archie pours another glass of sherry and offers one to Una.

"They thought we were having an affair."

"We were."

"What?"

"A musical affair."

"That's so true. I think I might have gone quite mad had I not met you, Archie. I might never have waited for Angus."

Archie sees a sudden melancholy come over Una's face. "But you did my dear. You did. And aren't you glad that you waited for him? He loved you to pieces. And now you have three delightful little scamps to keep you on your toes."

"And how they do Archie. There's something I want to show you." Una opens the drawer to the buffet and brings back a small leather bag. "Did I ever tell you about Rachel Little Feathers?"

"You may have mentioned her. You knew her when you were quite young as I recall."

"I called her Nokomis. That means grandmother. She gave me these tokens when I came of age." Una offers Archie the bear claw and goose feather. "Rachel told me so many stories about her people. I used to help her with her trap lines, and in the late summer we'd pick wild blueberries until my fingers turned purple." Una takes the feather back and holds it gently in the palm of her hand. "She told me that when I was born, she washed me in the lake. At that moment, she saw a goose land on the water, so she called me Nika, Little Goose. When she gave me this feather, she said that one day I would stretch my wings and fly away. I remember her very words. She said, 'Nika you going to take to flight. You going to have a great life journey.'"

Una places the bear claw and feather in the leather bag and pulls the drawstring tight.

"You know something, Arch?"

"What's that?"

"It's time for me to stretch my wings and fly."

AUTHOR'S NOTES

Unsayable Absence is a work of fiction made up of some secrets and truths, and many fabricated lies. It is true that my maternal grandmother, Bertha May Green, was born on a scow on the Lake of Bays near Huntsville, Ontario. During the First World War, she worked at a munitions plant in Nobel and afterward moved to Capreol where she married my grandfather Jack Wylie. She gave birth to three of her children in a converted boxcar.

My grandfather did serve with the Railway Troops. They were known as the 228th Battalion, and yes, they had a team of hockey players. My grandfather was not on that team, but it seemed to make for a good story. After the war he worked for the Canadian National Railway in northern Ontario. By the late 1920's he transferred to Brockville.

Following the tragic explosion of the J. B. King Drill Boat, my grandfather's body was never found. I was told that my grandmother was so overcome by shock that she had to be hospitalized, but no one said that it was at the Brockville Asylum.

In the early 1970's I attended York University in Toronto. The feminist movement was in full swing, and I was swept up by the prospect that there should be equality of the sexes. In 1970, TIME magazine published Gloria Steinem's article 'What It Would Be Like If Women Win'. She wrote: "In Women's Lib Utopia, there will be free access to good jobs, and decent pay for the bad jobs women have been performing all along, including housework."

At that time Feminism and the Women's Liberation Movement had already been around for decades, and I began to wonder what it must have been like for my grandmother in those early years. She passed away in the 1960s. In the mid-1970's I decided to ask my mother to fill in the blanks. Armed with a bulky reel-to-reel tape recorder I proceeded to record my mother's memories while seated on the front porch of our cottage. I have held onto that recording for several decades. In the background one can hear birds chirping, children laughing, and my dog whimpering for attention. A true field recording.

During my years at York, computers were enormous monsters that spit out cards the size of a small purse. Research meant perusing volumes of books in the stacks of the university library. Being a penny-poor student, I wrote copious notes on scraps of paper towels taken from the library washroom. Somehow, I managed to hold onto those cryptic notes to this very day. I checked online for those books that I had read but unfortunately, most are no longer in print. Still, I decided to include them in the bibliography because they are pivotal in my understanding of the role women played in the early 20th century.

Growing up, I heard rumors that, on the other side of my family, my father's grandmother was 'dark', a word that meant 'we don't talk about it'. After much probing, combined with the results of my DNA testing, I now know for certain that she was First Nation. Sadly, her assimilation remains a mystery. The character Rachel Little Feathers speaks to that lost memory. I was very careful to be historically accurate in the portrayal of Rachel and respectful of the Anishinaabe traditions.

Unusual publications that I have found over the years have also influenced my writing. Once, while visiting a flea market in Grey County,

Ontario, I rescued an old bible filled with pencil-written notes made by Maud McCoy. She was greatly opposed to the First World War. At one point in the novel, there is a lecture given at a church. In that chapter, I have quoted passages from Maud McCoy's writings.

Another invaluable book that I have treasured since the early 1970s is one that I discovered in the attic of Lord Beaverbrook's birthplace in Maple, Ontario. 'Enquire Within Upon Everything' was published in the late 1800s and offers advice on everything from how a housewife should greet her husband after a long day's work, to various methods for removing freckles.

"Unsayable Absence" has had a long gestation period and I find it quite ironic that I have lived more years than my grandmother did. I cherish my early memories of walking with her through fields of hay to collect berries for a wreath and learning how to make the call of a loon by blowing into my cupped hands. She was the first person to encourage me to play guitar, and as it turned out, I led a long successful career as a professional musician.

A bittersweet memory lingers. When I was sixteen my grandmother was hospitalized with heart problems. Some family members said it was all in her head. One afternoon I went to see her. She told me she was not afraid of dying. By morning she was gone.

It is with great affection that I give voice to what I imagine might have been a young woman's struggle in the first three decades of the 20th century and how she overcomes so many hardships, especially the tragic loss of a loved one.

This is Una's story.

PHOTOGRAPHS

My mother, Ernestine Robina Wylie, was a great storyteller. She told me so many things about her parents and what their lives were like in those early years of the 20th Century. My grandfather Jack Wylie married my grandmother, Bertha May Green on February 21, 1921, in Capreol, Ontario. The following photographs come from my mother's collection.

Bertha May Green and Jack Wylie around 1921.

The 228th Battalion known as the Railroad Troop, and others at Versailles, France, October 1, 1918. Jack Wylie, standing on the far right.

Up north on the CN line. My grandmother, Bertha in the center. Flanked by the cook and her daughter. Jack Jr. and Ernestine in front.

Unsayable Absence

Wells River, Vermont, 1927, during the flood where my grandfather worked on the reconstruction of the railway trestles.

My grandfather worked on a pile driver such as this one taken at Northfield, Vermont, December 1927.

"King", mascot on the J.B. King Drill Boat who saved my grandfather's life. "With a promptness that no human being could expel, this splendid animal sprang from the deck of the boat and dived after the drowning victim." *Toronto Globe 1930*.

The J. B. King drill boat. My grandfather worked as an oiler in the boiler room.

The J.B. Kind Drill Boat with crew. I believe the man seated with the dog is my grandfather, Jack Wylie.

Diver and rescuers looking for the bodies of the men killed in the explosion of the drill boat.

Cairn on Cockburn Island commemorating the 30 men who lost their lives in the explosion.

My grandmother Bertha Wylie in front of their apartment on George Street, circa 1930. Ernestine standing in the doorway. Jack pedaling with Grace on the back.

BIBLIOGRAPHY

ANNISHINABE - CHIPPAWA - OJIBWE

Anderson, Kim. *Life Stages and Native Women: Memory, Teachings and Story Medicine.* Winnipeg: University of Manitoba Press, 2011.

Author Unknown. *The Land of the Ojibwe.* Minnesota Historical Society

WEBSITES:

All Totems: https://alltotems.com/spirit-animals/goose-meaning-symbolism/

Muskrat Magazine. http://muskratmagazine.com/my-berry-fast/

Pitawanakwat, Lillian. *Ojibwe/Powawatomi (Anishinaabe)* http://www.fourdirectionsteachings.com/transcripts/ojibwe.pdf

Roy, Loriene. *Countries and Their Cultures: Ojibwa.* https://www.everyculture.com/multi/Le-Pa/Ojibwa.html

Tribal College Journal. https://tribalcollegejournal.org/nanaboozhoo-wiindigo-ojibwe-history-colonization-present/

BROCKVILLE

Emerton, Deborah (Editor). *Brockville Voices: An Oral History of Brockville 1900-1960.* Brockville, Ontario: Brockville Museum, 1994.

Thompson, Shawn. *River Rats, The People of the Thousand Islands.* Burnstown, Ontario: The General Store Publishing House, Inc., 1989.

CAPREOL

WEBSITES:

Capreol On Line. 2005. http://capreolonline.com/Looking/People/CapHist1936/history1936.html

Ontario Ghost Towns. http://www.ghosttownpix.com/ontario/intros/sellwood.html

Ontario Museums Association. http://www.museumsontario.ca/museum/Northern-Ontario-Railroad-Muse

FEMINISM

Barnes, Earl. *Women in Modern Society.* New York: B.W. Hueksch, 1912*

Booth, Meyrick. *Women and Society.* New York: Longmans, Green & Co., 1929*

Gilman, Charlotte Perkins. *The Man Made World.* New York: Source Book Press (1911) 1970.*

Lemons, J. Stanley. *The Woman Citizen - Social Feminism in the 1920s.* University of Illinois Press, 1973.*

Leutkens, Charlotte. *Women and a New Society.* New York: Essential Books, 1946.*

Mannin, Ethel. *Women and the Revolution.* New York: Dutton & Co. Inc., 1939*

FIRST WORLD WAR

Audette, A., 22nd Batt. and Audette, W. *Verses and History of the Great War 1914.* Copyright 1919.

Brewster, Hugh. *At Vimy Ridge: Canada's Greatest World War Victory.* Toronto: Scholastic Canada Ltd., 2006

Hebb, Ross. *Letters Home: Maritimers and the Great War, 1914-1918.* Halifax: Nimbus, 2014.

PRINT:

Magazine: Canadian Geographic. *The First World War 1914-1918: 100 Ways it Shaped Canada.* Canadian Geographic Enterprises, July/August 2014.

Magazine: Contributor: Granastein, J.L. *Vimy: The Birth of a Nation, Volume 1, Number 1, Winter 2017.* Kanata, Ontario: Canvet Publications Ltd., 2017.

Newspaper Article: *The Toronto Encyclopedia of World War One.* Toronto: Toronto Star, Saturday, August 2, 2014.

WEBSITES:

100th Anniversary of North Bay's National Hockey Team. Bay Today. November 28, 2016.
https://www.baytoday.ca/local-news/100th-anniversary-of-north-bays-national-hockey-team-475538

Broznitsky, Peter. Canadian Railway Troops. 2015.
http://www.russiansinthecef.ca/crt/index.shtml

Canada and the First World War. Library and Archives Canada. September 9, 2020.
https://www.bac-lac.gc.ca/eng/discover/military-heritage/first-world-war/canada-first-world-war/Pages/default.aspx/025005-2100-e.html

Canadian Rail, No. 437, November-December 1993. http://www.exporail.org/can_rail/Canadian%20Rail_no437_1993.pdf

Canadian Soldiers: Railway Troops. https://www.canadiansoldiers.com/insignia/brookerpdfs/Part%206b%20railway%20troops.pdf

https://www.bac-lac.gc.ca/eng/discover/military-heritage/first-world-war/Documents/canadian%20railway%20troops.pdf

Fouchard, Steven, Army Public Affairs. January 1, 2017.
https://www.facebook.com/notes/canadian-army/the-228th-centenary-an-army-hockey-story-part-one/1181391815286128/

Hockey Marching as to War - the228th Battalion. Library and Archives Canada. https://thediscoverblog.com/2016/01/05/hockey-marching-as-to-war-the-228th-battalion/

Jam Breakers, A Song for the Men of the 122nd. MuskokaRegion.com. Huntsville Forester. Feb. 17, 2010
https://www.muskokaregion.com/opinion-story/3643424-jam-breakers-a-song-for-the-men-of-the-122nd/

MacDonald, Bruce. Railroad Troops, February 2013. http://guysboroughgreatwar-veterans.blogspot.com/2013/02/canadian-railway-troops.html

Military Communication: Britannica.
https://www.britannica.com/technology/military-communication/From-World-War-I-to-1940

Muskoka Region: https://www.muskokaregion.com/opinion-story/3643424-jam-breakers-a-song-for-the-men-of-the-122nd/

Recruitment. Ministry of Government and Consumer Services, Ontario.
http://www.archives.gov.on.ca/en/explore/online/posters/recruitment.aspx
Royal Montreal Regiment.
https://royalmontrealregiment.com/communications-in-ww1/
Stark, William Redver (Artist).
https://www.bac-lac.gc.ca/eng/discover/military-heritage/first-world-war/stark/Pages/william-redver-stark.aspx

GREAT DEPRESSION
WEBSITES:
https://thecanadianencyclopedia.ca/en/article/the-great-crash-feature

HERBALISTS
WEBSITES:
Herbal Abortions.
https://io9.gizmodo.com/5933494/the-terrifying-history-of-herbal-abortion-medicines
The Telegraph.
https://www.telegraph.co.uk/gardening/3311533/Maybe-the-old-wives-knew-a-thing-or-two.html
Tiny Pioneer. https://www.tinypioneer.co.uk/tinys-blog/herbal-medicine-week

HOCKEY
WEBSITES:
Hockey Players on The Railway:
https://www.freewebs.com/hockeyrailroader/hockeyrailroaders.htm
Smith, Stephen. A Quirk of Canadian History: When War and Hockey Shared the Ice. December 30, 2016.
https://www.nytimes.com/2016/12/30/sports/hockey/wwi-canadian-soldiers-national-hockey-association-stanley-cup.html

MUNITIONS
Butlin, Susan. *Women Making Shells: Presence in Munitions Work 1914-1918: The*

Art of Francis Loring, Florence Wyle, Mabel May and Dorothy Stevens. Canadian Military History, Volume 5, Number 1, Spring 1996: Published by Scholars Commons, 1996.

Frager, Ruth A. *Discounted Labour: Women Workers in Canada*. Toronto: Ontario: University of Toronto Press, 2005

Author unknown. *The History of Munitions Supply in Canada 1914-1918*. London: Longmans, Green & Co., 1925*

Reader, W.J. *Imperial Chemical Industries, A History, Volume 1. The forerunners 1870-1926*. London: Oxford University Press, 1970*

Walter, Henrietta R. *Women as Munition Makers*. New York: Russell Sage Foundation, 1917.*

Yates, L.K. *The Woman's Part*. New York: George H. Doran Co. Date unknown.*

VIDEO:

Thomas, Rick. *Nobel, Ontario 1907-1984, Narrated by Dave Thomas*. West Parry Sound District Museum, date unknown.

WEBSITES:

Munitions Factories World War One:

Film: https://www.nfb.ca/film/and_we_knew_how_to_dance/

https://www.youtube.com/watch?v=czRMWEi4bAk

https://www.iwm.org.uk/history/9-women-reveal-the-dangers-of-working-in-a-first-world-war-munitions-factory

http://www.firstworldwar.com/features/womenww1_four.htm http://www.gumptioninc.org/2017/06/02/brief-history-nobelhttps://www.theguardian.com/society/2015/jan/06/girls-stirred-devils-porridge-first-world-war-remember-munitions-workers

https://www.theguardian.com/books/2015/may/16/brian-dillon-the-great-explosion-munitions-factory-uplees-faversham-kent-1915

http://www.doingourbit.ca/blog/8795

https://www.striking-women.org/module/women-and-work/world-war-i-1914-1918 https://www.firstworldwar.com/features/womenww1_four.htm

https://www.iwm.org.uk/history/voices-of-the-first-world-war-munitions

http://middx.net/articles/munitions.htm

http://wartimecanada.ca/document/world-war-i/manufacturing/

women-munitions-factories

MUSIC

Dalhart, Vernon. *Album of Songs*. New York: F.B. Haviland Publishing Company, 1928

Vincent, Elmore. *Lumber Jack Songs*. Chicago: M.M. Cole Publishing Company, 1932

WEBSITES:

Canadian Songs of the First World War. The Canadian Encyclopedia.https://www.thecanadianencyclopedia.ca/en/article/canadian-songs-of-the-first-world-war

Dance Halls. Acoustic Music Org. https://acousticmusic.org/research/history/musical-styles-and-venues-in-america/dance-halls/

History of Music In Canada. Library and Archives Canada. https://www.bac-lac.gc.ca/eng/discover/films-videos-sound-recordings/virtual-gramophone/Pages/history-music-canada.aspx#1916

MUSKOKA

Bartleman, James. *Out of Muskoka*. Newcastle, Ontario: Penumbra Press, 2002.

MacKay, Niall. *By Steam Boat and Steam Train*. Erin, Ontario: The Boston Mills Press, 1982

WEBSITES:

Baysville Heritage Walking Tour: https://lakeofbays.civicweb.net/document/33413

General Muskoka History: https://www.lakeofbays.on.ca/en/municipal-services/resources/Documents/Heritage---Ruth-Martin-Papers-book-1.pdf

Lake of Bays Heritage Foundation: https://www.lakeofbaysheritage.ca/

Lake of Bays Lane: https://lakeofbayslane.wordpress.com/category/our-place-in-history/

Land Grants: https://www.visitmuskoka.com/history.htm

Medical Records; Tuberculosis: http://www.archives.gov.on.ca/en/explore/online/health_records/tuberculosis.aspx

Muskoka Atlas 1879:https://www.arcgis.com/apps/MapSeries/index.html?appid=ccb1a65ab161460fb638c42212c9b85d

Steam Museum: https://www.muskokaheritageplace.ca/en/discover-the-museum/steam-museum.aspx#

PSYCHIATRY

Gay, Peter. *Freud, A Life For Our Time.* United Kingdom: J.M Denton & Sons Limited, 1988.

WEBSITES:

https://www.webmd.com/schizophrenia/what-is-catatonia#1

Brockville Psychiatric Hospital: http://www.archives.gov.on.ca/en/explore/online/health_records/psychiatric.aspx

https://www.asylumprojects.org/index.php/Brockville_Asylum_for_the_Insane

RAILWAYS

Atkins, Rebecca. *My Childhood in the Bush: Growing up in Brent on the CNR in Algonquin Provincial Park (1913-1919).* Toronto: Past Forward Heritage Limited, 2001.

Miku, Nick and Helma. *Railways in Canada.* Toronto: McGraw Hill Ryerson Limited, 1972.*

WEBSITES:

http://www.trha.ca/trha/history/railways/canadian-national-railway/

http://www.mactierrailroadheritagesociety.org/wp/

TORONTO

WEBSITES:

A City At War: https://www.ctvnews.ca/canada/a-city-at-war-reflections-of-toronto-s-military-past-1.1928368

Allan Gardens: https://tayloronhistory.com/2019/02/16/historic-greenhouses-in-allan-gardens-toronto/

CNE: https://theex.com/footer/about-the-cne/history/the-cne-and-the-great-war

Musical Theatre: https://www.thecanadianencyclopedia.ca/en/article/musical-theatre-emc

Patriotic Fervour: https://torontoist.com/2011/08/historicist-patriotic-fervour-at-the-cne-2/2/

Photographs: https://www.blogto.com/city/2010/12/toronto_of_the_1900s/
Toronto History Museums: https://www.toronto.ca/explore-enjoy/history-art-culture/museums/virtual-exhibits/history-of-toronto/the-first-half-of-the-20th-century-1901-51/

TRADITIONS

Armstrong, Audrey I. *Harness In The Parlour, A Book of Early Canadian Fact and Folklore.* Don Mills, Ontario: Musson Book Company, 1974.*

Armstrong, Audrey I. *Sulphur & Molasses.* Don Mills, Ontario: Musson Book Company, 1977.*

Author Unknown. *Enguire Within Upon Everything.* London: Holston and Sons, 1874.*

Day, Cindy. *Grandma Says, Weather Lore From Meterologists.* Halifax: Nimbus Publishing Limited, 2012.

Finnegan, Joan. *Some of the Stories I Told You Were True.* Ottawa: Deneau, 1981.

Fowke, Edith. *Folklore of Canada.* Toronto: McClelland and Stewart, 1976.

Johnson, Ben. *The History of Hogmanay.* United Kingdom: www.historic-uk.com, 2019.

Kalman, Bobby. *Early Pleasures and Pastimes.* Toronto: Crabtree publishing Company, 1983.

Marks, Lynne Sorrel. *Revivals and Roller Rinks: Religion, Leisure and Identity in Late Nineteenth Century Small Town Ontario.* Toronto: University of Toronto Press Inc., 1996.

McGovern, Una. *Lost Crafts - Rediscovering Traditional Skills.* Edinburgh: Chambers Harrap Publishers, 2008.

Ward, W. Peter. *Courtship, Love and Marriage in the Nineteenth-century English Canada.* McGill-Queen's University Press, 1990.

VERMONT FLOOD

FILMS:
Vermont's Great Flood: https://www.youtube.com/watch?v=2Um8UmQyLl8
Vermont's Super Flood 1927: https://www.youtube.com/watch?v=a9k80YezvWl

WEBSITES:

Central Vermont Railway:

http://images.techno-science.ca/?en/stories/central_vermont/c/page/1

https://www.canada-rail.com/quebec/railways/CV.html

History of the Flood:

https://glcp.uvm.edu/landscape_new/1927_flood/about_1927_flood.htm

Oral Transcriptions:

https://vermonthistory.org/documents/GrnMtnChronTranscripts/199-10BuxtonRoy.pdf

https://vermonthistory.org/documents/GrnMtnChronTranscripts/199-37KidderGeorgeV.pdf

* Reference books read in mid 1970s

Printed in Canada